John W. de Gruchy

Confessions of a
Christian
Humanist

Fortress Press
Minneapolis

To
ROZELLE
sister extraordinaire
and
in memory of our parents
HAROLD (1902–1986)
&
MABEL (1900–1993)

CONFESSIONS OF A CHRISTIAN HUMANIST

First Fortress Press Edition 2006.

Published in collaboration with SCM Press, London. Copyright © 2005 John W. de Gruchy. All rights reserved. Except for brief quotations in critical articles or reviews, no part of this book may be reproduced in any manner without prior written permission from the publisher. Visit http://www.augsburgfortress.org/copyrights/contact.asp or write to Permissions, Augsburg Fortress, Box 1209, Minneapolis, MN 55440.

Cover image: Face Collage © Noma / Images.com
Cover design: Laurie Ingram

Library of Congress Cataloging-in-Publication Data
De Gruchy, John W.
Confessions of a Christian humanist / John W. de Gruchy.
    p. cm.
Includes bibliographical references.
ISBN 0-8006-3824-7 (alk. paper)
1. Theological anthropology—Christianity. I. Title.
BT701.3.D44 2006
230'.046—dc22
                                        2005036159

The paper used in this publication meets the minimum requirements of American National Standard for Information Sciences—Permanence of Paper for Printed Library Materials, ANSI Z329.48-1984.

Manufactured in the U.S.A.
10   09   08   07   06   1   2   3   4   5   6   7   8   9   10

Contents

Preface

I began writing this book at the Rockefeller Foundation's Study Centre in Bellagio, Italy, where I was a scholar in residence in June 2004. The four weeks Isobel and I spent in that wonderfully congenial environment were a sheer delight. I am grateful to the Foundation for making this possible, for the gracious hospitality extended to us by the Director, Gianna Celli, for the friendship and stimulating conversation of all those who were in residence at the time. Subsequently I was able to share some of the substance of the book in a graduate seminar at the University of Cape Town; in lectures at Wesleyan University, Middletown, Connecticut; Union Theological Seminary, New York; the Center for Theological Inquiry, Princeton, New Jersey; Ghost Ranch Conference Center, New Mexico; and the University of the Third Age in Hermanus, and I am thankful to all who, on those occasions, contributed to improving my thoughts. In response, I was tempted at many points to elaborate my argument and indulge in more explanatory footnotes and references. I have tried to avoid this as much as possible. But, despite the danger of academic vanity, I have taken the liberty of referring to some of my other books where I have discussed such issues more fully.

Several friends read the manuscript prior to its final drafting: Carolyn Butler, James Gray, Lyn Holness, Steve de Gruchy, and Isobel de Gruchy. None of them can be held responsible for any mistakes in the text, or for the substance of what I have written, but all helped make the book far better than it might otherwise have been.

I am grateful to SCM Press in London, especially Barbara Laing, and Fortress Press in Minneapolis, especially Michael West, for agreeing to publish the book, and for the professional yet friendly and supportive manner in which they have helped bring it to completion.

The book is dedicated to my sister, Rozelle, whose friendship has been so warm, generous, and supportive over the years. She is, as all who know her well would confirm, an extraordinary person. Together we also want this book to be a memorial to our parents, Mabel and Harold, whose love and care we celebrate.

Hermanus, South Africa
The Feast Day of Thomas More,
Christian humanist and martyr

I

Prologue

Idle reader: Without my swearing to it, you can believe that I would like this book, the child of my understanding, to be the most beautiful, the most brilliant, and the most discreet that anyone could imagine. But I have not been able to contravene the natural order ...
Miguel de Cervantes[1]

The stories people hear and tell, the dramas they see performed, not to speak of the sacred stories that are absorbed without being directly heard or seen, shape in the most profound way the inner story of experience. Stephen Crites[2]

Always be ready to make your defence to anyone who demands from you an account of the hope that is in you. 1 Peter 3.15

As I write I am surrounded by images of people. At the entrance to my study there are two large collages of photographs of friends and colleagues I have known and worked with over the years, and a gallery of family pictures going back to my grandparents. Above my desk is a large portrait of Dietrich Bonhoeffer, the German theologian who died at the hands of the Gestapo, and nearby a photograph of his friend and colleague Eberhard Bethge on his ninetieth birthday. In front of me is a photograph of my wife, Isobel, taken 30 years ago when her hair was so beautifully red. On my desk stands a small carving of four tall Kikuyu tribesmen, a picture of my eldest granddaughter Thea as a young child, a Coptic icon of Mary, Jesus and St Anthony, the desert hermit, and a drawing by Leonardo da Vinci entitled 'The Vitruvian Man', a Renaissance icon of human perfection.

'The Vitruvian Man' is the 'ideal human' (though he is

---

1 Miguel de Cervantes, *Don Quixote* (London: Secker & Warburg, 2004), p. 3.
2 Stephen Crites, 'The Narrative Quality of Experience', *Journal of the American Academy of Religion*, September 1971, vol. 39, no. 3, p. 304.

plainly male), the prototype of being human, beautifully proportioned with outstretched arms and torso symmetrically balanced. Yet, as one modern-day commentator records: 'the whole idea of the drawing seems to be a physically realistic rendering of these abstract bio-geometrical symmetries, and so the stern looking man in the circle seems to be *someone*, rather than a cipher.'[3] There is no ideal human being, only real people like ourselves, those with whom we live and work, or meet on the street. As you read, I suspect images of people you know and love come to mind, people without whom life would lose much of its meaning. What attracts us to some people as models and mentors of the truly human life? This prompts further questions: is there a connection between 'The Vitruvian Man', someone we are most likely to meet in the gym or on the movie screen, and the icon of Jesus on the wall behind me as I write, whose arms are likewise outstretched, but nailed to a cross? And what is their relationship to the *Shona* sculpture, frontispiece of this book, a more maternal image of the human as relational and nurturing?

The question of the Hebrew psalmist, 'What are human beings?' (Psalm 8.4) is one that reverberates throughout the Scriptures and fills pages of philosophical and theological discourse. Is there an essence, for example, that makes us all human and therefore distinct from other forms of life? If so, what precisely is it? To whom or to what do we turn to find answers to such questions? Are we dependent on our own experience or is there something beyond ourselves, something transcendent that provides us with norms and guidelines for determining what it means to be human? If the latter, how do we discern what they are? And, given the immensity of the universe, how are we to understand ourselves who, according to the biblical tradition, are both made from dust, and yet have a dignity and responsibility within the universe that reflects 'the image of God'?

Answers to such questions are sometimes contradictory, sometimes complementary, but taken together they suggest

---

3 Charles Nicholl, *Leonardo Da Vinci: The Flights of Mind* (London: Allen Lane, 2004), p. 247.

a complexity and mystery that evokes constant exploration. As Michael Mayne, a former Dean of Westminster Abbey, suggests, 'We are most human, most what we are called to be, when we have one foot on the shore of what we know, and one foot in the mysterious unknown ocean.'[4] Mayne was not thinking solely of the mystery of the human unconscious but the mystery of being human as a whole. The truth is, the more we discover about ourselves, the more we recognize that we have only begun to scratch the surface. It makes a difference, then, whether our approach to being human is open or closed to this depth dimension of being human, one that defies neat formulae and definition and is often best explored through art, poetry, drama, music and religion.

Our understanding of what it means to be human, and to be more fully so, has changed considerably over the centuries, shaped by religious and philosophical traditions, refashioned by experience, exploration and experiment in ever changing contexts. Even though there are strong traditions that assert there is some unique human essence that demarcates the boundaries between the human and the animal world, there is no universal agreement on what that is. Many contemporary views suggest that our understanding of being human is something we construct, weaving together what we have received from the past with fresh insight. In recent times there has been a remarkable explosion in self-knowledge as a result of the rise of the social sciences, evolutionary biology and cosmology. The feminist critique of patriarchy has challenged the dominant male model of the human, and people who live in abject poverty or suffer disability daily challenge media models of human flourishing. This makes it impossible for anyone to write *the* definitive book on being human; it is certainly Quixotic to contemplate doing so.

What follows, then, is the sharing of some perspectives on being human and Christian drawn from my own experience and reflection after more than 30 years of teaching on the boundaries of theology, religion and the human and social

---

4 Michael Mayne, *Learning to Dance* (London: Darton, Longman & Todd, 2001), p. 213.

sciences, and many more years of Christian ministry. This exercise has been prompted by friends and former students who, on my mandatory retirement at the age of 65 in 2004, encouraged me to recount the journey that has led me to the conviction that being a Christian is about recovering our humanity, and therefore to elaborate on my understanding of what it means to be a Christian humanist.

In proceeding with this assignment I became aware of a major communications problem. Though written in South Africa, this book will be published in Britain and the United States. Presumably, then, there will be readers in each of these contexts, and possibly elsewhere in the world. Readers bring their own perspectives to the text, which invariably determines how they understand what is written. From my own experience of talking about the themes of this book in different contexts, I am aware that several key words and topics in what follows are differently understood. Even when there is a broad common understanding, there are nuances of meaning that indicate difference. Terms like liberal and conservative, fundamentalist and evangelical, religious and secular, creation and evolution, humanist and even Christian, are laden with diverse meanings as a result of different cultural experience. They are also very confusing at times for people dependent on the media for interpretation. It is too easy to box people into such categories without much thought or understanding. If some label me too liberal and others too conservative, I would be delighted by the ambiguity. I simply ask you not to jump too swiftly to conclusions, but to join me in exploring the issues in a way that might speak to your own situation.

Stories and grand narratives

From the beginning of history we humans have told stories, whether in word, dance, drama or painting, to make sense of our place in the world; stories about our origins, who we are, why the world is like it is, and how we should live. Such myths, epics and sagas began as oral tradition, stories told, heard and ritually performed rather than written and read.

And they have subsequently taken many different forms. The development of writing, printing and now electronic media have made it possible for us to share the stories of many people, many cultures and many traditions, as well as our own. Even though we may read them differently given our varied contexts, the great sagas that have shaped civilizations around the globe provide us with recognizable plots about good and evil, and equally recognizable portraits of villains, heroes and heroines. Cumulatively they help us explore the tragic and celebrate the triumphant, inspiring countless tales and lives that have drawn on them. Telling such stories is a necessary and potent way of handing on wisdom from one generation to another, one culture to another, about our common humanity and distinct personal identities.

Stories shape who we are, informing our values and directing our paths. Not that all stories are good and edifying; though even 'soaps' on TV tell us much about our humanity. Parents tell or read stories to their children, not just to put them to sleep, but to enthral them into a world of meaning, often conveyed through fantasy and fairy-tale. Responsible parents choose the stories with care, just as they also seek to monitor television programmes. Educators select poems, novels and dramas for the school curriculum to introduce learners to a canon of great literature, to stimulate their enjoyment and appreciation, and to empower them to be better human beings. Many people, myself included, relish reading biographies and autobiographies not just because we are interested in the lives of people, but also because they inform our experience, providing us with models of being – or not being – more truly human.

One of the most moving stories I have read in recent times is that told by Martha Beck in her book *Expecting Adam*. Martha and her husband John were graduate students at Harvard University well on their way to careers of academic distinction. Then Martha became pregnant for the second time and discovered that the baby would almost certainly have Down's Syndrome. Although not pro-life advocates, or religious in any formal sense, Martha and John decided not to terminate the pregnancy. *Expecting Adam* tells the story of their struggles, fears and pain. It also tells how the birth of Adam not only changed their understanding of what it means to be a 'normal' human being, but also transformed their lives. Near the end of the book Martha writes:

> I have discovered that many of the things I thought were priceless are as cheap as costume jewelry, and much of what I labelled worthless was, all the time, filled with the kind of beauty that directly nourishes my soul. Now I think that the vast majority of us 'normal' people spend our lives trashing our treasures and treasuring our trash.

She continues:

> Living with Adam, loving Adam, has taught me a lot about the truth. He has taught me to look at things in themselves, not at the value a brutal and often senseless world assigns to them. As Adam's mother I have been able to see quite clearly that he is no less beautiful for being called ugly, no less wise for appearing dull, no less precious for being seen as worthless. And neither am I. Neither are you. Neither is any of us.[5]

Expecting Adam raises many core questions for our understanding of being human and becoming more so. Are the advertising media images of human flourishing our guide to human well-being, or is there another way to approach the matter? Are 'disabled people', people with Down's Syndrome, for example, or those confined to a wheelchair, somehow less than what we mean by being 'fully human'? I don't think so. Indeed, to push 'sick people' out on to the boundaries of society where they are beyond public sight, as too often happens, is to 'turn the idea of health into an idol', robbing all of us of a true sense of what it means to be human.[6] The truth is, every one of us is 'on a health/sickness, ability/disability continuum'

---

5 Martha Beck, *Expecting Adam* (London: Piatkus, 2004), p. 317.
6 See the discussion in Jürgen Moltmann, *God in Creation: A New Theology of Creation and the Spirit of God* (San Francisco: Harper & Row, 1985), p. 273.

and our 'place on this continuum constantly changes; what matters is how we exercise our agency wherever we are on it'.[7] What is more, the way in which we learn to respond to suffering and pain, whether our own or that of others, will shape our humanity and personalities.

We cannot begin to understand our humanity or live humanely without such stories as *Expecting Adam*, whether they move us to tears, to love, to anger, to action, or bring about healing. I recall a workshop on HIV and AIDS in which sharing personal stories opened up fresh insight and enabled participants to discover fresh resources for coping. And who can forget the stories told by the victims of apartheid to the Truth and Reconciliation Commission (TRC) in South Africa, stories that unlocked the past and made healing possible even if not always immediately so? True story-telling, whether in the form of a parable, a novel, a drama, a film, a set of photographs, or shared personal experiences, is a reflection on or interpretation of life in its varied dimensions. Stories told with honesty, like all genuine works of art, break open reality, helping us to see things differently, to see ourselves differently and hopefully to live differently.

Story-telling is dependent upon memory, and is itself a way of remembering essential to being and remaining human. That is why we keep diaries and treasure photographs of significant moments that document the stages on our life's journey, bringing into focus people we love and respect, and recalling them in ways that help us savour the past in the present. That is why remembering the past rightly by a nation in search of a better future is so fundamental, and why the suppression of such memories is so dangerous. Stories evoke hope, whether personal or communal, without which we cannot be truly human. Thus story-telling links memory and expectation in a way that helps make sense of the present.

All of us have a story to tell. Even though most will remain unpublished, all are lived. We do, indeed, spend our years as a tale that is told. Not that all stories can be told, told easily or faithfully, for telling stories makes us vulnerable, is often

---

7 Alison Webster, *Wellbeing* (London: SCM Press, 2002), p. 79.

painful, and we are prone to forgetfulness and self-deception. The stories we tell, whether about ourselves or about others, reveal how we see life and understand what it means to be human. But they do much more. Without telling our story it is difficult to enter into meaningful relationships, even if it is only the sharing of selected snippets over coffee. Stories open our lives to others, inviting them to share in our journey, as we might enter theirs. Antjie Krog's account of the TRC in *Country of my Skull*[8] is evocative reading because she recounts the stories told by apartheid's victims in a way that not only draws us into them after the event, but also into the story of her own experience of what she saw and heard.

Many stories are suddenly and tragically terminated, or run meaninglessly into the sand, lacking significance, or they remain fragmentary, lacking coherence. Unlike classic novels that have a discernible plot and a satisfying conclusion, they find an echo in modern novels that convey the apparent meaninglessness of so many lives. Not all are as bizarre as Franz Kafka's *Metamorphosis* in which a human turns into a cockroach, but many are banal, lives lived on the surface like insects scurrying along the pseudo-marble corridors of a shopping mall. Like Ulysses in the Homeric tale, we wander around not knowing quite where we are or where we are going. How important it is, then, to stop and reflect on our story, for we never quite know how or when it will end.

The fragmentary nature of our stories is part of the reason why many of us find it helpful and necessary to locate our lives within the context of some larger story, or 'grand narrative' such as our national saga or, on a larger scale, the biblical story of paradise lost and regained. Such 'grand narratives' not only give us a shared identity nurtured by a religious tradition or the history of clan and nation, but they also help us to interpret our own journey. Dante's *Divine Comedy* has fulfilled that role for many in the past, as has John Bunyan's *Pilgrim's Progress*, translated into 200 languages, 80 of them African. For many influenced by evangelical missions, *Pilgrim's Progress* became the means for integrating the

---

8 Antjie Krog, *Country of my Skull* (Johannesburg: Random House, 1998).

stages of one's own life into the biblical story, fused together with the lives of many others around the world.[9] In Stephen Crites' words: 'A sacred story in particular infuses experience at its root, linking a man's individual consciousness with ultimate powers and also with the inner lives of those with whom he shared a common soil.'[10] We are drawn into a living tradition. Lesser narratives, but no less important for us, are the genealogies depicted in our own family tree, or the absence of such narratives that tell a different story, one of uprooting, displacement and enslavement. And sometimes, unlikely personal genealogies, as in the biblical story of Ruth, become foundational for an emerging nation.

My paternal ancestors originally came from France and then settled on Jersey, one of the Channel Islands, in the fourteenth century. My grandfather, a master mariner, captained a sailing ship that traded tea between England and China. Eventually after an adventurous life at sea, which included being attacked by pirates and spending weeks adrift on a raft in the Pacific Ocean, he settled in Cape Town in 1883. There he married my grandmother who had arrived at the Cape that same year, from Sussex, England. Both my maternal grandparents came from England and settled in Port Elizabeth in the Eastern Cape at the turn of the nineteenth century. Devout Methodists, grandpa Herbert Hurd became the mayor of Walmer. My mother, as an elder daughter, had responsibilities that denied her an education beyond primary school; my father became a telephone engineer. I was what is called a 'laat lammetjie' in Afrikaans, born six years after my only sibling and sister, Rozelle, with whom I now share a friendship enriched by remembering the stories of the past. My parents were by no means wealthy, willingly selling their car to help pay the fees when the time came for me to go to university. I was the only member of a large extended family to receive such an education.

---

9 Isabel Hofmeyr, *The Portable Bunyan: A Transnational History of The Pilgrim's Progress* (Princeton: Princeton University Press, 2004).

10 Stephen Crites, 'The Narrative Quality of Experience', *Journal of the American Academy of Religion*, p. 304.

I am also privileged to know where I came from. There were many others who came to Cape Town as slaves in the eighteenth and nineteenth centuries, wrenched from the soil, families and communities in which they had been nurtured in East Africa and the Dutch East Indies. Deprived of the relationships that gave meaning to life, not least those with the ancestors or 'living dead', they were depersonalized, robbed of their identities, given derogatory names not of their own choosing, and forced to forge new identities as slaves or free persons. The slave trade was not only a crime against humanity because of the untold suffering it caused, it was also a crime because of the way in which it broke these connections and obliterated identity. Discovering or recovering our roots is part of becoming ourselves. Modern secular individualism simply does not appreciate this sense of interconnectedness or the significance of roots and ancestral memories in shaping personhood.

The idea of the 'grand narrative' is suspect today. Tribalism, jingoism, imperialism and religious intolerance are but some of its offspring that refuse to entertain the possibility that others have the right to live by different stories. White South Africans like myself were, from an early age, introduced to the story of Jan van Riebeeck, the first Dutch governor at the Cape of Good Hope, and to the subsequent saga of European colonization leading up to the Great Trek in the early part of the nineteenth century. This not so 'grand' narrative was meant to shape our identity as white South Africans, giving us a reason for being in Africa, and providing guidelines for the way in which we should relate to indigenous peoples – all of which provided the 'historical' justification for apartheid. There are many other similar narratives of conquest and colonialism.

Yet not all grand narratives are of that kind. Some, like the story of the struggle against colonialism, slavery and apartheid, have a different character, one that applauds human freedom, dignity and equality rather than justifying oppression, racism and discrimination. Likewise, the biblical grand narrative, from the story of creation to the final coming of

God's kingdom, has been read in different ways. For some, it has provided the basis for domination, whether religious, political or environmental; for others, it has been a text that has inspired the struggle for justice, liberation and reconciliation. Despite the justifiable antipathy towards grand narratives, it does seem that we cannot easily live without them; hence there is a ready market for *Star Wars* and *Lord of the Rings*. We need them to help us make sense of our own stories and those of others.

My own story certainly cannot be told or understood except in relation to the South African story of much of the twentieth century. Nor can it be told without reference to the gospel story that has shaped my Christian identity. I still recall how, in Sunday school those many years ago, we used to belt out the children's hymn:

> Tell me the stories of Jesus
>   I love to hear,
> Things I would ask him to tell me
>   If he were here.

The way in which I have grown to understand 'the Jesus story' has changed over the years, just as it has been appropriated in different ways through the centuries. Each of the many Christian traditions is an interpretation of that story, the way in which its adherents relate to the 'grand narrative' of the Christian tradition as a whole. The term 'Christian humanism' suggests one way of interpreting the story, a way that I and others find compelling. Although chiefly associated with scholars of the European Renaissance and some twentieth-century, mainly Catholic, advocates, humanist impulses akin to the spirit of Christian humanism have provided a vibrant cord which has threaded its way through the history of the Church from the prophets of Israel and Jesus of Nazareth to the present day. How I understand that story within the greater Christian grand narrative, and even more, within the human story as a whole, is what this book is about. It is not, let me stress, a theoretical study on what it means to be

human, an anthroplogy, but a confession of faith that being
a Christian is being truly human. This, I suggest, goes to the
heart of Christian humanism.

Confessions, apologia and testimony

Those familiar with St Augustine's *Confessions*[11] will know
that it bears little resemblance to the back pages of a Sunday
newspaper where celebrities tell us about their sexual exploits.
Augustine bares his soul, but he does so with great circum-
spection, not to titillate but to convert the reader. His *Confessions* are autobiographical but not an autobiography. A great
deal we might want to know about his life is alluded to, but
much is left unsaid. What Augustine gives us is a journal of
lived experience cast in the form of a prayer, documenting
memories of a restless heart in search of truth and love, having
been encountered by the beauty of God in whom he discovers
both himself and his peace. In sharing his story, Augustine
reconstructs his life from the perspective of his newly found
faith, locating it within the 'grand narrative' of the history of
sin and redemption. In doing so he indelibly shaped the interpretation of Christianity in the Western world for generations
to come.

The title of my book was conceived while re-reading the
Confessions, an exercise that further encouraged me to draw
on my own life story in order to anchor and communicate
what I wished to say. Let me pause to stress the point. I am
not attempting to write a comprehensive autobiography, or
to tell my story in a linear way, as the reader will soon discover. The bits and pieces told are intended as catalysts for
comment and reflection on the themes of the book. But I also
understand these fragments within a framework larger than
my own life, the story of twentieth-century South Africa, the
church struggle against apartheid,[12] the ecumenical movement

---

11 The edition that I use is in volume VII of *The Library of Christian Classics*
(London: SCM Press, 1955).

12 See John W. de Gruchy with Steve de Gruchy, *The Church Struggle in
South Africa: 25th Anniversary Edition* (London: SCM Press, 2004).

and the academy. What follows, then, is less autobiography and more of a confession, apologia or testimony drawing on selected episodes from my experience mediated by Christian faith. This will help show what I mean by being human, being Christian and being a Christian humanist. In some ways it also reveals my own personal struggles with faith and doubt, with truth and falsehood, with injustice and the sins of privilege, and the ever-present tendency to self-deception.

I was born on 18 March 1939 in Hatfield, then a small, insignificant suburb of Pretoria, now Tswane. Soon after birth, I was baptized in the local Methodist church and given the names John Wesley, as insisted on by my maternal grandparents. On moving to Cape Town in 1943 my parents joined the local Congregational church in which I was later confirmed. But my faith journey only consciously began when, as a teenager, I made a commitment to Jesus Christ as saviour and Lord at a Christian youth camp. At that stage my experience of life was, to say the least, limited and callow, the very opposite of that of Augustine who only came to faith after many years of free living and intellectual searching. I sometimes wonder whether it might have been better if I had waited, as he did, to have some real sins to confess before making that decisive commitment. Decisive it nevertheless was. However others or I might assess it now, whether psychologically or theologically, it was a decision that affected the rest of my life. Many years later I was deeply moved by the former United Nations' General Secretary, Dag Hammarskjöld's account of his own 'conversion':

> I don't know Who – or what – put the question, I don't know when it was put. I don't even remembering answering. But at some moment I did answer Yes to Someone – or Something – and from that hour I was certain that, therefore, my life, in self-surrender, had a goal.[13]

Unlike Hammarskjöld, I could give time and date, and believed I knew who had put the question; but like him, I had a sense that life had a purpose.

---

13 Dag Hammarskjöld, *Markings* (London: Faber and Faber, 1964), p. 169.

Much has happened since that youthful act of commitment made around a campfire in the Western Cape mountains. Interestingly I have thought more about it in recent years than previously, which may have to do with age and the flowering of long-term memory. Undoubtedly my understanding of what Christian commitment means has changed over the years, and many of Augustine's pre-conversion struggles have dogged my post-conversion steps. The same is true for others who have had a similar adolescent experience. I recall some whose faith soon stagnated as though they were in a religious time warp; instead of opening them up to life in its fullness, conversion closed them to its possibilities. I also know of others who gradually or suddenly turned away, regarding their conversion either as a misleading diversion in the process of growing up, or as something that was no longer helpful. Some of my most dogmatic and evangelical friends of those years became ardent 'born again' atheists and secular humanists. I, too, have shared many of the doubts that led to their 'de-conversion', and have discovered that there is sometimes only a thin line dividing genuine faith and honest doubt.

My earliest steps in Christian faith were undoubtedly naïve. How could they have been otherwise? Adolescence is not necessarily the best of times in which to make life-changing, long-lasting decisions. Yet it is the time in which many of us make them, and often have to do so. And there is profound truth in Jesus' teaching that certain things are more evident to children than to adults. In any case, it is sometimes better to make certain commitments before we know too much about what might result. Magellan, young and adventurous, would probably never have set off to find the Spice Islands if he had known what lay ahead of his globe-encircling armada. But it is never good to live without thoughtfully reflecting back upon one's decisions, learning from mistakes and capitalizing on what was good. Isobel and I married young; we had children young; and I was young when ordained to the Christian ministry and began to serve as a pastor of a congregation. I shudder to think back on how naïve we were. But I have grown to recognize the difference between naïveté, a childlike innocence, and what Paul Ricoeur called a 'second naïveté', one that is honed and refined by experience, and yet child-like in its capacity for wonder, appreciation, creativity. I like Sara Maitland's description of 'second naïveté' as a recovery of innocence:

> open-minded, simple-minded without loss of knowledge or integrity, becoming as a child again without the security blanket of lack of data; with a determination to find the world beautiful, magical, wild beyond dreams, dancing its complex patterns of truth, weaving its multicoloured threads of discourse so that all things can be true and we can once more be ravished by the beauty of God as revealed by choice, by loving power, in the whole dense, disorderly, chaotic and joyful universe.[14]

In Christian tradition, baptism (and the confession of faith in Christ that belongs with it) has been understood as the means for restoring our innocence as children of Adam, a 'second birth'. In Catholic tradition, the sacrament of penance, or confession, is the means for its renewal along the journey of life. While these sacraments can become mechanical, performed out of a sense of duty, they are rich in meaning and, as many can tell, often life changing, restoring the innocence of which Maitland writes, or awakening the second naïveté of which I have just spoken. In his deeply moving *A Sorrowful Joy*, Albert Raboteau, great-grandchild of a slave and now a Princeton University professor, tells of his recovery of faith and his reception into the Orthodox Church, symbolized by the 'merciful oil of chrismation, binding together my colors and bringing out their depth'. All the memories of his Catholic childhood, his awareness of nature's beauty, his connection with those who had gone before, including his father killed by white men in the Deep South, and the people who refused 'to demean their human dignity' were 'confirmed, renewed and fulfilled'.[15] Raboteau, as he tells us, discovered the

---

14 Sara Maitland, *A Big-Enough God* (London: Mowbray, 1995), p. 189.
15 Albert Raboteau, *A Sorrowful Joy* (New York: Paulist Press, 2002), p. 51.

reality of forgiveness and reconciliation, and began to write with new vigour and insight, seeing the world with new eyes. In 1964 I was privileged to spend an unplanned week on silent retreat at the Taizé Community in France. As a young pastor fresh from graduate studies in Chicago, I was simply interested in visiting a place about which I had heard so much, on my first visit to Europe. But the Dutch brother in charge of my stay insisted that I go on retreat and 'search my soul' in preparation for confession. Not exactly what I had in mind. As a Protestant unschooled in such practices, it was a tough assignment, but an important one on my journey. It also brought back to mind that part of the process in my adolescent conversion was a mandatory 'confession of sins' without which one could not even begin the journey of faith. Not that I had as much to confess then as I do now, or even had at Taizé after a week of rigorous soul searching.

If confessing that I was a sinner was part of the conversion process, telling others about my new-found faith in Jesus was another essential element. Such testimony is a form of story-telling, and can become as egocentric. Although I was never very good at it and often embarrassed when asked to give it, I shudder to think how arrogant my 'testimony' must have sounded when I did. This notwithstanding, being a Christian does require giving an account of one's faith. That is what is traditionally meant by an *apologia*. It is not an apology for what we are or what we think or do, but a reasoned account of the faith we hold and the hope we have for the world. My confessions in this book are much more an *apologia* or, better, a testimony, rather than a confession of sins. Nonetheless, both are necessary in the Christian journey towards human wholeness. Confession of sin reminds us of human fallibility and failure, while a confession of faith points us towards the restoration of our humanity, human well-being, and the birth of a new humanity. In many respects, what follows is an account of what I, as a Christian, believe, my credo, if you like; but I do not claim that it covers all aspects of Christian faith or truth. It is theological testimony rather than systematic theology.

My understanding of theology as testimony has been shaped by the fact that for much of my life I was engaged in the Church struggle against apartheid, inspired in part by those involved in a similar struggle against Nazism. Let me make it clear, however, that I was no hero courageously manning the trenches, as some were. Like many another pastor and theologian in the situation, my involvement was more within the Church than directly on the political terrain, though obviously the two could not be kept apart in different water-tight compartments.

Many theological voices contributed to my understanding of the Church struggle against apartheid, but those of Karl Barth and Dietrich Bonhoeffer were particularly significant. Barth, a Swiss Reformed theologian, was the foremost Protestant theologian of the twentieth century, and his thought remains influential. His early liberal Christianity and optimistic view of human nature was shattered by the spectre of 'Christian nations' fighting each other in the First World War, and later reinforced by the failure of the churches in Germany to resist Hitler. During the Nazi period, while teaching in Germany, he became a leading member of the Confessing Church until deported by Hitler, and in the post-war years his theology had a major influence on those engaged in the ecumenical struggle for justice and peace. Bonhoeffer, a German Lutheran who was murdered by the Gestapo at the age of 39 in the closing weeks of the Second World War, has left a legacy that continues to influence many Christians of all traditions. He was one of the few theologians who did oppose Hitler from the beginning and showed solidarity with the Jews. 'Confessing Christ' against dehumanizing ideologies and practices was at the heart of the Church struggle in both Germany and South Africa.

I wrote my doctoral dissertation on Barth and Bonhoeffer while I was working for the South African Council of Churches (1967–73), comparing their understandings of the Church.[16] My engagement with Bonhoeffer, in particular, turned out to

---

16 John W. de Gruchy, *The Dynamic Structure of the Church: A Comparative Study of the Ecclesiologies of Karl Barth and Dietrich Bonhoeffer*, unpublished dissertation, University of South Africa, 1971.

be a life-long dialogue, which may help explain the frequency with which I refer to him in what follows.[17] Indeed, my involvement over the years with scholars in the International Bonhoeffer Society has been one of the most stimulating and enriching aspects of my theological journey, connecting me with friends and colleagues around the world who share the same interest in Bonhoeffer's legacy.

As apartheid became the formal policy of government nine years after I was born, and remained the ruling ideology until I was 55, most of my life was lived under its dominance. This obviously influenced greatly the way in which I came to understand the Christian faith, as it also shaped the contours of my life. As the transition to democracy began to transform South Africa in the early 1990s, so my focus shifted from themes of confessing Christ in the struggle for liberation, to the relationship between Christian faith and democratic transformation, to the relationship between faith and art as allies in the renewal of society and the Church, and to reconciliation and the restoration of justice.[18] All of this I would now bring together under the rubric of Christian humanism, 'a critical humanism' that arises out of the Christian gospel, challenging the dehumanizing powers of the world, whether secular or religious, in the interests of human well-being.

There are undoubtedly discontinuities between confessing Christ against apartheid and Christian witness today in a different global and local context. Yet some continuities remain, not least among them being the need to combat violence, racism and poverty.[19] But over and above these challenges, many of us share a concern about the ideological alternatives facing us today irrespective of our particular context or faith commitment. These are no longer defined by the opposing

---

17 See, *inter alia*, John W. de Gruchy, *Bonhoeffer and South Africa: Theology in Dialogue* (Grand Rapids: Eerdmans, 1984).

18 See my three books, *Christianity and Democracy* (Cambridge: Cambridge University Press, 1995), *Christianity, Art and Transformation* (Cambridge: Cambridge University Press, 2001) and *Reconciliation: Restoring Justice* (London: SCM Press, 2002).

19 See the final chapter in de Gruchy, *The Church Struggle in South Africa: 25th Anniversary Edition*, pp. 223–60.

ideologies of the Cold War, but by global economic forces that disadvantage developing nations, by politically dangerous polarizing religious ideologies we broadly and indiscriminately label religious fundamentalism or extremism, and by a pervasive secularism characterized by individual and corporate greed and selfishness. Just as Nazism and apartheid were dehumanizing ideologies, so much of what we now face, not least rampant consumerism, runs counter to the Christian vision of what it means to be human. Today, as during the years of apartheid, confessing Christ has to confront the fact that too often Christianity is co-opted for purposes that contradict the gospel, sanctioning militarism, nationalism and sectarianism in the name of Christ.

Part of the challenge facing those of us who claim to be Christian today is the increasing tendency for the word to be used in the media to imply right-wing 'Christian fundamentalism'. Christian fundamentalists have, in many ways, highjacked the term. As Christian fundamentalism is an issue that I will discuss at some length later on, let me acknowledge at the outset that it is a slippery term, as is 'Muslim fundamentalism', and that not all of it is right-wing or extremist in character. Unfortunately the various theological and historical nuances that scholars attach to the word are generally lost on most people, even though they may be reasonably well informed about the Church and Christianity. Whatever Christian fundamentalism might have meant in the past, today, as I have discovered in different contexts where I have lectured on these themes, most people immediately think of the fundamentalism associated with the southern States of the United States, the so-called 'Bible Belt'. And, by extension, to those forms of Christianity that have a similar flavour or ethos in their contexts.[20] As such, Christian fundamentalism

20 On the history of Christian fundamentalism in the United States, see, for example, George Marsden, *Fundamentalism and American Culture* (Oxford: Oxford University Press, 1980); and in South Africa, see Allan Lance Jansen, *The Influence of Fundamentalism on Evangelicalism in South Africa,* unpublished PhD dissertation, University of Cape Town, 2002. On Fundamentalism more generally, see *Fundamentalisms Observed*, Martin Marty and R. Scott Appelby, eds (Chicago: University of Chicago, 1991).

is not the same as Orthodoxy or Evangelicalism, but a powerful religious sub-culture that is actively engaged in promoting a right-wing political agenda.

Christian fundamentalists are not alone in doing so, and have the right to their convictions as well as to pursuing them in the public arena. But too often such Christian fundamentalism, like that of other faiths, shows little respect for difference. As a result, it rides roughshod over issues of human rights, and gives its support to political programmes that are jingoistic and militaristic in character. No one has expressed this more clearly in recent times than Jonathan Sacks, the Chief Rabbi in Britain, in his book, *The Dignity of Difference*. 'Fundamentalism,' he writes there, 'like imperialism, is the attempt to impose a single way of life on a plural world. It is the Tower of Babel of our time.'[21] In discussing fundamentalism later I will develop this a little more, especially when I refer to my own conversion and experience. But whether fundamentalist or not, much Christianity gives the word 'Christian' a bad name. The sad truth is that Christians and churches do not always live up to their calling, alienating many who might still venerate Jesus but who have little time for his representatives.

Fortunately there is another side to this sobering, disturbing story of the way in which Christianity is so often perceived and experienced, one that meets some of these objections, though never justifying any of them. One that offers more of what unbelievers rightly expect of those who are Christian. There are many Christians who are what Jesus called 'the salt of the earth'; there is a record of Christian service in the world that speaks for itself; there are contemporary Christian prophets who speak out against oppression, and martyrs who have been killed because of their witness to truth and justice; there are Christian scholars whose account of their faith and hope is equal to the most searching questions of its critics; and there is a Christian humanist tradition that expresses the gospel in ways that affirm our common humanity and enable

---

21 Jonathan Sacks, *The Dignity of Difference: How to Avoid the Clash of Civilizations* (London: Continuum, 2003), p. 201.

human flourishing. For the purpose of Christian faith is not to make us religious, but to make us more truly human.

I wish I could simply describe myself as a Christian. But, sadly, there are too many 'Christianities' for us to simply speak about Christianity or being a Christian. For immediately we do we are pressed to declare or confess more precisely what kind of Christianity we espouse. There are many available options: some denominational, such as Catholic, Presbyterian or Baptist, others referring to a transdenominational theological position, such as evangelical or liberal. All such labels beg further clarification once we begin to examine them more carefully. Along with others, I am encouraging the retrieval from the past of another term, namely Christian humanist, a description that I believe has considerable value in the current situation, and one with which I would increasingly wish to identify myself. But how have I arrived at this description of myself, and what does it mean?

There have been many influences, apart from those already mentioned, that have shaped the way in which I understand what it means to be a Christian. The earliest was undoubtedly the liberal Protestantism of the local Congregational church in which I spent my childhood and teen years. My involvement with more fundamentalist-evangelical Christianity at high school and during my early student years at the University of Cape Town (1956) challenged that liberalism and gave greater definition to what Christian commitment is about. Theological study at Rhodes University (1957–60) challenged both my liberal background and my fundamentalist convictions, expanding my Christian horizons by opening my eyes to a more critical but also more dynamic and challenging approach to the Bible, introducing me to the ecumenical movement and the rich liturgical resources of the wider Christian tradition. I was also attracted to the Scottish Congregationalist theologian P. T. Forsyth, whose books, though now dated, I regularly return to for inspiration. This was at a time well before liberation, black and feminist theologies erupted onto the scene and challenged many of my presuppositions.

Isobel and I were married in January 1961 and went to live

in Durban where I became the minister of the Sea View Congregational Church. In 1963 we were given leave of absence to take up a World Council of Churches sponsored Church World Fellowship at Chicago Theological Seminary and, together with our young son Steve, spent a year in that very stimulating environment. We travelled first by boat from Durban to New York via Southampton. Looking back, I still think it is amazing that as late as 1963 it never occurred to us to travel by aeroplane. But landing at New York harbour late in the evening with no one to meet us, nowhere to go, and no plans for getting to Chicago, was just the beginning – a rather disconcerting beginning – of a year of cultural shock. This was, after all, the first time I had been outside South Africa. I have no doubt that the experience of living in a different culture, and taking courses both at the Seminary and at the University of Chicago, were seminal in my own intellectual and personal journey. Equally significant was the fact that we were there at the height of the Civil Rights Movement. This gave me a new perspective on apartheid back home, and made the connection between faith and the struggle for justice more decisive.

On our return to Durban we joined the newly established Christian Institute (CI) led by Beyers Naudé. A Dutch Reformed pastor and moderator of the Southern Transvaal synod, Naudé had decisively broken with his church's support for apartheid and was subsequently defrocked. A former member of the Broederbond, the all-powerful secret society that dominated Afrikanerdom, Naudé became the leading figure in the struggle against apartheid. Though widely acknowledged around the world for his stand, at that time he was a prophet without honour in (white) South Africa. But he was a great example to many of us who were seeking to find our way. He was, I now discern, a true Christian humanist whose ecumenical vision, solidarity with the victims of apartheid and concern for justice and peace arose out of a deep faith in the gospel. There were others who also influenced my life along similar lines during these Sea View years, including Alex Boraine with whom I worked on several projects, and who would later become President of the Methodist Church of Southern Africa, a member of Parliament, and *inter alia* the vice-chair of the Truth and Reconciliation Commission.

In Sea View I organized a CI Bible study group in our church that attracted people from various denominations, including the priest of a nearby Catholic parish. Such study groups were intended to examine the current situation in South Africa from a biblical standpoint and to provide support for people engaged in opposing apartheid. In this heyday of the Second Vatican Council, I gained a new appreciation for the Roman Catholic Church, not least through the influence of Archbishop Denis Hurley, an outstanding progressive voice in South Africa. My increasing involvement in ecumenical initiatives eventually led to my appointment as the Director of Studies and Communications for the South African Council of Churches (SACC) in 1968, based in Johannesburg. At that time Anglican Bishop Bill Burnett was its General Secretary, someone who combined a deep spirituality with prophetic leadership. Burnett later became Archbishop of Cape Town and a major figure in the charismatic movement. During the five years I worked at the SACC, I was also the first Secretary of the Church Unity Commission established in 1967 to seek the union of the Anglican, Congregational, Methodist and Presbyterian Churches in Southern Africa.

Working for the SACC plunged me more deeply into the church struggle against apartheid, and made participation possible in ecumenical events around the country, in various parts of Africa (at that time a difficult enterprise for South Africans), and the wider world. This exposed me to a wonderful range of Christian insight and some remarkable church leaders and theologians. Looking back I can detect the influence of Roman Catholics, Eastern Orthodox, Anglicans, Lutherans, Mennonites, Methodists and of course, many within the various branches of my own Reformed family of churches. And, although I understood myself, and still do, broadly speaking to be a Reformed theologian,[22] increasingly

---

22 See my Warfield Lectures at Princeton Theological Seminary in 1990. John W. de Gruchy, *Liberating Reformed Theology: A South African Contribution to an Ecumenical Debate* (Grand Rapids; Cape Town: Eerdmans; David Philip, 1991).

I found my identity within the ecumenical movement, and especially with those who sought to relate matters of faith and order to those of justice and peace, and those for whom liturgical renewal and the Church's mission were informed both by lively tradition and by contemporary insight. Thus my own personal story gained a new dimension and frame of reference. I became what might be described as a theological and ecclesiastical hybrid. Such hybridity sometimes leads to a loss of roots and sense of tradition, but it immeasurably enriched my understanding and experience of being Christian – and being human.

In 1973 I began my formal teaching career in the Department of Religious Studies at the University of Cape Town. This opened up different vistas, forced me to wrestle more decidedly with the challenge of other religious traditions, and made me clarify my own beliefs and convictions. It also provided a stimulating environment in which to explore the relationship between Christianity and the human and social sciences. But it was only towards the end of my formal academic career, and especially following my appointment as the first director of the Graduate School in Humanities in 1999, that I began to think of myself specifically as a Christian humanist and to reflect on what this might mean in post-apartheid South Africa.

Christian humanism: retrieving a legacy

When I started working on this project and endeavoured to explain to interested friends, both Christian and secular, what I was doing many of them expressed puzzlement and surprise. Could one be both a Christian and a humanist, they would ask? Can the term Christian humanist be meaningfully retrieved today whether within our global or any particular local context? Is there any reason for doing so? Given the history of humanism in general is it not too confusing, misleading and generally unhelpful, especially with a Christian prefix? Has not the Church been more against than supportive of humanist values? In short, for secularists, the term 'Christian humanist' is an oxymoron; for religious fundamentalists it is a betrayal of the gospel; and for many of us, 'isms' hold little attraction. And seeing that Barth, to whom I often turn for inspiration, regarded the term 'Christian humanism' 'an awkward tool' or 'flawed steel',[23] should we not rather affirm a Christian identity and forget about all suffixes, whether humanist or otherwise?

Although the substance of Christian humanism existed long before the European Renaissance, the term is historically identified with a loosely knit group of Renaissance scholars. In many respects, the Renaissance was an era, as Peter Gay reminds us, 'of pagan Christianity'. By that he meant a blending of the best in classical Greek and Roman culture with Christianity, and not the kind of neo-paganism that we would now associate, for example, with Nazism. There was, he writes, 'nothing incongruous about the sight of a Christian Humanist, a Christian Stoic, a Christian Platonist, or even a Christian skeptic'.[24] The truth is, Christianity was the matrix within which the Renaissance was born and nurtured, and many Renaissance humanists were devout Catholics.[25] Thus, what we refer to specifically as Christian humanism had to do initially with the recovery, within a Christian framework, of the legacy of ancient classical traditions, and especially its literature. It is usually traced back to the influence of Francesco Petrarch in the fourteenth century, and then to other notable Italian scholars, Lorenzo Valla and Pico della Mirandola among them, into the next century,[26] before spreading more widely through Europe, evolving differently depending on circumstances and personality. A common denominator was the revival of learning through the study of the Bible, the church fathers, and classical texts in their original languages.

23 As in Eberhard Busch, *Karl Barth: His Life from Letters and Autobiographical Texts* (Minneapolis: Fortress, 1976), p. 366.

24 Peter Gay, *The Rise of Modern Paganism*, The Enlightenment: An Interpretation, vol. 1 (London: Wildwood House, 1973), pp. 256–7.

25 Timothy G. McCarthy, *Christianity and Humanism: From Their Biblical Foundations Into the Third Millennium* (Chicago: Loyola Press, 1996).

26 See See E. Harris Harbison, *The Christian Scholar in the Age of the Reformation* (New York: Charles Scribner's Sons, 1956), pp. 31–68.

In this way Christian humanists sought the transformation of a moribund medieval scholastic culture and the renewal of the Church. This, in turn, prepared the ground for the Protestant Reformation. Indeed, the leading Reformers, Martin Luther, Huldrych Zwingli and John Calvin, along with many of their close associates, were all products of Christian humanism.

Christian humanists were not only scholars and church reformers, but also deeply involved in public life; they were what we now call 'public theologians'. And like John Colet, Dean of St Paul's Cathedral in London at that time, and Erasmus of Rotterdam, they were sometimes also pacifists. Erasmus was undoubtedly the paradigmatic Christian humanist of the Renaissance, someone whose advice was sought by kings, popes and princes. An ordained priest, committed Christian, peacemaker and cosmopolitan scholar, he was remarkably influential in both Church and political circles, though arguably his greatest achievement was his biblical scholarship. In this respect he provided key resources for the Reformation. An initial admirer of Luther, he eventually withdrew his support when schism seemed an inevitable outcome of the Reformer's activity. This was one reason why Protestant theologians have exalted Luther and Calvin at the expense of Erasmus, despite a sneaking admiration of his contribution held by many, Barth and Bonhoeffer included.

Not much was heard about Christian humanism by that name following the Reformation, but the phrase resurfaced in the twentieth century, notably in the writings of the French Catholic philosopher Jacques Maritain, for whom it provided an alternative to the dehumanizing totalitarian ideologies of his day.[27] Three remarkable Jesuits of the twentieth century have likewise referred to themselves as Christian humanists: the palaeontologist Teilhard de Chardin, the martyr Alfred Delp, and the theologian Karl Rahner. For Teilhard, to whom I will refer frequently in what follows, Christian humanism expressed his conviction that the advances of evolutionary science and cosmology needed to be integrated into Christian faith; for Delp, who like Bonhoeffer died at the hands of

---

27 Jacques Maritain, *Integral Humanism* (1938).

the Gestapo, it provided the starting point for a new movement within the Church that took human beings rather than
religion as its starting point;[28] and for Rahner it referred to
the conviction that 'Christianity proclaims a genuine and
"radical humanism"'.[29] There is also much in Bonhoeffer's
legacy to suggest that it is an appropriate term to describe
his own position as it developed,[30] and it has likewise been
used to describe Hans Urs von Balthasar, another theologian
whose contemporary influence has become widespread.[31]
This should suffice, not only to establish the credentials of the
Christian humanist tradition, but also to indicate something
of its diverse character yet common core.

A salutary reason why Christian humanism became a
subject of interest to some during the twentieth century was
because of the dehumanizing impact of totalitarian ideologies
and devastating world wars. Indeed, the topic of humanism as
such engendered much discussion among European intellectuals in the aftermath of the Second World War. One indication of this was a conference held near Geneva, Switzerland,
in 1949 to develop what was dubbed 'A New Humanism'.
Attended by a broad cross-section of European philosophers,
historians, orientalists, natural scientists, theologians and
Marxists, who shared a common concern for the future of
Europe, it was hoped that they would together reach some
consensus on what this 'new humanism' might be. For Barth,
who was one of only two theologians invited to participate,
the conference resulted in a genuine encounter between those
who gathered to discuss the subject. But 'the *concept* of humanism and its definition were surrounded by the deepest obscur-
ity and contradiction'.[32] Invariably associated with some form

---

28 Alfred Delp, *Prison Writings* (Maryknoll, NY: Orbis, 2004), p. 94.

29 Karl Rahner, 'Christian Humanism', in *Theological Investigations
Volume IX* (London: Darton, Longman & Todd, 1972).

30 See my unpublished paper 'Dietrich Bonhoeffer as Christian Humanist',
presented at the International Bonhoeffer Congress, Rome, 2004.

31 See Edgardo Antonio Colón-Emeric, 'Symphonic Truth: Van Balthasar
and Christian Humanism', *The Christian Century*, 31 May 2005, pp. 30–4.

32 Karl Barth, *God Here and Now* (London: Routledge and Kegan Paul,
1964), p. 95.

of secular rather than religious humanism, its meaning then as now was ambiguous, 'lost in a confusion of tongues and interpretations'.[33]

According to Barth's account, two dominant positions emerged in the course of the Geneva conference. The first reaffirmed 'classical humanism' with its roots in ancient Greece and Rome, and the European Renaissance. Conference participants who affirmed this position sought to develop it by integrating the achievements of modern science, together with the humanism of other cultures, in a 'planetary humanism'. The second position that emerged conceived of humanism more in terms of the absence of 'exclusive dogmas' and the advocacy of human freedom. This assumed that the world was intelligible and humans perfectible, though it ended up rather less optimistic about humanity's ability to achieve rational goals.[34] Barth's critique of the conference was not indicative of any opposition to the theme on his part. As he would later write in his *Church Dogmatics*, the Second World War had raised questions about human dignity, human rights and the relationship between people in a new and urgent way.[35] But he was doubtful that the proposed 'new humanism' had the capacity to counter the forces of dehumanization, and so provide genuine hope for the future of humanity. And, as we have seen, he was equally sceptical about the term 'Christian humanism', though not, I suggest, about what it really signifies.

The demise of apartheid, hailed by some as a victory for humanism, has led to much discussion about the need for a continent-wide African Renaissance. Within South Africa itself there are voices advocating a critical humanism that builds on a 'politics of hope' able to face the challenges ahead. Such a humanism, it is argued, must affirm both human dignity and obligation, seek to overcome past hatreds as well as present challenges that threaten human existence, accept

---

33 Puledda Salvatore, *On Being Human: Interpretations of Humanism from the Renaissance to the Present* (San Diego, CA: Latitude Press, 1997), p. 4.

34 Barth, *God Here and Now*, p. 97.

35 Karl Barth, *Church Dogmatics: The Doctrine of Creation*, Church Dogmatics, vol. III/2 (Edinburgh: T&T Clark, 1960), p. 228.

others beyond national borders, be committed to the reconciliation of sameness and difference in the realm of law, and recognize both the risks and opportunities of the new global connectedness that we presently experience.[36] Whether such a critical humanism has, in the long term, the capacity to achieve its goals, it signals a recognition that the future depends on the recovery and affirmation of values and concerns that are humanist in character and quality. But how does this vision of a 'critical humanism' of hope relate to Christianity and the witness of the Church today, both in my own context and more globally – an era so powerfully shaped by the horrendous events of 11 September 2001, and their aftermath?

The term Christian humanist is particularly apposite within the post-colonial, post-apartheid southern African context. Kenneth Kaunda, a former President of Zambia, described himself as such in a book published in 1966 entitled *A Humanist in Africa*. He spoke of a humanist revolution spreading across Africa which aimed at restoring the dignity and national pride of the peoples of the continent who, for so long, had been dehumanized by the forces of slavery and colonialism.[37] He wrote as an African, deeply rooted in its culture and tradition; he also wrote as a Christian, the product of a missionary education. The humanism of which he spoke was not the secular humanism of the West; it was Christian, not one based on a Christianity that contributed to the misery and enslavement of African people but to the renewal of the continent. But perhaps no one has encapsulated the term more, both in terms of his theology and his life, than Desmond Tutu. His theology of *Ubuntu* is precisely what a genuine Christian humanism is about, and his life of courageous struggle on behalf of human dignity and rights, irrespective of ethnicity, religion or gender, has been a beacon of compassion and sanity.[38]

---

36 Achille Mbembe and Deborah Posel, 'A Critical Humanism', editorial, *The Wiser Review*, Wits Institute for Social and Economic Research, Johannesburg, no. 1, July 2004.

37 Kenneth D. Kaunda, *A Humanist in Africa: Letters to Colin M. Morris* (London: Longmans, 1966).

38 See Michael Battle, *Reconciliation: The Ubuntu Theology of Desmond Tutu* (Cleveland, Ohio: Pilgrim Press, 1997).

Christian humanism today cannot simply be an uncritical restatement of past forms unchastened by contemporary struggles for truth and justice, nor can it be a secular humanism with a Christian veneer. Rather it must necessarily be a retrieval of Christianity's core theological convictions and moral values in ways that are critical of and yet constructively engaged with secular culture in serving the well-being of global humanity as embedded in local contexts.

If I were to draft a preliminary manifesto of such a Christian humanism, these would be among the major points that I would make. The rest of my book is an elaboration of them:

Christian humanists affirm the integrity of creation, recognizing that human life is rooted in and dependent on the earth. In a time of environmental crisis, Christian humanists are concerned about the well-being of the earth in all its variety within the universe. Acknowledging the whole cosmos as God's creation, Christian humanists recognize that all of life is bound together in an amazingly complex evolutionary web that evokes humility and awe.

Christian humanists believe that we share a common humanity with all other human beings. We are human beings first, and then only Christian by choice. The biggest threat to the world derives from a refusal by so many, including many Christians, to honour this common humanity and therefore to respect difference. This is demonstrated in every sphere of life, from global economic and environmental policies to gender relationships, from international affairs to the way we relate to the disabled.

Christian humanists believe that we should join with secular humanists and people of other faiths in the struggle for human rights, freedom, dignity, justice and peace, and sustainable policies for the environment. Christian humanists nonetheless affirm a humanism that is distinct because it is shaped by faith in Christ. Being a Christian *humanist* implies that one is committed to human dignity, rights and freedom, and has some real hope for humanity; and being a *Christian* humanist suggests that these commitments and this hope are inseparable from one's faith in Jesus Christ.

Christian humanists believe that the salvation we have in Christ is not about making us more religious but more fully human, reconciling relationships, restoring human wholeness and well-being, and unlocking potential and creativity. Central to this process of humanization is a spirituality rooted in the Bible, worship and prayer, a spirituality of struggle both personal and social for those things that make for genuine peace.

Christian humanists believe that the Christian Church is called to be a sign of the 'new humanity' God has brought into being through the death and resurrection of Christ; and therefore to live, act and hope in ways that contribute to human well-being in all its dimensions, countering the dehumanizing and depersonalizing tendencies of bad religion, secularism and scientism. Christian humanists are ecumenical rather than narrowly denominational in their vision, but recognize that the unity of the Church is as much, if not more about overcoming divisions of ethnicity, nationality, class and gender, as it is about resolving ecclesiastical differences.

Christian humanists today, like those of the past, have a love of learning in search of practical wisdom; a respect for difference yet a commitment to truth; a passion for justice and peace that transcends the confines of national loyalties; and a sensibility to the aesthetic that espouses beauty and encourages creativity. As such, Christian humanists, like those of the Renaissance, seek to relate Christian faith to the best in human culture, whether classical or cultural, whether local or global, whether European or African or Asian.

At a time when many secular people are aware of the pitfalls of modernity and are turning elsewhere for meaning and hope, it may well be that the insights of a critically reworked Christian humanism provide both the language and the perspective for which they are searching – a humanism that affirms genuine transcendence and human well-being rather than one that promotes religiosity or fundamentalist ideas and values; a humanism that is both embodied in the world, and yet driven by a sense of the transcendent. Indeed, a radical human ism that affirms what is true, good, beautiful and human, and seeks the transformation of all that is false, bad, ugly and inhuman.[39] Certainly, people of other faith traditions, Jewish or Muslim for example, with whom I have spoken, respond positively to this position in terms of their own faith commitments. And they do so because it represents a timely counter and alternative to the rampant secularism and religious fundamentalisms that surround us. If such concerns are kept in the foreground, we may yet find Christian humanism a useful tool rather than one of flawed steel.

---

39 See Hans Küng, *On Being a Christian* (London: Collins, 1976), p. 602.

2

Being Human

The readiness of lovers to disregard prudence, to love and to suffer
for it despite status, class, race, nationality and moral merit,
conditions and awakens in us a sense of the mystery and
preciousness of human beings. Raimond Gaita[1]

To be human is to make, to create, and to live out new ways of
being in history. Rebecca S. Chopp[2]

Homo sum: humani nil a me alienum puto.
I am a man, and reckon nothing human alien to me. Terence[3]

God created humankind in his image ... male and female
God created them. Genesis 1.27

We are made from dust. A more lowly origin is hardly imagin-
able. Yet this is what both the Bible and modern science tell
us. All life has its origins in cosmic dust. The Hebrew word
'Adam' derives from 'adamah', which means 'from the earth'.
And there is apparently a distant linguistic connection between 'human' and 'humus' reminding us of our humble roots
in the soil. This is a good place to start our self-investigation,
for it reminds us that we are an integral part of the rest of
creation, and that our present and future well-being is inextricably bound up with the well-being of planet earth. As
St Francis of Assisi exclaimed in his 'Canticle of the Sun', the
earth is 'our mother who sustains and keeps us'. As humans
we have a special status within creation, but we dare not deny
or ignore our earthliness, or abrogate our role as stewards of

---

1 Raimond Gaita, *A Common Humanity: Thinking About Love and Truth
and Justice* (London: Routledge, 2002), p. 27.
2 Rebecca Chopp, *The Praxis of Suffering* (Maryknoll, NY: Orbis, 1986),
p. 125.
3 From Terence's *Heauton Timoroumenos*, 25, quoted in *The Penguin
Dictionary of Quotations*, eds J. M. and M. J. Cohen (London: Penguin, 1960),
p. 392.

the earth's bounty. To do the latter is crass irresponsibility, to do the former is sheer arrogance, pride or 'hubris', widely regarded in Christian theology as the primal sin. A young Bonhoeffer put this with startling clarity: 'The earth remains our mother, just as God remains our Father, and our mother will only lay in the Father's arms those who remain true to her.'[4] This connectedness to the earth is assumed even if not always stated in all that follows; so too are its theological and moral implications. It is an affirmation of our bodily existence, our interdependence with all of creation, and the earthiness of the humanity we share in common with all other human beings, the theme I now wish to explore more fully.

A common humanity

Teaching in the Department of Religious Studies at the University of Cape Town (1973–2004) was an enriching and challenging experience, both because of the subject matter and the varied composition and interest of my students. This variety was mirrored in the department as a whole. Believers and non-believers, devotees and sceptics, rubbed shoulders with each other, as did priests, ministers, rabbis and imams, some lecturers, others students. We did not ask anyone to declare their faith or lack of it; we regarded everyone as a human being interested in exploring the great religious traditions of the world, their texts and beliefs, their rites and ethics, and the many issues that such enquiries inevitably raise about the nature of religion, of life, and of what it means to be human. Although challenged by many other perspectives, at no time was it necessary for me to deny my Christian identity or convictions; rather I grew to respect the convictions of others and the common humanity we shared in seeking the truth and its implications.

However real such academic experiences of common humanity might be, the full recognition of what it means is

---

4 Dietrich Bonhoeffer, 'What is a Christian Ethic?', an address given in Barcelona in 1929, published in *No Rusty Swords* (London: Collins, 1965), p. 47.

never more evident than in times of crisis that override difference. We discovered this more in the struggle against apartheid than we did in the classroom as people of different faiths and none at all joined forces in opposing dehumanizing policies and practices. More conservative Christians, as well as those of other religious traditions, may find it difficult to appreciate the extent to which such sharing together in a common struggle for human dignity and equality challenges and changes one's perceptions, and creates awareness of the priority of being human together.

Experiences of common humanity have occurred in many other times of crisis and struggle, especially when facing natural disasters such as the Asian Tsunami that occurred on Sunday 26 December 2004, killing hundreds of thousands, displacing millions, and causing massive devastation. The terrifying power and fury of a surging ocean unleashed on those Indian Ocean coastlines, the scale of the disaster and extent of the destruction, were almost beyond comprehension. But it was the immensity of the suffering, anguish and pain of injury and death, and the loss of loved ones, livelihoods and futures that was overwhelming and called forth unprecedented humanitarian aid motivated by a profound sense of human solidarity and compassion. Did it really matter that some were Hindu, others Buddhist or Christian, and yet others secular Westerners on holiday?

Like the Lisbon earthquake of 1755 that resulted in a huge death toll, sending shock waves through European society and shattering the optimism of Enlightenment elites, the Asian Tsunami revealed much about our common human nature, not least its frailty within a cosmic and natural order that both sustains and destroys life. We were also reminded that such disasters bring out the best in people. The Tsunami demonstrated the human capacity for courage and heroism, for survival and, against enormous odds, the determination to rebuild shattered lives and communities. Within a week of the disaster babies were born into a new year, one of them named Tsunami, a sign that even that dreaded name could become a symbol of new life and new hopes. It therefore seems churlish to note, though we must, that amidst this abundance of human good was evidence of twisted minds, trafficking in children, corruption and profiteering from the plight of others. This is part of the mystery of being human: the heights to which we can reach, and the depths to which we can sink. As we pondered the Tsunami many of us thought, by way of contrast, of those regions and countries engulfed in violent struggles, and especially of the war in Iraq. If only the billions of dollars that were being poured into weapons and acts of human destruction could be channelled into instruments of human well-being, not just in times of disaster but as a matter of daily policy, the world would be transformed. But this requires a vision of being human that is sadly lacking in many centres of power and terror. It demands a 'will to serve the common good' rather than the 'will to power', a global commitment to justice rather than the pursuit of greed.

It is tragic that some people lose the ability to recognize others as human or human life as sacred. One of the most telling moments in the hearings of the Truth and Reconciliation Commission (TRC) in South Africa came when the lawyer for the family of one of the victims of torture asked the defendant: 'Did you not think that what you were doing was inhuman?' The security policeman's reply said it all: 'I do now!' Black people, so apartheid ideologists propounded, did not have the same needs, feelings and aspirations as Europeans, so they could be paid less, endure pain more, and be educated in an inferior way. There was little acknowledgement that sharing a common humanity bound people together rather than separated them by race and religion; that denying the humanity of others inevitably leads to a denying of one's own humanity; that dehumanizing others dehumanizes oneself. We learnt this in the struggle against apartheid. As long as some people are not free, all are in bondage. Thus it was that the liberation of black people from oppression paved the way for the liberation of white people from being oppressors. Not all white people grasped this opportunity of grace and freedom. Those who did have discovered their humanity in a new way.

The stories told to the South African TRC remind us that

crimes against humanity, in this age of human rights, are by no means something of a past dark age. World wars, the Holocaust, apartheid, ethnic cleansing and genocide were twentieth-century realities, and the new millennium has not started well in this regard. Daily we are confronted by examples of the human propensity for acting inhumanely, deflating any notion we might have of inevitable moral progress. Each time we are tempted to believe that the world is morally improving, calamity strikes, and violence spirals into terror and war. The 'will to power' and the inclination to choose what is not in the interests of the common good are everywhere apparent, continually threatening human well-being and the future of our planet. Acts of sheer brutality, in which the human capacity for evil is so evident, so perennial and so universal, is evidence of something gone radically wrong. We sense our own entanglement in a history of human failure, and know we have an inherent tendency to choose what is neither good nor right for others or us. So to understand what it means to be human we have to recognize this dark shadow side that too often erupts in our personal and corporate lives.

St Augustine, acutely aware of his own faults, described this moral bondage as 'original sin', tracing it back to Adam and propounding that it was sexually transmitted to the rest of us. No one to my knowledge believes the latter any longer, and many have difficulty with the notion of 'original sin' brought about by some primordial Fall from innocence. Clearly a literal reading of the Genesis account, something that Augustine himself quite explicitly rejected, cannot be reconciled with what we know of the cosmos and the emergence of human life. After all, how does an initial Fall with all its consequences, literally understood, fit into current views of an expanding universe if it presupposes an initial perfect world, a paradise lost as a result of our first parents' sin? But the biblical authors, despite their pre-scientific world-view, were not as naïve as many who read the story. Their majestic account of our being made from the dust of the earth in the 'image of God', of our loss of innocence through ignorance, arrogant wilfulness, and a desire to 'play God', remains a truthful depiction of how we experience the world and ourselves. It also tallies well with the gradual awakening of consciousness and moral responsibility towards each other and the earth. You do not have to believe in 'total corruption' to recognize the reality of human nature as 'fallen', and therefore in need of healing and wholeness. No matter how good any of us may be, there is always a corner somewhere in our lives that cries out for forgiveness and grace.

Few debates in recent times have raised such issues more heatedly than those to do with Adolf Hitler. Was he in some sense unique, the personification of evil, or was he human like the rest of us, capable of loving and appreciating music, art and nature, but capable also of mass murder? Both are undoubtedly true. If we deny the second view, we fail to recognize much of the evidence, and avoid the sobering truth that 'normal' human beings like ourselves can engage in acts that dehumanize others as well as ourselves. The truth in the first view is that sometimes human beings can become the embodiment of evil, people who represent and express the cumulative power of the demonic that has been gestating in the womb of a nation or ethnic group, perhaps over centuries. That is why we should always deal timeously and rightly with past violations of human dignity and rights. The way to combat terror is not to wait until it explodes in our faces, but constantly to deal with its causes; not to exacerbate it through accelerating the spiral of violence, but to undermine its potency through pursuing justice.

Although we should always be wary of excuses that deny human choice and responsibility, or somehow shift the blame from our shoulders onto those of others, or the devil, we can discern in history how forces are unleashed that create human monsters given the right circumstances. The truth is that Hitler, like all dictators and demagogues, was not alone. Many people regarded him as a great leader, a hero and a saviour; he had massive support from the populace, and even people of learning, culture and piety succumbed to his spell. They were seemingly impotent in withstanding the Nazi onslaught, incapable, as Bonhoeffer put it, of seeing 'the abyss of evil or the abyss of holiness'.[5] For, indeed, there were others who opposed Hitler and became his victims, among them communists, secular humanists, Jews, Catholic priests and members of the Confessing Church, who exemplify the other, the better, the holy side of being human. But such exceptions prove the rule. Confronted by evil, we human beings frequently capitulate and abscond on our responsibility, too often with spurious religious justification.

We do not need Holocausts or Hitlers, Tsunamis or TRCs to remind us of human sin and corruption, or human courage and compassion in resisting evil and doing good. Daily we are reminded of human fallibility and folly, selfishness and pride, of selfless service and sacrifice, resilience, hope and holiness – all dimensions of being human, some of them sobering, others encouraging and sometimes simply astounding. Coupled with what we know about the human body and mind, about the processes of evolution and the achievements of culture, we are amazed by the complexity of being human; by the range of difference that enriches life and yet produces conflict; by the sameness that is evident in our shared fears, foibles and failures; and by the solidarity that unites us in compassion and motivates deeds of courage and kindness. In all this we recognize bonds that bind us together as human beings despite differences that sometimes tear us apart.

A matter of birth and death

Our humanity is a birthright, the result of an act of procreation. How that birthright is understood by society determines a great deal of our well-being, for it makes a huge difference whether we are all regarded as born equal, or whether some are regarded as less human than others. Holocausts, apartheid and ethnic cleansing are all premised on the latter. But so too is the way in which people have been treated through the centuries because of disability, gender, age, colour or social status. Our definition of 'being human' has

---

5 Dietrich Bonhoeffer, *Ethics*, Dietrich Bonhoeffer Works, vol. 6 (Minneapolis: Fortress, 2005), p. 78.

far-reaching practical consequences, but it is not easy to come by. There is not even consensus on when anyone becomes human. Is it at conception, or at some later, indefinable moment in the womb, or at birth? And when, we might equally ask, is someone no longer human? These are important questions, as anyone who has struggled with such boundary moral issues as abortion or euthanasia will know.

While birth and death are everyday occurrences, everyone who has witnessed either will recognize something of a mystery that cannot be clinically described. But of this we can be sure: we all share a common beginning – birth – and a common ending – death. As certain as our birth unites us in a common humanity, so too does the more sobering certainty of our death. We all die equal even if the circumstances of our death and burial vary considerably in character and quality. The Asian Tsunami killed rich and poor, tourist and fisherman and subsistence farmer alike, with a merciless suddenness that numbed all who witnessed it. But whether we die peacefully or violently, whether we die poor or rich, the awareness of death's inevitability is part of being human. As the years pass, for me now seemingly more quickly than previously, an awareness of the encroachment of death is more pronounced as friends, colleagues and loved ones age and pass on. Age makes us more aware of finitude and temporality, though anyone who has survived life-threatening danger irrespective of age will already have had a foretaste of what is inevitable.

Philosophers from at least Plato onwards have taught us that meditation on death helps us understand and appreciate being human. Birth and death taken together are defining moments in helping us understand what it means to be human and to be part of the universe in which we live. There is a rhythm and purpose in the life cycle that is built into the universe. After all, the universe was born out of cosmic dust generated by the death of the first generation of stars, and the evolution of life has ever since presupposed decay and death in order to bring the new into being. We are made from that dust. So life is not possible without death, without the pain of shedding blood and tears that accompanies both birth and death. That is a rule as real for the well-being of the universe, even if not our immediate personal well-being, as is the law of gravity. Like birth, death unites us with both the cosmos and all living creatures, and especially with all other human beings in a common bond mixed with sorrow, hope and sometimes relief.

Among other things, birth and death remind us that being human involves both being alone and being in relationship. The birthing process begins through a relationship, good or bad as it may be, and one is normally born into a family circle of some kind through which life is nurtured. And whether or not one chooses to marry, family relationships, whether surrogate or natural, are an essential part of being human. Yet, while gestation in the womb is the most intimate of all relationships, the trauma of being born and the cutting of the umbilical cord is the beginning of a life in which parting and painful separation from others becomes a norm. In the end, separation is the most tragic element in death, even if some believe in a promised reunion with loved ones beyond the grave.

Although friends, family or travellers on a fated aircraft may surround us at the time of death, death is experienced by us all as individuals. Not only do we die alone; in dying we are isolated from those with whom we have shared life. Thousands upon thousands may die together as a result of natural disasters, but each of us dies *alone* in an act that separates us from others. This sundering of contact with those who remain is in large measure the sting of death. One friend whom I visited a few hours before her death told me that the hardest part of dying was not living long enough to see her grandchildren grow up and achieve their goals in life. She would not live to see the story told by their lives. While being alone is often something longed for, cherished and sometimes needed, the dread of loneliness and the fear of death are on the same continuum. So, too, is the fear of being forgotten.

By focusing on birth and death, then, we are able to discern one of the deepest dimensions of being human, namely being in relation to others. While relationships are often destructive they constitute an essential element of what it means to be human; while times of being alone may be essential for our well-being, they are only so within the context of life lived in community with others. The *Shona* sculpture, frontispiece of this book, well expresses this relational character of being human, something so profoundly expressed in the Xhosa phrase *Umntu Ngumntu Ngabantu*: we exist as humans in and through others, a concept abbreviated in the word *Ubuntu*. We exist through others, and we find ourselves, as well as define ourselves, in relation to them. Even those who pride themselves on being 'self-made individuals' cannot exist except in relationships, however good or bad, close or distant. The fact is, we all had mothers, and we all live in spaces inhabited by others; even hermits cannot escape entirely from this, and prisoners in solitary confinement hunger for human companionship.

In the first Genesis creation narrative (1.26–7), the acknowledgement that humanity is created 'male and female' reminds us that relationality is fundamental to the biblical understanding of being human. Among the many Christian interpretations of human beings created in the 'image of God' (the *imago* Dei), the idea that this reflects God's own relational character as triune, and therefore our innate capacity for a relationship with God and other humans, is compelling. But in the Western world from the time of the Enlightenment to the present, an undue emphasis on the individual has compromised our sense of relationality and thus undermined our humanity and connectedness to earth. So we need some clarity on what it means to be both an individual and a person in sharing a common humanity.

Individuals, persons and being human

The post-Enlightenment emphasis on the individual in the West was necessary in the struggle for human rights against the dehumanizing injustices of authoritarian and totalitarian cultures and regimes. Today we rightly applaud individual initiative and creativity, the taking of individual responsibility for our actions, and protesting against anything that makes us simply part of a mass, cogs in a giant wheel, controlled from above. We often say of someone that she or he is a real individual, by which we mean that they stand out in a crowd, they go against the stream, they 'do their own thing' rather than obey convention. But such individualism is ambiguous. It may well express a laudable spirit of nonconformity; it may also show little concern for others. Individual rights, a necessary term in law, can be misused in ways that defend unjust structures and policies, as we have discovered in South Africa where such rights can be abused in denying the more basic rights of others both as human beings and persons. Such individualism betrays that essential element in being truly human, namely being in relation to others. Self-interested individualism, such as we often associate with North American society, was never endorsed by its great social philosophers.[6] Individualism made absolute is fraught with dangers for society, as it is for us as human beings.

Martin Buber, the Jewish scholar who once described himself as a 'Hebrew humanist',[7] taught many of my generation the difference between relating to the other person as an 'it' or object rather than a person or 'Thou'.[8] But his analysis of the 'I–Thou' relationship is more complex than is often thought, for he understood how demanding it is to maintain the intensity of a direct 'Thou' relationship with anyone. Almost inevitably the routine of life results in the other becoming an 'it' in some sense. Regarding another as an 'it', that is, as an object that makes no transcendent demands on us, often happens in the world of business or the academy where the other is reduced to an e-mail address, a cipher or a disembodied mind. This may not be dehumanizing in the same way as torture, but it is depersonalizing, and can so easily deteriorate into the abuse and manipulation of others. I have made this distinction

6 See Robert Bellah, et al., *The Good Society* (New York: Alfred A. Knopf, 1991), p. 294.

7 Aubrey Hodes, *Encounter with Martin Buber* (London: Allen Lane, 1972), p. 82.

8 Martin Buber, *I and Thou* (Edinburgh: T&T Clark, 1958).

between depersonalizing and dehumanizing intentionally, for it draws attention to a difference between being human and being a person, and the rights that are attached to both. But I am aware that we must not make such distinctions too rigidly, for every human being is a person, and every person a human being.

Whereas being human is a birthright, personal identity is constructed during the course of our lives, from the moment of birth until death, distinguishing each of us from everyone else. It is the particular story that we live, the construction of our humanity as a person. Such personal identity, which can be traced among other things to our particular genes, is therefore inseparable from our bodies, our gender and sexuality, the culture and context in which we live. That is why simply relating to the other in some disembodied way as an 'it', or 'spirit', or 'universal human being' unrelated to a particular culture or context, is less than personal and therefore less than being human.

This notion of being a person goes back to antiquity and derives in part from Christian tradition, especially from the way in which the doctrine of the Trinity was formulated in the early centuries of the Church's life. When Christians speak of God as triune, we do not mean that 'Father, Son and Spirit' are three individual gods, but three persons; that is, their identity is distinct but never in isolation from each other. God is not an Absolute Monad, an impersonal force, but some One who is by nature relational and who relates to creation and to human beings. This understanding of God helps us discern that being personal is always interpersonal, which, as I have already suggested, is one way of thinking about what it means for us to be created in the 'image of God'. Understanding God and ourselves in this way also helps us grasp the importance of affirming both sameness and difference as essential to relationships.

I am often more amazed by how different human beings can be, than by the common humanity we share. Whales and baboons, which abound where we live, may have some individual traits, but I am not sure their parents are as amazed as Isobel and I are by the differences between our children, Steve, Jeanelle and Anton. We often wonder how we could have given birth to people who have developed so differently into their own unique selves. Yet there is also a sameness that makes them part of the family, expressing bonds that are deeper than difference. The same is true of us as parents. Husband and wife, though 'one flesh' according to the Bible, are invariably different in personality and character, something that should and usually does enrich their separate personalities rather than alienate them from each other. Certainly I would have been a different person if I had not married my wife and if I had not been father to my children – all of whom taught me so much, perhaps without knowing it. The same is true, though in different ways, with regard to friendships. Without such relationships we lose something of our humanity. As Bonhoeffer wrote to his close friend Bethge near the end of his life:

> But what is the finest book, or picture, or house, or estate, to me, compared with my wife, my parents, or my friend? One can, of course, speak like that only if one has found others in one's life. For many today man is just a part of the world of things, because the experience of the human simply eludes them.[9]

In making distinctions between 'being human', 'being a person' and 'being an individual', and perhaps especially in trying to define what we mean by *person*, I know that I am entering a minefield of debates and theories that have occupied scholars over the years. Not only are there conflicting metaphysical, anthropological and biological views that inject into the debate such notions as soul, species and genes, but also questions that have to do with embodiment. My discussion is informed in part by such debates, though I do not intend to enter into them here. But it is necessary and helpful to make and keep in mind the distinction between being human in

---

9 Dietrich Bonhoeffer, *Letters and Papers from Prison* (London: SCM Press, 1971), p. 386.

common with others, yet different as persons who embody that humanity. And, to go further and insist that while being a person and being human are inseparable, there is something more fundamental about being *human*, something that binds us together despite personal difference.

Personal identity has to do in part with our individual uniqueness, our difference from others, while being human is contingent on sameness. If every human being were entirely different, sharing no basic characteristics, it would be impossible to live together in society, to be human. Rather than distinguishing us from others, our humanity unites us with others. Geneticists tell us that the differences between human beings, irrespective of where they come from, are biologically virtually negligible, even though each of us is uniquely stamped by our DNA. They also tell us, incidentally, that our relationship to the animal world is much closer than was previously thought, and we share 99 per cent of our genes with chimpanzees. Some animals, dolphins for example, also appear more intelligent than humans in certain respects. This may be corroborated by the fact that few animals died in the Asian Tsunami, suggesting a 'sixth sense' that warned them of danger, prompting them to move speedily to higher ground.

'Being human' expresses a commonality that has been and continues to be variously described, but whatever the terminology and discourse used, we discern common propensities in all humans. Each of these may be understood and described differently, and they may be displayed in various ways and to varying degrees from person to person, and especially from culture to culture. We are all aware of the human capacity to love and to hate, to share and to greedily hoard, to speak the truth and to lie, to serve and to dominate, to hope and despair, to express joy and sadness, to embrace and shun others, to feel guilty or ashamed, and to relish acceptance and forgiveness. In this sense, we all share a common humanity, even though we all have distinct personalities in and through which that humanity is expressed.

To affirm the distinct ways in which our humanity is embodied in us as persons is not to reject the sameness that unites us, but to recognize that every human being is also different *and that these differences matter.* They define who we are as human beings. We have names, a sense of where we have come from and where we belong. Many also have titles to demarcate identity and establish status, differentiate us from others, and identify us with peers, colleagues or other social and cultural groups. We define ourselves, and others may do so as well, in terms of family, religion, culture, gender, nation, business, education, occupation, as well as in terms of interests, sport or hobbies. We are not disembodied souls, and these dimensions of our existence make a difference to who we are as persons. The fact that I am a white male South African is part of who I am, and also who I have become in the process of my life. A major indicator of our well-being or wholeness is the extent to which we have become integrated personalities; that is, persons in whom the various elements that make us who we are, are embodied in a way that enables meaningful relationships with others who are different from us.

The denial of the personal identity of others, just like regarding them as less than human, has a long and painful history that needs no further documentation here. But it is sobering to remember that it was the influence of such great minds as the Roman senator Pliny the Elder whose fantasizing about inhabitants in other parts of the world had such a negative influence on the attitudes of Europeans well into the Renaissance. The 'other' was simply inhuman by European criteria, and was given a name that became a stereotype. Such thinking undoubtedly shaped the attitudes of those who embarked on voyages of 'discovery', and even though evidence indicated the opposite, colonialists and settlers who followed the first explorers retained many preconceived jaundiced views. Many still do. Prejudging others in terms of our own self-understanding and cultural norms is universal – a negative trait of being human that we all share. Such stereotyping is depersonalizing, something that feeds xenophobia, and sometimes results in genocide and ethnic cleansing; that is, crimes against humanity.

Depersonalizing is not precisely the same as dehumanizing, though they are undoubtedly very similar and often merge. For this reason I hesitate to distinguish between them. But by doing so, we get a better sense of the difference between being a person and being human. Being in prison is depersonalizing, but prisoners have human rights; being tortured is dehumanizing, it is a denial of those rights as human beings. Depersonalizing is traditionally part of prison, army and other forms of institutional life, including so-called mental institutions or even hospitals, where people are often reduced to numbers and ciphers, or where they are known by demeaning names, described by tasteless epithets, and dressed in drab uniforms. Such depersonalizing is almost inevitable and, though by no means ideal or to be encouraged, it is a step or two away from dehumanizing others. Dehumanization occurs when, for example, prisoners are denied the human rights they do have, as when they are tortured, raped, maimed and lynched. Dehumanizing is not simply physical abuse, it is also emotional and psychological.

Apartheid became a crime against humanity because it made personal identities and differences absolute, thereby denying a common humanity and, in the process, degrading the identity people had; in short, dehumanizing them. Segregating people into racial groups defined by physical appearance and cultural difference, then codifying this in identity documents that determined where people could live, what kind of education they could receive, what work they could do, and who they could marry, both depersonalized and dehumanized the other. And it all began by a refusal to accept that all shared a common humanity. The Black Consciousness Movement, led by Steve Biko in South Africa, was an affirmation of a common humanity through recovering an identity that had been abused.

A sense of being human together, of sharing a common humanity, shapes the way in which we live, behave and act towards each other. Consider for a moment Jesus' parable of the Good Samaritan (Luke 10.25–37). Some of those who passed by on the other side, religious types, might have regarded the wounded traveller as an 'it', an object by the side of the road. Some might have acknowledged him as a person with a name and an identity. But religious duties demanded that they should not stop to help, and perhaps the identity of the victim was such that he was not regarded as worthy of attention. What if the wounded person had been a Pharisee or a priest, might that not have altered the reaction of the Pharisee and priest who passed by? But the Good Samaritan, a person whose ethnicity and religion should, according to current stereotypes, have led him to pass by on the other side, recognized a fellow human being. This bound them together as humans and laid an obligation upon the Samaritan to offer help and support. In other words, the recognition of a common humanity became the basis for a moral act. So being human is not simply something given at birth, something we share with every other person, it is also something we have to strive for, appropriate, make our own; and we do so not least in treating others as we would have them treat us – as human beings. In this process we become more truly human – and, inseparably and invariably so, more truly our individual, personal selves.

Human well-being

During the year Isobel and I spent in Chicago, I was privileged to listen to many great scholars, including the philosopher Gabriel Marcel, and Paul Tillich, who was the major contemporary theologian I had studied during my final year at Rhodes. But perhaps the person who had the most influence on me was Ross Snyder, a professor of Christian education, who was appointed my mentor. He was a remarkable human being, something of a homespun theologian rather than an academic one, who believed that much 'theological talk' took one away from reality into the realm of abstraction. His aim was to develop theological insights incarnate in human life. I well recall his first seminar. After five years of formal training in the humanities and theology at South African universities, I was accustomed to listening to lectures and making copious notes. Such discussion as there was, was largely cerebral, the interaction of minds. So I was taken by surprise when Snyder began his first seminar by asking each of us to write a response to the question: 'Who am I?' Snyder got me thinking much more deeply than I had before about my identity as a person, human being and pastor. Several years later he published a little book entitled *On Becoming Human*. In the opening paragraph, he wrote: 'This is a book about becoming human. Something we are always about, but never finish.'[10]

If, as Alexander Pope once observed, 'to err is human', it might be inferred that becoming 'more human' implies that we are even more prone to making mistakes. But what it really means is that, to use this example, we are more able to learn from our mistakes, and more willing to forgive others who make mistakes to our disadvantage. In other words, the acknowledgement of our erring, or confessing our sins, is an essential part of becoming more truly ourselves, of building sound relationships with others, and of learning from our experience. It certainly is a precondition for reconciling people who have been estranged, whether at a personal level or more broadly within a society that, like South Africa, has been long characterized by racism and injustice. Confession of sins is good for the soul not least because it opens us up to the possibility of forgiveness and renewal. As I have suggested elsewhere, the process of such confession is similar, whether before God, between persons, or more broadly within society, as in the Truth and Reconciliation process in South Africa.[11] So, too, are the dynamics of forgiveness that restore human dignity and worth, and rebuild relationships.

Becoming more human has to do with the development of our capacity to love, to trust, to forgive, and to be angry when it is right to be so, even if these are expressed in ways that are different. Alongside these is the deepening of the capacity to imagine, to experience awe, to sense injustice, to recognize

10 Ross Snyder, *On Becoming Human* (Nashville, Tenn: Abingdon, 1967), p. 9.

11 John W. de Gruchy, *Reconciliation: Restoring Justice* (London: SCM Press, 2002), pp. 106–11.

beauty, to distinguish wisdom from knowledge, to discover joy, to laugh, to live responsibly, and to risk vulnerability. Human well-being has to do with the development of such human capacities in each person in ways that are appropriate to that person, ways that enrich life, enable self-worth, heal, restore and promote mental and bodily health, and develop a sense of connectedness to the earth. I like Alison Webster's description of human well-being:

> It has to do with the interweaving of the psychological, the physical and the spiritual; it includes an element of how we inhabit our personal histories and how we negotiate these in our present; it depends upon our inter-relationships with others – relationships which offer the possibility of harm and of flourishing – and, finally, it involves questions of identity. Well-being must be about naming oneself, not being named by others; naming our limitations as we understand them, not as others do. And living with them, while also extending ourselves in ways that do not undermine our naming.[12]

From a specifically Christian perspective, the guidelines for becoming more human are found in Jesus' Sermon on the Mount and especially the Beatitudes (Matthew 5), for they reflect Jesus' own embodiment of what it means to be truly human. I will say more about this later.

Becoming more truly human, and in the process becoming more truly ourselves, is largely about changes, some great and others imperceptible. It is learning to know ourselves, recognizing strengths and weaknesses, and knowing how to deal with both in ways that enable maturity. 'To live,' wrote John Henry Newman in another connection, 'is to change, and to be perfect is to have changed often.'[13] Becoming more truly human, then, is a life-long task, like learning a craft. We are given our humanity in the womb, but the project of becoming more truly human, and therefore more truly ourselves, of

---

12 Alison Webster, *Wellbeing*, p. 21.

13 John Henry Newman, *An Essay on the Development of Christian Doctrine* (London: Penguin, 1973), p. 100.

achieving well-being, remains with us to the end. If being human is something given, becoming more truly human is a 'work in progress', something 'we are always about' as Snyder put it. And this is inextricably bound up with our development as persons.

Academics use the phrase 'work in progress' to refer to the research they are doing, not its eventual outcome. It has to do with process, with the recognition that there is much still to be done before publishing the result of their research. All that can be said thus far is tentative, even though at a certain stage the research takes a form that anticipates its outcome. The writing of a book is much the same. It is often a messy process, starting with an idea, then trying to discover direction and finally weaving a coherent pattern. Alan Paton once told me that he seldom found it necessary to revise a manuscript after he had written it. But that is not true for most of us. Writing essays and books does not come easily or quickly. In a similar way, before the birth of a baby there is a necessary period of gestation during which the outline emerges and the various parts take shape and become more clearly defined. It is much the same with becoming more truly human and more truly ourselves: it is a life's work in progress, a mixture of pain and elation. One that is determined by a variety of factors, some given – genes, social environment and the like, that may well limit options – and others chosen. If our common humanity is something given, everyone's birthright, becoming more truly human is shaped by choices and responses we make, in which we become more fully ourselves, more aware of our common humanity, and when we nurture the humanity of others. The wonder in all this is that as people become more truly human, their different personalities are enhanced in terms of their own capacities – they become more distinctly themselves yet more aware of their relationship to others.

We do not have control over all the changes that take place in our lives. Other people, outside factors, the social environment in which we live, and our own bodies keep on changing us. Ageing, for example, is part of being human, and there is not a great deal we can do to prevent it from happening even if we can slow the process. We can remain, as some would say, 'young at heart and in mind', an art that Ross Snyder himself perfected. So while we cannot avoid growing older, we can learn to handle change better. Personal growth towards maturity is about learning from past mistakes and making better choices, of learning about our strengths and weaknesses, and learning to master our wills rather than being at their mercy. Privilege is about having more choices than most others, and the resources to pursue those made. It carries with it greater responsibility for what we do with our lives.

Privileged people, and I count myself among them, are not necessarily the most adept at becoming more truly human despite all the opportunities available to them. In fact it is quite often the reverse, for becoming more truly human is about character not status, wisdom not degree certificates, relationships not self-made or inherited wealth. So it is often people who are disadvantaged, people who struggle against great adversity, who help us to discern best what it means to be truly human. Examples of this abound in South Africa where suffering and struggle have so often brought out the best in people, and where so many have demonstrated such a remarkable capacity to be truly human without privilege, and to become wonderful people.

The German word *Mensch* helps capture something of the sense of what I am getting at. When we say of someone, that he or she is a genuine human being, a *Mensch*, we are not denying their personality, we are affirming a quality of being that we can discern in all such people, a quality of being that shines through and shapes who they are in themselves. Referring to someone as a genuine *Mensch* indicates a special quality of being human that is *embodied in that person*. I can think of several people I know well who are, for me, genuine human beings even though they are all very different people. Yet while their common humanity is expressed variously, there is an almost tangible, luminous quality they have in common, the quality of being truly a *Mensch*. But, we must now ask, does 'being religious' help or hinder us in becoming more fully human, more truly ourselves?

3

Being Religious

... religion can be defined, with greater or lesser success, more than fifty ways. Jonathan Z. Smith[1]

A theological evaluation of religion and religions must be characterized primarily by the great cautiousness and charity of its assessments and judgments. Karl Barth[2]

Religion that is pure and undefiled before God, the Father, is this: to care for orphans and widows in their distress, and to keep oneself unstained by the world. James 1.27

The Durban suburb of Sea View where I began my ministry in 1961 comprised both Indians and Europeans (as white people were then called). There was at least one Hindu temple in the vicinity and several more in nearby Cato Manor. For that reason I became interested in studying the relationship between Hinduism and Christianity and registered for a doctoral degree at the University of Natal on the Indian philosopher Savarapalli Radhakrishnan. Radhakrishnan, a devout Hindu, had been a professor of philosophy at Oxford University, and was particularly well known for his attempt to show how Hinduism represented the kernel of all religions. So I set myself the task of studying his thought and did so for a year or two during which time I also had conversations with Hindu swamis of the Divine Life Society. These studies came to a halt when I went to Chicago, though they did influence the future course of my life, as I shall now tell.

Towards the end of my time as director of studies and communications on the staff of the South African Council

---

1 Jonathan Z. Smith, 'Religion, Religions, Religious', in *Critical Terms for Religious Studies*, ed. Mark C. Taylor (Chicago: University of Chicago Press, 1998), p. 281.

2 Karl Barth, *Church Dogmatics I/2: The Doctrine of the Word of God* (Edinburgh: T&T Clark, 1970), p. 297.

of Churches (SACC), I launched the *Journal of Theology for Southern Africa*. The *JTSA*, which first appeared in December 1972, incorporated the Lutheran journal *Credo* and the journal *Ministry*, published in Lesotho, but soon took on an identity of its own as a leading theological journal in the region. In an attempt to gain authors and subscribers, I travelled around the country and further afield, eventually visiting the Department of Religious Studies at the University of Cape Town. In the course of conversation, the Head of Department, John Cumpsty, expressed interest in my earlier studies on Hinduism, and invited me to teach on a one-year contract. This took me by surprise. I was not planning to leave the SACC, but I did have a sense of calling to teach theology. Was that possible in a department of Religious Studies, I asked myself, especially when contracted to teach the Indian Religious tradition? But it was an irresistible opportunity even though it meant leaving Johannesburg as a family without much sense of security for the future.

Looking back, I must confess to a certain embarrassment, as I was by no means an expert in Indian religion. But for several years I immersed myself in the literature and entered into discussion and friendship with people who knew far more than I did. It was a rewarding experience. In the end I had a reasonable grasp of the subject, with a new respect for the religious traditions of others, and the way that people of other faiths perceive Christianity. I also came to appreciate why some students brought up in the Christian tradition were, at that time, finding Eastern religions more attractive. Many had never experienced a vibrant Christian spirituality, and others were alienated from Christian fundamentalism. They were searching for something authentic, more spiritually satisfying. All of this helped prepare me in unanticipated ways for teaching Christian studies, to which most of my academic career was subsequently devoted.

I recall one undergraduate student, early on in my teaching career, asking whether she had to be 'religious' in order to study 'religion'. If she had not been so earnest I think all of us around the registration table would have laughed out loud. Not at her, or because her query was unreasonable, but because it demonstrated an understandable but wrong conception of what a department of Religious Studies is about: namely, to introduce students to the various religious traditions, their practices, values and beliefs, and to explore the questions about life and death they seek to answer. You do not have to be religious or have faith in God to do that. Religious studies can assist in the study of theology in a variety of ways, but doing theology, and specifically Christian theology, is different from the study of religion; it is 'faith seeking understanding', as St Anselm put it.

Perhaps the major reason why we reassured our enquiring student that she did not have to be religious in order to study religion was our awareness that previous or present religious experience sometimes prevented people from doing so openly and honestly. There were students whose religious piety and conviction made them suspicious of and antagonistic towards what we were teaching, fearful that they would lose their faith. But there were others who would have nothing to do with Religious Studies for the very opposite reason; they had had bad experiences of religion, whether at home, school or church, that had turned them against religion of any kind, and especially for most, against Christianity. This was particularly true of those who had been brought up in strict religious homes or churches, irrespective of denomination, or those who had been 'converted' as teenagers, as I had, but who had begun to have serious doubts about the claims of evangelical or fundamentalist Christianity. For many of these students, coming to university was a liberating experience, not always for the good, but often as a step towards responsible maturity. In the process, some found a more satisfying faith, while others became more alienated from religion, confirmed in their secular lifestyle and world-view.

I could identify with many of these students, whether religious or secular, because I had myself travelled along a similar path. I had come to study at the University of Cape Town in 1956 in preparation for becoming a teacher or possibly a minister, something encouraged more by my mother than my father. There was no department of Religious Studies in those days, so studying religion as such was not an option. But the study of the humanities was, for me, the beginning of a journey not away from faith but more deeply into faith. It could have been otherwise. Nonetheless, I do understand why, for many, exposure to classical and critical contemporary thought leads them away from Christian faith and the Church. For them it often seems that in order to become fully human they have to break free from the apron strings that have previously tied them to their religious upbringing or to adolescent religious conversion.

As it turned out, teaching Christian Studies in a department of Religious Studies proved to be deeply worthwhile. Although theology was not really what the Department was about, the situation in which we then lived, the needs of many pastors and priests in the community, and the lack of other options, made it a necessity. Together with my friend and colleague, Charles Villa-Vicencio, we developed a graduate programme that attracted students from far and near, many of them already ordained, who were committed to doing theology rigorously in a South Africa that was then, so it seemed, descending rapidly into civil war. This was during the 1980s when we lived through two states of emergency. The programme did not compromise on academic toughness and was as thorough as any other comparable to it, but it had a contextual flavour that proved to be significant for our students, many of whom spent time in prison during their years of study because of their anti-apartheid activities.

These were the years during which the *Belhar Confession* and *Kairos Document* were published,[3] texts that became seminal for what we were doing; years when the liberation theologians of Latin America, and the black theologians of both North America and South Africa spoke to us in such a decisive way. Nonetheless, we took seriously our responsibilities as members of a department of Religious Studies, territory that would have been alien to many of our theological heroes, but a location that proved to be of great value. Theology has

---

3 See de Gruchy, *The Church Struggle in South Africa*, pp. 187–200.

a great deal to learn, I believe, from the more general study of religion, just as it has from the social sciences as a whole. But what precisely is religion? And is being religious part of being human, or necessary for being more fully so?

Religion and piety

Words like 'religion' and 'religious' are notoriously difficult to define. We speak about world religions such as Judaism, Buddhism or Christianity because they have certain things in common. There are strong family resemblances between some of them as among the Indian religious traditions (Hinduism, Jainism and Buddhism), or those that derive from the Abrahamic tradition (Judaism, Christianity and Islam), or those traditional to sub-Saharan Africa and Native America. And there is a certain affinity between people who share religious moral convictions, mystics of all traditions, and religious leaders who join together in efforts to promote peace and justice in the world. Inter-faith forums and the World Parliament of Religions are realities because there is something that relates religions and distinguishes them from other movements and institutions. But to lump world religions together in some undifferentiated mass is unhelpful and an injustice to all.

Particular religions have views, but not religion as such. Indeed, speaking about world religions in general, or talking about a religious view on some subject, soon runs into difficulty. To speak of religion *in general*, for example, as 'the opiate of the people', as Karl Marx did, is problematic, for it was a view shaped by a particular historical context. Similarly, the distinction made between 'true religion' and 'false religion', or between 'revealed' and 'natural' religion, as used within Christian history, makes sense within that tradition, but cannot be applied to religion as a whole. Even within Christianity, such value judgements are hotly contested. And I am certain that my understanding of 'bad religion' as dehumanizing, and 'good religion' as humanizing, whether applied to Christianity or other religions, is by no means universally acceptable. Robertson Davies, a distinguished Canadian novelist, provides a good example of the problem in *The Merry Heart*, a book of his mature reflections. Posing the question: 'What do we mean by religion?' he answers: 'Many people cannot separate the words from orthodoxy – some code of belief that has been laid down to which the religious person tries to adhere as best he may.' He then cites Christianity as the dominant example of such religion in his country, saying: 'Christianity asks its followers to strive for human perfection, thereby bringing nearer the Kingdom of God which will bring peace and perfection to our world.'[4] While this may be a popular view of Christianity and contains more than an element of truth, few, if any, Christian theologians would agree that it is a wholly satisfactory one, or one that is true of religion in general.

One of the books that helped me most to clarify the use of the term 'religion' was Wilfred Cantwell Smith's classic study on *The Meaning and End of Religion*. In it he shows how we use the word 'religion' in four distinct ways. The first way has to do with personal piety; the second way refers to a system of beliefs, practices and values expressive of what some scholars refer to as particular religious 'world-views'; the third way describes religion as a social and historical phenomenon embodied in institutions; and the fourth way distinguishes 'religion in general' from other things such as art or politics.[5] With the exception of the first use, religion as piety, Smith proposed that we drop the use of the word because it is misleading and unnecessary. Religion, he argued, is best understood in terms of faith commitment or personal piety; that is, religion as 'being religious'. Otherwise we should talk about particular faith traditions or faith communities, and speak of the cumulative tradition of religious experience. These are helpful distinctions and on the whole I follow them. But what about the adjective 'religious', Cantwell Smith's preferred word, as distinct from the noun 'religion'?

While I was writing this chapter I heard a radio interviewer

4 Robertson Smith, *The Merry Heart* (New York: Viking, 1997), p. 280.
5 Wilfred Cantwell Smith, *The Meaning and End of Religion* (New York: Mentor Books, 1964), pp. 47–8.

describe a well-known singer as being very religious about her music. People can be religious about many things like music, sport or stamp collecting and presumably they can be religious about studying world religions. The *Concise Oxford Dictionary* does not make it any easier for us when it defines 'religious' with several other terms, each of which needs its own clarification. It is, we are told, being pious, God-fearing, scrupulous and conscientious. Being religious, in other words, is a subjective attitude; it is all about our affections; it does not necessarily refer to any particular object of devotion whether sport, music, stamp collecting or God. Hopefully, students in Religious Studies are conscientious, but not many are 'pious', nor need they be. But does one have to be 'pious' or 'religious' in order to be Christian – or human?

Having said all this, it is actually very difficult to avoid using the words 'religion' or 'religions'. And people usually know what is meant, even if they may not be able to say so with scholarly precision. So I am not suggesting that we avoid speaking of Christianity or Buddhism, for example, as religions. Nor that we should refrain from speaking about 'bad religion' or 'good', 'sick religion' or 'healthy', to use William James' categories as in his celebrated lectures on *The Varieties of Religious Experience*.[6] There are forms of religion, James argued, that may be earnest, sincere and devout, but which lead to a soul sickness or morbidity that demeans people, stunting their growth as human beings. This may not be dehumanizing in the sense of physical torture, though the Inquisition certainly was; but it may, for example, take the form of emotional manipulation, keeping someone in bondage to a religious authority, or inculcating attitudes and values in the devout that lead to the dehumanizing of others through acts of violence, terror or crusade. No wonder, then, that many people turn to psychology and therapy as a better alternative to becoming more truly human, and better integrated people. As anyone who has examined the books on 'religion' in bookshops will know, many of them today are about 'self-help'

6 William James, *The Varieties of Religious Experience* (London: Fontana, 1960), pp. 94–171.

popular psychology and 'new age' religion, rather than the classic religious traditions, or Christian spirituality.

For me, a major criterion in deciding whether they are the one or the other is precisely whether they help make us more truly human. Of course, I can already hear critics say: 'But what about truth? Should not that be the criterion by which we make such decisions?' Yes, that is so, but truth claims also need to be evaluated, and one important, indeed, biblical evaluation is the end result. If a particular doctrine leads to violence against others, or myself for that matter, can it be true? The Bible is outspoken about religion gone wrong, whether it is idolatry or hypocritical lip-service to God. True religion, as the letter of St James puts it, is meant to express genuine love through serving those in need (1.27).

Michelangelo's famous sculpture of Jesus lying in the arms of Mary, located near the entrance to St Peter's Basilica in Rome, is called the *Pieta* because it radiates the warm, loving devotion shown by Mary towards her crucified son. That beautifully sums up the original meaning of piety: the mutual love shared between parents and children, and by extension between lovers. True religious piety is something that 'flames within the heart', as Dante put it,[7] echoed in John Wesley's account of his conversion as an experience in which he felt his heart 'strangely warmed'. But true piety, as both Dante and Wesley knew, is not simply a subjective affection; it is something to do with the will and a 'sense of measure'; that is, a love that is guided and expressed in day-to-day practice. So to love God with heart, soul and mind, and to express that love towards others in a practical way, is the essence of true piety. That is good religion.

Pietism, a Christian movement in eighteenth-century Europe associated with the Moravian Brethren, was so called precisely because it emphasized the warm, loving devotion of a believer to Jesus as saviour in reaction to the cold rationalism of Enlightenment Christianity. This piety was not just inward looking or otherworldly, but expressed itself in loving

---

7 *The Divine Comedy of Dante Alighieri*, *Purgatorio* (New York: Bantam, 1982) viii/82, p. 73.

service to others. The Moravians played a role in Wesley's conversion, and there can be no doubt that the Evangelical Revival that resulted from Wesley's ministry combined that deep sense of piety with social responsibility. The evangelical tradition has a long record of ministry to the needy and downtrodden. Many other examples of such piety come to mind, not least Mother Teresa of Calcutta whose compassion numbered her among the saints of the twentieth century. Such piety or holiness belongs to the essence of what the New Testament calls 'true religion', the religion that cares for those in need. There is, in other words, a way of 'being religious' that is affirmed as profound in its spirituality and genuinely humanist in its concern and compassion.

But the way in which 'pious' and 'pietistic' are often used today suggests the contrary, carrying the stigma of a self-righteous narrowness of spirit that lacks concern for the world. I think it is probably for such reasons that we now prefer to use the word 'spirituality' to express 'piety' and the spiritual disciplines, such as prayer, meditation and worship that help make it possible. One of the reasons why I, as a young evangelical Christian, reacted against being called 'religious' (or pious) was because of what the word seemed to communicate rather than what it actually meant. Used in a positive sense it implies a passion and commitment for something or someone, but used more pejoratively it suggests a kind of saccharine unworldly piety. My parents were church-goers but certainly not religious in that latter sense, and few of my friends were religious in any sense at all except in their passion for girls and rugby. If it were not for my adolescent conversion I would not have been any different. But even so, as much as I was becoming religious in the commonsense use of the word, I did not like being described as such because it always suggested a kind of piety or religiosity with which I did not wish to be identified. I suspect many other Christians, or believers in other faith communities, feel much the same. But in any case, describing someone as 'being religious' does not indicate whether it is something good and humanizing, or the reverse.

Depersonalizing religion

Since Vatican II, Catholics have spoken of 'spiritual formation' to describe the way in which priests, nuns and monks are trained for the religious life. Such formation, especially today, takes into account both the traditional disciplines of the past and contemporary insights on personal development informed by the social and human sciences. Prior to Vatican II, however, the process was sometimes rigorously designed to break down one's former personality in order to create a new one, as though you had enlisted into the religious equivalent of the Marines. Mary, the mother of Jesus, portrayed as totally docile and obedient to the will of God, with little will of her own, was the prototype for training nuns. This process undoubtedly produced remarkable women, Mother Teresa among them. But that is not how Karen Armstrong experienced her life as a nun, told so graphically in the first volume of her autobiography *Through the Narrow Gate*.[8] As a devout adolescent she went in honest search of God, but was forced to deny everything she was as a person, friendships included. She survived seven years of training. But in the end, broken at heart, mentally ill and in deep despair at her failure to realize her dream, she left the convent, her vows annulled by the Vatican.

In the early years of her 'secularization' Karen, in deep depression, visited one of her former convent sisters who had, despite everything stacked against them, become her closest friend. Rebecca was in hospital suffering from acute *anorexia nervosa*. The reason was attributed to her training as a nun. In response to Karen's wistful comment during her visit that Jesus was, after all, a man of passion and sensitivity, Rebecca replied: 'I know. But, you know, I wanted to change ... I wanted to be another kind of person' – not her former passionate self, but a serene and obedient member of a religious order. Karen Armstrong writes:

> I thought of Jesus on Mount Tabor when, the gospels tell us, his disciples had seen him transfigured: light streamed from

8 Karen Armstrong, *Through the Narrow Gate: A Nun's Story* (London: HarperCollins, 1997).

his face, his garments had shone white as snow. He had not been diminished but enhanced. His personality and body remained intact but, transfused with divine power, he had perfected his humanity.

Then she blurted out: 'They didn't have to get rid of us; they could have perfected what we were.'[9]

'They didn't have to get rid of *us*!' Their religious training was aimed precisely at that. In the case of Karen Armstrong it led to her leaving the convent and, for several years, struggling to find her self again. Rebecca stayed within the convent, but became a pale shadow of what she was before she, too, finally left. 'They could have perfected what we were.' Instead of becoming 'religious', fundamentally remoulded into someone else, they could have become more fully themselves, not egocentric, but ego-matured, and therefore more radiantly human. Their spiritual formation was, on the contrary, depersonalizing rather than personally fulfilling as one would expect the 'search for God' should be.

In *The Spiral Staircase*, the sequel to that first autobiographical volume, Armstrong continued her story after she was 'secularized'. It is a deeply moving story, full of pathos and passion, as she tried to live a 'normal' life as a student at Oxford, and then as a teacher, and finally as a minor TV celebrity but with a growing status as an author of books on religion. It is a story of losing faith in God, angrily turning her back on the Church and everything religious and then, slowly and painfully recovering faith in a very different kind of God, a God of great compassion, and gradually finding her way to a more positive appreciation of religion. In doing so, she rediscovered herself and her humanity. Towards the end of *The Spiral Staircase*, Armstrong writes:

> In the course of my studies, I have discovered that the religious quest is not about discovering 'the truth' or 'the meaning of life', but about living as intensely as possible in the here and now. The idea is not to latch on to some super-

---

9 Karen Armstrong, *The Spiral Staircase: A Memoir* (London: HarperCollins, 2004), p. 129.

human personality or to get to heaven, but to discover how to be fully human ...[10]

She went on to say: 'In the past, my own experience of religion had diminished me, whereas true faith, I now believe, should make me more human than before.'[11] That, I believe, is what spiritual formation is about. And, we might add, that really is the point of such practices as 'going on retreat' or seeking the advice of a 'spiritual director'. As one modern expositor of the classic *Spiritual Exercise of St Ignatius Loyola* puts it, 'they foster such humanist values as respect for individual experience, freedom, and human dignity'[12] rather than getting rid of human personality in the desire to be or make someone 'religious'. But there are many others who, like Karen Armstrong, lose their faith in God, having been hurt by bad religion. Instead of enhancing and fulfilling their lives, religion has boxed them in by rules and demands that have led them away from the good news of the God revealed in Jesus Christ.

Growing beyond fundamentalism

My experience was different from that of Armstrong, perhaps because it was Protestant rather than Catholic. I was certainly not intent on pursuing a 'religious' life in a convent or monastery searching for God under rigorous discipline. Yet in some respects there were similarities, not least the danger that my conversion into the orbit of evangelical-fundamentalism – a term I will explain in a moment – had the potential to affect me as her religious formation affected her. Though I never liked being called 'religious', I was, in fact, becoming religious in a way that threatened to close down rather than open up possibilities for growth as a human being. Fortunately I was able to grow beyond the constricted boundaries of evangelical-fundamentalism and discover a new and enriching world of

---

10 Armstrong, *The Spiral Staircase*, p. 304.
11 Armstrong, *The Spiral Staircase*, p. 305.
12 Ronald Modras, *Ignatian Humanism: A Dynamic Spirituality for the 21st Century* (Chicago: Loyola Press, 2004), p. 68.

Christian community and faith, though without the traumas
Armstrong endured.

The term 'evangelical' is historically used to describe the
churches that grew out of the Protestant Reformation, both
Lutheran and Reformed. In Germany, the Protestant churches
are still referred to as *evangelisch* to distinguish them from
the Roman Catholic Church. In the Anglo-Saxon world, however, 'evangelical' has been more variously understood. Strict-
ly speaking it has been used to describe those who conservatively uphold the classic faith of the Protestant Reformation.
But it has also been used more colloquially to refer to those
who, among Protestants, emphasize the need for a personal
conversion to Jesus Christ as their saviour. This emphasis
characterized the Evangelical Revival led by John Wesley in
eighteenth-century England.

The term 'fundamentalism', while often similar to 'evangelical' in meaning, has a different history and ethos. It was
first coined in the United States in the 1920s to describe those
Christians who wanted to defend the 'fundamentals' of Protestant Christianity against liberal theologians and secular
humanism. The struggle was not around 'religious experience', but truth; being 'born again' was not a leap of faith into
the unknown, but based on revealed truths reasonably demonstrated and based on the authority of the Bible: creation not
evolution, the virgin birth, the divinity of Christ, the substitu-
tionary doctrine of the atonement, the bodily resurrection of
the dead, and the second coming. All of these have their foundation in Scripture and the Christian creed, and while traditions differ in their interpretation, they represent something
of a common core of belief. But the 'fundamentals' were very
narrowly conceived and interpreted by conservative scholars
engaged in their battle with liberals who, they claimed, had
sold out their Christian birthright to the prevailing culture.
Since then historic Protestant fundamentalism has developed
in a variety of directions. Today it is a difficult word to define because it is used in ways that embrace many Christian
groups and movements, some revivalist, others Pentecostal,
some charismatic, others conservatively Evangelical, some

counter-cultural and politically peripheral, others politically and culturally dominant. Many contemporary evangelicals shudder at being called fundamentalists, and resent the way in which fundamentalism has hijacked the term. Yet looking back I do not recall any distinction made between 'being evangelical' and 'being fundamentalist' in those early days of my spiritual journey. The two seemed synonymous, hence my description evangelical-fundamentalism.

The evangelical-fundamentalism I experienced as a teenager was not 'bad religion' as such; indeed, I was wary of the word 'religion' as this seemed a substitute for a living faith. Yet, like any religion, it was potentially so. Indeed, it was my growing sense of this potential that gradually led me away from it. But at the outset, my conversion gave life and church-going a new significance. I came to see things differently, with new eyes, though without much wisdom. I was instructed in how to pray and introduced to reading the Bible in a new, regular and more personal way that became part of my life's daily rhythm. In effect, my conversion provided a religious grid, inadequate though it may have been, from which I began to understand myself.

It all began at a camp organized by Scripture Union, an organization dedicated to evangelism and encouraging Bible reading among young people. There were fine people involved in those circles in which my newly found faith was nurtured, people whose piety was expressed in a genuine love for others, and whose faith and integrity I continue to respect. For many of us teenagers, their strong Christian convictions, their concern for us, and the challenge of their teaching stood in strong contrast to what seemed the rather tepid Christianity that many found in their home congregations where the preaching and worship seldom made any connection with our experience. This remains true today as many young people – and also the not so young – look beyond mainline denominations for a more authentic, lively and meaningful Christian experience. Our younger son, Anton and his wife Esther, belong to a Pentecostal church for this very reason. Others again are attracted to more Catholic forms of Christianity, with their apparent certainty of faith and morality, and the mystery and tangibility of their liturgy.

I was already a confirmed member of the Church when I was converted as a teenager. Far too often conversions of this kind fail to appreciate all that preceded them, and therefore ride roughshod over personal development in pressuring everyone into the same mould. My life would have been very different if my parents had not been Christians, if I had not been baptized as a child, or nurtured within a church and family that cared for me. That surely prepared the ground for what was yet to be. So what did that conversion really mean? What could it possibly mean? It did not mean being converted from one religious faith to another, as it does for some, nor did it mean becoming a member of the Church. The term used in those circles was 'being born again'. This is a graphic and appropriate way of describing what happened, though the term 'born again' is often misunderstood and misused.

The expression comes from the story, recounted in John's Gospel (3.1–10), of Nicodemus the Pharisee who came to Jesus by night. In response to Nicodemus' searching question about 'entering the kingdom of God', Jesus tells him of the need to be 'born again' or 'born from above'. What Jesus meant was that in order for anyone to live under the reign of God, it was necessary to undergo a rebirth, a change of direction, a conversion or, to use the Greek word used by Paul to describe the process, *metanoia* (Romans 12.1–2). This means a change of heart and mind, or personal transformation. Only then would we begin to discern or 'see the kingdom of God' that was present in Jesus himself. 'To see the kingdom of heaven' (a substitute word for God in Judaism and the Gospels) thus meant discerning the rule of God in the world and seeking to live accordingly. That is what it means, as Jesus taught, to 'seek first God's kingdom'. It is not a way of escaping from the world by becoming religious – the Pharisee was certainly that – but a new way of living *in the world* according to the values of God's reign. But it took me a while to discover that 'being born again' was not a ticket to heaven, but a way of becoming more fully human as a follower of Christ in this world.

By the end of my first year as an undergraduate university student my short involvement in evangelical-fundamentalism was coming to an end. There were various reasons for this, the first of which had to do with its lifestyle. 'Worldliness', almost more so than being called doctrinally 'unsound', was the worst epithet that could be uttered against Christians who did not conform to fundamentalist standards of behaviour and belief. 'Unworldliness' meant, in short, not smoking or drinking alcoholic beverages, not wearing make-up if you were a girl (the thought that males might want to do this was far beyond comprehension), not dancing or going to the cinema, not dating non-Christians, and certainly not engaging in sexual activities outside marriage, the details of which were implied rather than stated. In at least one instance it forced a promising young sportsman friend of mine to withdraw from playing rugby and cricket. That was somewhat extreme, of course, as some of the most appealing evangelists for this form of Christianity were sportsmen and women who demonstrated that Christianity was not for wimps.

Fundamentalist teachers were correct about the dangers of smoking, and who can deny the dangers of alcohol abuse and sexual promiscuity. But there were, and are, serious shortcomings and dangers in the fundamentalist code and the pressures used to enforce its brand of behaviour and belief: cutting people off from exploring the richness of culture; repressing sexuality in a way that sometimes induces a sense of false guilt; and separating people from those of other faiths and traditions, or those 'beyond the pale', resulting in a lack of understanding and prejudice. Another pressure, at that time at least, discouraged us from political involvement and social responsibility. But not least among the dangers of such fundamentalism, was the way in which these pressures so often led to a backlash, a rejecting of moral values and of Christianity itself.

I recall being sent early in my ministry as a denominational representative to the National Conference of the Temperance Alliance, held in Durban. While most of those present would have regarded drinking alcohol as sinful, they thought nothing of segregating at meal times, even if this meant sending the one and only black participant elsewhere for his meal. I raised an objection, but was told that the missionary institution where our meals were to be served was segregated in accordance with the dictates of apartheid. It was appalling to me that Christians, evangelicals and fundamentalists to a man (yes, they were all male), could spend days discussing moral issues, and fail to recognize the immorality of treating another human being and fellow Christian and leading Methodist minister, Enos Sikakhane, in that way. Enos and I ate together and both of us left the Conference soon after.

There is irony in the fact that many fundamentalist preachers and their followers are, today, far more 'worldly' than fundamentalists of a previous generation. What was frowned on then is frowned on no more as Christians pursue prosperity and try to outdo and impress their neighbours in lifestyle. Now it is often the case that Christians who have broken away from fundamentalism and become more radical in their convictions about politics and the environment are more counter-cultural in a way that earlier generations of fundamentalists would recognize. My own church tradition, the Congregational, is part of what was in England called 'Nonconformity', because of a refusal to conform to dictates of the established Church of England in the sixteenth century. But all Christians are called to be 'non-conformists'; that is, not being conformed to cultural values that are contrary to Christian norms.

The second reason why my association with evangelical-fundamentalism came to an end was as a result of awareness that it required a closed mind; above all, it was not prepared to examine critically Christian belief or the Bible, any more than behaviour codes. You either accepted the whole doctrinal package without question, or you did not belong. Critical enquiry had no place in this scheme of things; doubt was a sin that needed to be expunged or at least suppressed the moment it arose. I recall the day I bought my first serious theological book. It was a moment in which a sense of guilt mixed with one of liberation. I had joined the evangelical university SCA (Student Christian Association) and participated in its meetings, though I must confess I never felt quite at home nor regarded myself as belonging to the hard core membership. In all probability I was also regarded with some suspicion by the SCA leadership for not being theologically sound. One of the senior students in the SCA, sensing that I had something of an independent mind and was being influenced by unsound views, warned me never to read books published by the British SCM Press for they were invariably modernist. I should stick to those with the IVF label, many of which I had, incidentally, found very helpful. So there I was, browsing in the Methodist Bookshop in Cape Town where I discovered a copy of *Christian Apologetics* by Alan Richardson. Horror upon horrors I noticed it was published by SCM Press. Eagerly yet surreptitiously, as though I was smoking my first cigarette (I only did ever smoke one, preferring a pipe in those days), I glanced at its table of contents and decided that I would buy it. It was an act of defiance that clearly signified a change of mind. But what was Christian apologetics all about? That I still had to find out, but at least it sounded deliciously unsound.

Christian apologetics played a very important role in the early days of fundamentalist Christianity; it was, after all, born out of a defence of Protestant orthodoxy. But Richardson's apologetic approach to theology was very different, though one that was, in turn, subject to strong criticisms by Barth who believed that the best form of apologetic was to proclaim the Word of God revealed in Scripture rather than engage culture on its terms. While this may appear to be fundamentalist in character, Barth's understanding of the Bible was certainly not. His focus of attack was the liberal Christianity in which he had been trained because it had become the religious veneer of Western bourgeois culture rather than a witness to God's revelation in Jesus Christ. Such religion was really a human attempt to justify itself and, as such, idolatry. According to Barth as I first encountered him, the great nineteenth-century critics of religion, like Friedrich Nietzsche, Karl Marx and Sigmund Freud were right: religion is a human construct, human pretension, a means of oppressing others, and the fulfilling of wishful thinking.

God's revelation, culminating in Jesus Christ, is something quite different. Such revelation proclaimed in the gospel and witnessed to in Scripture, judges religion and awakens faith in God. Scripture, for Barth, was therefore testimony or witness to Jesus Christ, and thus became the Word of God as the Spirit pointed to Christ through its pages. This is very different from verbal inerrancy as propounded by fundamentalists, and while not without its own problems, it helped me to break free from the narrow constraints of fundamentalism without surrendering biblical authority. In fact the Bible came alive in a new way. But any challenge to the fundamentalist doctrine of biblical infallibility and inerrancy – that is, every word in the Bible was dictated by God, even in the interests of trying to understand the Bible better – put one beyond the fundamentalist pale.

It is certainly true that the critical study of the Bible, especially in its more radical forms, has subsequently led some Christians to lose their faith (usually fundamentalist in character). But defending the Bible uncritically, as fundamentalists do, contributes to even more misunderstanding and disparagement. And to say that Christians who are not fundamentalists do not take the Bible seriously or are theological and moral relativists is generally not true. Walter Brueggemann, whose biblical scholarship has so magnificently demonstrated the point, speaks rather of the need to find a way beyond both 'fideism and scepticism'.[13] That is, beyond an unreflective faith in the Bible (fideism), to a recognition that the biblical text requires critical reflection if faith is to understand itself; and, at the same time, beyond the scepticism that characterizes much biblical criticism, and often betrays a hostility to Christianity on the part of those who once believed, but no longer do so.

The fundamentalists' claim that their authority derives from the Bible *alone* simply does not stand up to scrutiny. For one thing, they refuse to recognize or take account of the historical process that led to the writing of the various, often disparate, parts of the Bible, and to the selection of the

---

13 Walter Brueggemann, *Theology of the Old Testament: Testimony, Dispute, Advocacy* (Minneapolis: Fortress Press, 1997), p. 729.

books that comprise the canon. Fundamentalists are therefore experts at 'proving' their position by bringing together a range of texts taken indiscriminately from the Bible irrespective of their original context, on the basis of their particular world-view. This method can be used to prove most things from the Bible. So it is not surprising that fundamentalists disagree among themselves on certain issues even though they all claim to base their views on the 'Bible alone'. But another problem is the fact that fundamentalists, in reading the Bible, are not critically aware of their presuppositions shaped by past religious conflict, cultural norms and social experience. Everyone who reads the Bible inevitably makes choices as to what are the most important and significant passages. The difference is that fundamentalists seldom acknowledge what they are doing or seek ways to deal with the problem.

Fundamentalists also insist on reading the Bible literally. There is an unwillingness to distinguish between history and myth, metaphor and analogy, poetry and prose in interpreting the Bible. Of course, there are times when we must take the Bible literally. When the prophets call on us to do justice and love mercy, or when Jesus teaches us to be peacemakers, or when Paul reminds us that we are saved by grace and not by our own righteousness, then Scripture is literally true for us. But fundamentalists extend the literal reading of Scripture to texts and passages that are patently not meant to be taken in that way. There is a symbolic blindness or block in their approach that prevents them from actually hearing what the Bible is saying. Like anyone else, fundamentalists have the right to read the Bible in whatever way they choose. But they need to be challenged when they use it to justify attitudes and policies that oppress and dehumanize people. Whether intentionally or not, this has happened too often in the past, and continues in the present. Biblical texts have been used to sanction slavery, racism, the oppression of women and today, to support sexual discrimination, homophobia, xenophobia and global expansionism. Which brings me to my third reason for breaking with evangelical-fundamentalism.

Religion as ideology of crusade

My home congregation as I grew up, Union Congregational Church in Kloof Street, Cape Town, might not have been as dynamic and appealing to young people as the circles in which I was converted, but it had a long history of social conscience going back to its first minister, Dr John Philip, the early nineteenth-century missionary who had led the campaign against slavery at the Cape. I remember attending an early anti-apartheid protest meeting in the City Hall at which my own minister, Basil Brown, who was later to become the General Secretary of the Christian Council of South Africa (forerunner to the SACC) was present and sitting on the stage. This made a considerable impression on me. But it was at Rhodes University that political sensitivities were sharpened. This was partly as a result of contact with black students at Fort Hare University, and partly due to Professor Leslie Hewson's lectures on South African church history. I recall the first anti-apartheid protest march in which Isobel and I participated, along High Street in Grahamstown in 1959. Hewson, one of the most saintly people I have ever met (a true model of holiness) was among its leaders. Early the next year, on 21 March, the Sharpeville massacre sent shock waves around the country. That was a critical turning point for me as it was for many others, but few in the evangelical-fundamentalist camp seemed to take much notice. Indeed, evangelical-fundamentalists in South Africa refused to get involved in opposing apartheid, and many of them openly or tacitly supported it. Ideologically, they had identified themselves as right-wing supporters of the status quo.

I became more politically aware, and a little more radicalized, as a pastor in Durban during the years following Sharpeville, and especially as I have mentioned, on my return from Chicago when I became involved in the Christian Institute. I recall reading Albert Luthuli's *Let My People Go!* and having the opportunity to visit him in Groutville where he was a deacon in our church. At the time Luthuli was President of the banned African National Congress. Try as I might,

I could not get my colleague white ministers to read Luthuli's book or to think of him as a Christian leader. All they could see was a 'communist', an epithet that was by association also aimed at me. Much later in 1980, on a visit to Namibia (then South West Africa) during my term of office as President of the United Congregational Church, I discovered that one of the leading evangelical-fundamentalist church leaders in South Africa, someone who was most harsh on those who deviated in belief or behaviour, was an ardent supporter of apartheid and personally involved with the South African security police and military on the Angolan border.

Churches opposed to apartheid were often vilified by the more right-wing fundamentalist churches, who were also used by the state to undermine their influence. Many pastors and priests known to me were harassed by right-wing fundamentalists, sometimes in their congregations, some of whom acted as informers for the security police.[14] I had personal experience of such activity, and know of others who were arrested and imprisoned as a result of such surveillance. In principle, it is good that evangelical-fundamentalist Christians today have become more socially and politically concerned, and many of their churches are more racially integrated and involved in social outreach than the more established denominations. But it is deeply disturbing that those who kept silent during the struggle against apartheid, or supported it, now advocate policies that are sometimes equally at variance with human rights.

Much religion through the ages has been for the good of humanity, but much has also been misused in justifying political programmes that have been dehumanizing. This is as true of many religious traditions, as it is of religious movements whether identified as left-wing, right-wing, or establishment in their ideological alignments. But such movements have become particularly dangerous when they have regarded themselves or their nations in Messianic terms, seeking to

---

14 On right-wing Christianity during the apartheid era, see the special edition of the *Journal of Theology for Southern Africa*, no. 69, December 1989.

overthrow perceived enemies and establish the kingdom of God on earth by whatever means. We are only too familiar with such forms of religion in our own day, as we witness the outbursts of terror perpetrated by Muslim extremists and the crusades that have followed to combat them, often explicitly in the name of Christ. I am equally concerned about all these forms of bad religion, but my focus here is on right-wing Christian fundamentalism, both because of the way in which such religion gave its support to apartheid, and because it has now become a global ideology of crusade.[15]

The current rhetoric that promotes this view, proclaimed by many fundamentalist leaders, whether preachers or politicians, portrays the United States as the nation chosen by God to wage war against the powers of evil. It has a divine mandate to rule the world. Such claims have been made for many nations in the course of history to justify their imperial designs and colonial exploits, and they have invariably drawn on biblical texts to justify their actions. The notion that the United States (or Britain, Germany, France, Russia, Japan, apartheid South Africa) has a special place in the providence of God, a mandate to govern, is nothing new. But it has taken on ominous tones in recent times as tensions in the Middle East have heightened, the notion of 'a clash of civilizations' become widespread, and the 'war on terror' given a religious aura. According to the fundamentalist ideology of 'righteous empire', not unlike that of the medieval justification of crusade, we are now living in the 'end times' during which the 'war on Satan' (now synonymous with the 'war on terror') will intensify prior to the final victory of Christ over all anti-Christian forces. The war in Iraq signals the beginning of the battle of Armageddon that will hasten the return of Christ. This scenario is premised and justified on what is referred to as a 'dispensationalist' reading of Scripture. Using selected texts from Daniel, Revelation and Mark 13, dispensationalists impose an interpretative grid on the Bible that, they claim, enables them to predict the unfolding of world events.

---

15 See *Exporting the American Gospel*, Steve Brouwer, Paul Gifford and Susan D. Rose (eds) (New York: Routledge, 1996).

I was introduced to this way of reading the Bible by friends in the Plymouth Brethren soon after my conversion, and recall a series of lectures that graphically depicted by way of charts the fact that we were living in the end times. This is the 'grand narrative' by which we can make sense of a world in crisis and turmoil. Such dispensationalism is widespread in fundamentalist circles, and spills over well beyond them, reinforced by apocalyptic movies and popular religious books. Whereas previously it was a belief on the fringes of Christianity and mainstream society, now it is increasingly influential and aligned with political power. Whereas previously it led to a withdrawal from the world of politics in anticipation of God's coming kingdom, now it provides the ideological basis for strident political engagement in righteous crusade against the unrighteousness of others who are different.

Christians are engaged in a struggle, but it is not a struggle between religions and civilizations, but against what the letter to the Ephesians calls 'principalities and powers' (6.10–17) and these are operative as much in our own backyard as they are anywhere else. Indeed, the struggle between good and evil, as Bunyan's pilgrim knew only too well, is more often within us than outside us. But, of course, there is a global battle to be waged, a struggle against injustice and oppression, a struggle for truth against falsehood, a struggle to overcome hatred in the name of the God who loves the world and seeks its redemption. There is also a war to be waged against drug trafficking, corruption and crime, against the abuse of women and children, and against poverty and hunger. But fundamentalist right-wing religionists have a very different understanding of what this global battle is about, tying it to their conviction that the battle of Armageddon has begun. To hasten the 'end of the world' through military action and crusades therefore seems commendable, something to be advocated and supported. In doing so, alliances are made with economic and anti-environmental lobbies that promote global policies that are to the disadvantage of the poor and ravage the earth. Seeing that everything is coming to an end anyway, such concerns are at best secondary. My antipathy towards such Messianic fundamentalism began long before the 'war on terror' brought it to such prominence.

Right-wing Christian fundamentalism may not have the same extreme militant character we now associate with radical forms of Islam, but its unqualified support of Western militarism is certainly perceived by many Muslims as a threat to global peace and their own well-being. Many Muslims regard globalization as the means whereby the West is seeking to spread its secularist views, and see Western military enterprises as the new Christian crusade to overthrow Muslim lands. Of course, this contemporary scenario has a long history stretching back into the Middle Ages, so the problem is not simply one that can be laid at the door of Christian fundamentalism today. Most sections of what was called Christendom have been at fault in this respect, whether Catholic, Orthodox or Protestant. The litany of their failures makes appalling reading when one considers the legacy of inquisition and crusade, and more recently, of holocaust and apartheid, all carried out in the name of Christ. When Christianity is bad, whether fundamentalist or not, like all bad religion of whatever creed, it can be awful.

Such bad religion is ugly, violent and dehumanizing both in its character and its consequences. It leads to hatred, self-righteousness and idolatry. Christianity has at times certainly betrayed its origins and ethos in this way, and it is not alone in doing so. The Lordship of Christ as the suffering servant who gives his life for the sake of the world must surely mean something different from the triumphalist spirit of ideological self-interest wherever it surfaces within the Christian Church. Whereas Muslim extremists engage in acts of violence, shouting 'Allah is great', Christians too often, like the crusaders of old, do battle against terror, crying 'Jesus is Lord'. Such triumphalism is certainly not Christian. As George Lindbeck put it, the 'crusader's battle cry "*Christus est Dominus* (Christ is Lord)" ... is false when used to authorize cleaving the skull of an infidel',[16] even though in other contexts it may

---

16 George Lindbeck, *The Nature of Doctrine: Religion and Theology in a Postliberal Age* (Philadelphia: John Knox, 1984), p. 64.

be true. To confess Christ against dehumanizing and idolatrous power is not the same as confessing Christ in support
of one's own political and material interests. To use Luther's
terminology, the first is a theology of the cross, the second a
theology of glory.[17] Which brings me to my final bother about
fundamentalism – its virulent opposition to anything that
smacks of humanism. Humanism, of whatever hue or kind,
is the 'enemy within', weakening the resolve to fight the anti-
Christ and thus its agents. Such rhetoric is not new to those
who lived in Nazi Germany or apartheid South Africa, but it
is no less disconcerting to hear it again today.

During the early years of apartheid, both National Party
government propaganda and the pronouncements of the Dutch
Reformed Church portrayed 'liberalisme, kommunisme, en
humanisme' as the common enemies of South Africa and
signs of the anti-Christ. This litany was not original to South
Africa; it was one repeatedly uttered by conservative forces
in Europe during the first half of the twentieth century, not
least in Holland, Germany, Spain and Italy. And it prepared
the ground for the rise of Nazism, Fascism and apartheid.
While communism as *the* enemy has virtually disappeared,
liberalism and humanism remain agents of the anti-Christ for
many conservative and fundamentalist Christians, and are
often attacked with venom. The danger with this is not the
criticism of liberalism and humanism as such, for criticism is
always necessary and often appropriate, but the creation of an
atmosphere which breeds anti-humanist tendencies that can
and often do lead to dehumanizing actions.

In the early 1980s, Eberhard Bethge, Bonhoeffer's friend,
biographer and interpreter, spent a semester at Lynchburg
College in Virginia, at a time when the 'Moral Majority' movement was at its height. A Sunday visit to Jerry Falwell's church
deeply disturbed Bethge because it reminded him so much of
the German Christianity he had experienced during the Nazi
period. Christ had become identified with the national cause.
In Bethge's words, the battle lines had been drawn between

---

17 *The Heidelberg Disputation* (1518) article 21. See *Martin Luther's Basic
Theological Writings*, ed. Timothy F. Lull (Minneapolis: Fortress, 1989), p. 44.

'a "Christian nation" and humanism'.[18] Bethge did not define precisely what he meant by 'humanism', nor did he qualify it with the word 'Christian'. But he had in mind that tradition in German history that had long sought to provide an alternative vision and set of values to those of the uncritical nationalism that led to National Socialism with its rabid anti-Semitism and denial of human rights. For Bethge, Christians had an obligation to take a stand with secular humanists in defence of the values for which they both stood, even if on different grounds.

Both Christian fundamentalists and Muslim extremists regard humanism, whatever its form, as one of the major ideologies of the enemy, and they regard liberal versions of their respective faiths as sell-outs to and lackeys of secularism, evolutionism and scientism. For this reason, they are opposed to secular democratic forms of government that do not privilege their religion. Secular humanism is, for fundamentalists, a rival religion bent on governing the world and, in the process, destroying its moral and cultural values. So fundamentalism as a 'popular religion' gains much of its appeal by its ability to portray intellectuals and scholars, including evangelicals who are critical of the fundamentalist world-view, as Godless enemies of the common people and their values. And, as always in history, this mass appeal is something politicians harness against their critics and opponents whether they believe in its truth or not. Such alliances rightly fill us with alarm for the spectre they raise of a new wave of wars of religion, crusades and genocide. Irrespective of the brand, whether Christian, Jewish, Muslim or Hindu, such religion is simply bad religion. No wonder students ask whether they have to be 'religious' in order to study religion, and so often turn away from religion in search of a better way of being human. No wonder, too, that concerned people put their hope in a more enlightened secular world order. But is secular humanism the answer to the global search for peace, justice and human dignity?

---

18 See John W. de Gruchy, *Daring, Trusting Spirit: Bonhoeffer's Friend Eberhard Bethge* (London: SCM Press, 2005), p. 201.

4

Being Secular

*Secularization is the process of social change in which religion
loses its social significance.* Bryan Wilson[1]

*Secularism is the name for an ideology, a new closed world-view
which functions very much like a new religion.* Harvey Cox[2]

*I hate, I despise your festivals,
and I take no delight in your solemn assemblies.* Amos 5.21

In the North American Fall of 1963 I was one of many graduate students who crowded into the common room of the
Divinity School at the University of Chicago to listen to the
English Bishop John Robinson speak about his recently published book *Honest to God*. *Honest to God* had become a
media event in Britain, but it was only one of several books at
that time (Harvey Cox's *Secular City* was another) that made
the views of Tillich, Rudolf Bultmann and Bonhoeffer more
widely accessible, giving support to the notion of a secular or
'non-religious' Christianity. 'The time when people could be
told everything by means of words, whether theological or
pious is over', Bonhoeffer had written from prison:

> Even those who honestly describe themselves as 'religious'
> do not in the least act up to it, and so they presumably mean
> something quite different by 'religious' ... Are there religion
> less Christians? If religion is only a garment of Christianity
> – and this garment has looked very different at different
> times – then what is religionless Christianity?[3]

---

1 Bryan R. Wilson, 'Secularization', in *Dictionary of Ethics, Theology and
Society*, ed. Paul Barry Clarke and Andrew Linzey (London: Routledge, 1996),
p. 747.

2 Harvey E. Cox, *The Secular City* (London: SCM Press, 1965), pp. 20–1.

3 Bonhoeffer, *Letters and Papers from Prison*, pp. 279–80.

Having already cut my theological teeth on such thinking, I was now entranced to be part of a discussion that included, among others, Tillich himself.

I had avidly read *Honest to God* on board the *Southern Cross*, the ocean liner that had taken us from Durban to South-ampton en route for New York. I recall discussing it excitedly with another passenger from Durban, a medical doctor and outspoken atheist. What Robinson was saying spoke directly to the issues that my new friend raised against Christianity. They also spoke to me as a young pastor, as they did to many others at the time, who were disenchanted with a Christianity that seemed out of touch with the challenges, both intellec-tual and moral, that were facing us. I kept on coming across people, usually students, who could not reconcile Christian-ity and being a Christian with what they knew about science, with their sense of obligation to working for social justice, or simply with their growing up as human beings. They were tired of the religious clichés they too-often heard preached in their churches.

The 1960s was a time of considerable ferment in the Church as these issues came to the fore, and we all either struggled to hold on to our faith or simply let it go. It was the time of the Civil Rights Movement in the United States, of student revolt in Europe, and of liberation struggles in Latin America, each of which made an impact on South Africa and on the way in which we did theology. 'Being secular' within that historical context, so Robinson and others taught us, was not some-thing to be rejected as un-Christian, but rather to be affirmed as consonant with biblical faith. Cox spoke of an 'authentic secularity', and counselled us 'not to be dismayed by the fact that fewer and fewer people are pressing what we have nor-mally called "religious" questions'.

> The fact that urban-secular man is incurably and irrevers-ibly pragmatic, that he is less and less concerned with reli-gious questions, is in no sense a disaster. It means that he is shedding the lifeless cuticles of the mythical and ontological periods and stepping into the functional age. He is leaving

behind the styles of the tribe and the town and becoming a technopolitan man. As such he may now be in a position to hear certain notes in the biblical message that he missed before. He may be ready, in some respects, to 'do the truth' in a way his superstitious and religious forerunners were not.[4]

Surely, I thought at the time, I must be a 'secular believer'. Strange as it sounded, the idea was tempting, challenging and not without merit. But was that what I really was or wanted to be? More especially, did I want to be associated with the 'death of God' theology that soon emerged on the more radical wing of this loosely defined theological enterprise? My evangelical background reacted against moving in that direction. So too did my further exploration of Bonhoeffer's theology which gathered momentum during that time. Nonetheless, I was intrigued by the implications of secularization for Christian faith and life. How were we to understand this process, and what were its fruits? Is 'being secular' rather than 'being religious' a more appropriate adjunct to being Christian, and more akin to 'being human'?

Looking back to those heady times and discussions, I recognize that much of the talk about secularity was faddish, and that the resurgence of religion as a political force in the late twentieth century belies the notion that we were entering a time when religion would no longer play a role in public life. 'Secular Christianity' held little appeal for many of those engaged at the grass roots of society, for whom fundamentalism and Pentecostalism were far more attractive options, or for those who began to seek a home in the doctrinal certainty and liturgical splendour of Eastern Orthodoxy or the Catholic Church. Neither did it convert my atheist doctor friend. But did this mean that the vision of Christianity we associate with Bonhoeffer and others who shared it was invalid or served no purpose? As Cox suggested in a later book, *Religion in a Secular Society*, only 'a theology that has taken the modern age seriously will be able to take seriously what is coming

4 Cox, *The Secular City*, pp. 69–70.

next'. 'No one' he continued, 'can move beyond the secular city who has not first passed through it.'[5] What, then, can we now say about secularization, its outcomes and its implications for both being human and being Christian?

Secularization and its outcomes

In most traditional societies the distinction between the religious and the secular is seldom made. Such dualistic thinking about reality divided into two spheres, the one religious and the other secular, is not in the biblical mainstream either. It developed much later when secular came to refer to the affairs of the world, the temporal and profane as distinct from the religious, eternal and sacred. Although God ruled over the whole cosmos, God's kingdom was really located in the next world rather than this. Or, as the more pious read Jesus' words, the kingdom was 'within us' rather than something that made a transforming impact on social and political realities.

Within the Catholic Church a distinction is also made between 'religious', meaning those priests, monks and nuns who belong to religious orders separated from the world, and 'secular' or diocesan clergy who live fully in the world. Martin Luther's historic and traumatic move from being a monk, that is 'religious', to becoming a Reformer living fully in the world (i.e. 'secular') married to Kate, a former nun and admirable brewer of beer, was unintentionally a major moment in the journey towards the secularization of Europe. It provided a personal paradigm for what more perceptive Catholic leaders and theologians feared would become a social avalanche leading to the demise of Christendom.

Mainstream Protestantism sought to retain and even reinforce the benefits of Christendom by establishing national churches. There were, Luther insisted, two distinct realms. The Church, responsible for the spiritual life of the nation, and the state, for its secular well-being. A corollary of this separation of Church and state was that the two should not

---

5 Harvey Cox, *Religion in the Secular City: Toward a Postmodern Theology* (New York: Simon and Schuster, 1984), p. 268.

interfere in each other's affairs. This was not intended to loosen the bonds between Christianity and society, for the Protestant Princes were, after all, Christian. But it did set them free to govern without interference from the Church. Even though John Calvin sought ways to ensure that the Church continued to exercise a social and political role in those territories where his version of the Reformation took root, the break-up of medieval Christendom, together with Luther's teaching on the two realms, set the stage for the secularization of Europe and the emergence of the secular state. But while the Reformation was an unwitting catalyst for secularization, the process as such was more complex and contextually varied, gaining momentum from other sources and forces in the centuries that followed. Chief among these were the rapid advances in scientific achievement, the political and social upheavals signalled by the French and Industrial Revolutions, and the intellectual ferment that stretched from the Renaissance through to the Enlightenment.

The Enlightenment was an elitist development largely affecting the intelligentsia. Reason was separated from faith. The authority of the Bible, the Church and Christian creeds were set aside. Human goodness, self-sufficiency and dignity were affirmed. The outcome, described by the German philosopher Immanuel Kant, was a 'world come of age', a new historical epoch in Europe, loosely called 'modernity', in which people, hypothetically at least, became personally responsible for their lives, depending on reason and science rather than on God. To be properly human meant that human beings should establish truth, rules and laws by reason alone. This was the milieu in which what we now refer to as secular humanism was born, a form of humanism unlike that of the Renaissance, one that had decisively cast off its Christian heritage. Varying between agnosticism and atheism, it was wary of any absolutes whether religious, political or otherwise, and protective of human freedom and rights. Secular humanists saw no need for recourse to any power or meaning beyond being human; religion within the limits of reason was possible as a moral code, but religion otherwise understood kept humans in bondage to superstition, giving them a false sense of security.

Apart from a more engaged response from liberal theologians, Church traditions and movements, the response of both the Catholic Church and the major Protestant denominations to secular humanism was one of unqualified opposition. Any sign of modernist or liberal tendencies was frowned upon and often punished. This meant, in effect, that the major churches became reactionary on many issues that were part of the liberal and humanist agenda. In turn, secular humanism became the defender of values that were previously advocated by Christians in the High Middle Ages and Renaissance. Reason, culture, humanity, tolerance and freedom became 'battle cries against the church, against Christianity, even against Jesus Christ'.[6] Secular humanism emerged as the rational defender of humanity and the common good, standing against religious dogmatism, ecclesiastical triumphalism and popular superstition.

Whereas the Enlightenment was largely an elite affair, the process of secularization it helped engender ensured that what was previously confined to the few began to impact on the many.[7] Growing numbers of people lost whatever sense of religion or piety they or their parents and grandparents might have had. This did not mean that religious belief or practice disappeared. Popular piety remained entrenched in many places, churches fought a rearguard action against the eroding acids of modernity, and many people remained nominally members of established churches. Many lived their lives in two spheres, the one religious with its discredited world-view and inward-looking piety, and the other where they took for granted the advances in science, as in seeking medical help; and, if they engaged in social and political affairs, they did not do so in terms of their faith convictions. Secularization and scientific advancement had changed the religious consciousness of Europe, the way people thought about the world

---

6 Bonhoeffer, *Ethics*, p. 340.

7 Owen Chadwick, *The Secularization of the European Mind in the Nineteenth Century* (Cambridge: Cambridge University Press, 1975).

and themselves. Christianity was privatized, the Church mar-
ginalized, and religion trivialized. Secularization had a further outcome that has had far-reaching consequences in the
modern world, namely secularism. Whereas secular humanism cherished values that enhanced the well-being of society,
secularism refers to a self-centred individualism that has little
concern for the common good. This is an important distinction about which I will say more shortly.

The consequences of this separation of religion and the secular, or what Bonhoeffer described as 'thinking in two spheres'
were far-reaching. Eventually, on the basis of such thinking,
the Protestant Church in Germany found it very difficult to
oppose Hitler and, likewise, many Christians in apartheid
South Africa believed that they should not oppose the government's policies. Christianity had nothing to do with politics;
it was a matter of saving souls and not getting one's hands
dirty in the affairs of the world. I vividly recall the month
I joined the staff of the South African Council of Churches
– August 1968. My first responsibility was to arrange a press
conference for the launching of 'The Message to the People
of South Africa', a 'confessing' document prepared by the
SACC and the Christian Institute in which apartheid was
condemned as a 'false gospel' which promised security on
the basis of segregation. 'The Message' attracted widespread
media attention and, as a result, opened up the floodgates of
criticism and attack. Prime Minister John Vorster led the way,
warning the SACC not to think it could follow the example
of Martin Luther King Jr in the United States and so 'disrupt
order in South Africa under the cloak of religion'.[8] In short,
the Church had no right to be involved in the political arena,
nor did its message have anything to do with the way in which
society was structured.

Bonhoeffer's thoughts about 'non-religious Christianity'
were an attempt to address this problem in his own context, so
that Christianity might make an impact on reality as a whole,
not just some religious part of life. But his prognosis that the
world was moving towards a time of no religion seems to have

---

8 See de Gruchy, *The Church Struggle in South Africa*, p. 115.

been proved wrong, especially if we look beyond Western Europe. In 1991 Gilles Kepel, a Parisian-based political scientist, published a book with the evocative title *The Revenge of God* in which he documented the resurgence of Islam, Christianity and Judaism in the late twentieth century.[9] After two centuries in which religion had been on the retreat, centuries during which the 'death of God' had gradually but inexorably become a presupposition of modern life, suddenly, so it seemed, God had returned with a vengeance. Religion, irrespective of its particular faith tradition, had bounced back from the sidelines to which it had been relegated by secularization. Once again it had become a major political force that could not be ignored. The main types of religion that emerged with a vengeance were varied in character, from 'new age' to more traditional forms of the major religions and, of course, evangelicalism and fundamentalism. Parallel to this was the decline of more liberal, more secularized versions of the major faith traditions, notably as embodied in main-line and more ecumenically orientated Christian denominations.

But even though religion has proved amazingly persistent, and returned to life with fresh vigour across the globe, it has done so in tandem and tension with global forces that remain powerfully secularizing in character. Several key questions thus arise. Is secularization an inevitable global force that will eventually reshape the lives of every human being, or is (was) it simply a transitory Western European phenomenon? If it is more global, is the process and its outcomes the same or similar in every context? And are these outcomes good or bad for society and humans? Is it a process that has now run its course, or as post-modernist theory suggests, one that co-exists with other social forces and realities that are traditional and religious in some sense? Indeed, in many modern states, religious and secular constituencies vie with each other for social and political power. In some societies, such as the United States, where religion is encouraged but where secularization is equally rampant, a strange blend of the secular

9 Gilles Kepel, *The Revenge of God: The Resurgence of Islam, Christianity and Judaism in the Modern World* (Cambridge: Polity Press, 1994).

and the religious is evident in both private and public life, something akin to what we also find in South Africa.

South Africa makes an interesting case study in these dynamics. What is referred to as African traditional religion continues to provide the bedrock of the culture of the majority of citizens, even though more than 70 per cent of the population are Christian by allegiance, and many have become secular in outlook. White, English-speaking South Africans have long been marked by a blend of Christianity and secularity, while their Afrikaner counterparts have traditionally been noted for their Reformed Christianity piety. Apartheid was justified as a policy that protected Christian values and would ensure the survival of Christendom in South Africa. It was almost unthinkable to be an Afrikaner and not a Christian. Today this is no longer the case. Many Afrikaner intellectuals have turned away from Christianity and become secular in their world-view and lifestyle, reacting against the kind of religion in which they were nurtured, and against a Church that had misled them in so strongly supporting apartheid.[10]

Yet even though secularization is taking place at a startling pace, South Africa remains a very religious country. Nothing demonstrated this blend of the religious and the secular more publicly than the ceremony on 10 May 1994 in the grand amphitheatre of the Union Buildings in Pretoria inaugurating Nelson Mandela as President. Diverse, even disparate and conflicting cultural elements blended together in remarkable harmony. Representatives of the secular state – a judge, generals, the President and his deputies; and representatives of religious tradition – a Xhosa *imbongi* (praise singer), Hindu priest, Muslim imam, Jewish rabbi and Christian bishop – each fulfilling a role irrespective of the differences that have traditionally kept them apart. In many ways, this was the first 'post-modern' inauguration of a democratically elected President played out before a world audience. The secular and the

---

10 See the discussion in Jaap Durand, 'Secularism, Pluralism and the Afrikaner Churches in the Twenty-First Century', in *Theology in Dialogue*, ed. Lyn Holness and Ralf K. Wüstenberg (Grand Rapids: Eerdmans, 2002), pp. 175–89.

religious, the universal and the particular, the public and the private, flowed together in a way seldom if ever seen before, and setting a precedent for the future.

Not all faith communities welcome this acknowledgement of religious pluralism, any more than they accept the notion of a secular state. For many Christian fundamentalists, a secular state is nothing less than anti-Christian. This reveals a widespread misunderstanding of the necessarily secular (not secularist) nature of modern democracy. In trying to untangle the confused threads of the often very heated debate, it is important to recognize that secular states vary in character and constitution. We also need to distinguish between a *secular* state, that is, one which is not beholden to any religious tradition, and a *secularist* state which rejects religious values and denies religious traditions their rightful place in the public domain. In the former Soviet Union, for example, it was not sufficient to let the process of secularization run its course and produce 'secular humans'; religion was outlawed and social engineering put in place to ensure its extinction. That experiment has largely backfired. The survival of Orthodoxy in Russia and other Eastern European countries, as well as of the churches in China and Cuba, provides one of the most remarkable contemporary accounts of religious endurance despite sustained attempts by the state to stamp it out.

None of this should blind us to the reality of secularization as a process that continues to make its impact on our lives. There are undoubtedly many millions of people world-wide today who do not see the need for religion, spirituality or God, however defined, just as there are many others who might say they believe in God, but for whom it makes no practical difference. Their lives are bounded by material reality, the mundane, this world: they are 'being secular'. There is no, or little, sense of the transcendent or recognition of spiritual reality. Which leads me to re-emphasize the important distinction between secularism and secular humanism, or what is often referred to today as neo-humanism, for the latter is a choice made on grounds of moral and philosophical principle. Secularism, by way of contrast, is driven by individual self-interest.

Secularism asserts individual freedom without social responsibility, promoting a pragmatic lifestyle of relative moral value, an individualism that rides roughshod over the common good and the interests of others, and a cynicism that has no concern for future generations. Secularism is, in short, a-moral, fostering greed and corruption whether in the private or public sphere. It is reflected in the outrageous salaries paid to some business executives, to media and sports stars, in the ugly flaunting of wealth in a world of great poverty, in the disregard for the vulnerable and the worship of the powerful, in religion that exalts wealth as a sign of divine favour and blesses military might as a means to achieve God's goals. Secularists can suddenly become very religious, especially if it suits their interests. By contrast, secular humanism is a principled position, one that has a genuine concern for human well-being, and therefore presents a particular challenge to religion. But before examining it more fully, we must take a detour and consider the role of science in the process of secularization, its relation to religion and offer a critique of scientism, the bedfellow of secularism.

Science and scientism

The remarkable advances of scientific endeavour were critical to the process of secularization, demystifying the world, replacing traditional/religious understandings of healing with scientific medicine, and supplanting faith with rationality. However, the fact that scientific achievement has discredited certain religious world-views and set people free to be responsible for their own lives, does not mean that, as a result, the world has become a better place morally speaking, that modern scientific achievement has all been good, or that modern technology alone can cure human ills. Despite the enormous advances of science, and the huge improvements these have made to the quality of life for many people, science and technology has often been misused to transgress boundaries and provide the tools of death and destruction. Science is a wonderful servant in our quest for human well-being, but it is a terrifying master. When we allow that shift we have bowed the knee to the idol of scientism.

Scientism is letting science dominate in ways that rob us of our humanity and undermine the common good. It turns science into an absolute creed, blindly and uncritically expecting science to deliver far more than it reasonably can. Scientism reflects a failure to recognize the limitations of science and draws conclusions that do not logically follow. For example, using Darwinian evolutionary theory, socio-biologists of an earlier generation concocted what was called 'Social Darwinism'. This not only meant that the fittest survive (which is not always true), but that only the fittest *should* survive. There was only a short step to the Nazi programme to exterminate what were regarded as 'lesser' breeds of human beings, and to racist policies the world over, including apartheid. Scientific theories are too often regarded as facts, and used to fashion political and social policies to the detriment of human beings and the environment. Scientism denies that there are other ways to arrive at truth than through empirical investigation alone – a view seriously challenged by many philosophers, artists and religious believers of the past and the present, as well as many scientists themselves.

And, on top of these extravagant and dangerous claims, its critique of religion and religious values is often naïve, based on a crude understanding of what is believed, and a contempt for those who believe. As I have already indicated, there is much in religion and in Christian tradition that needs to be criticized and some jettisoned. But there is a world of difference between the informed critique of theologians who usually have a better grasp of the failures of their tradition, and the ill-informed criticism of secularists who make little effort to respond to what the traditions at their best actually teach. Scientism, in fact, not only ignores a great deal of universal cultural experience as embodied, not least in religious traditions and the best accounts of what they mean, but in doing so also reveals the same kind of closed mind that we find in religious fundamentalism and totalitarian ideologies. As Huston Smith reminds us, science 'is as fallible as other social efforts.

False starts, blind alleys, in-house vendettas and outright dishonesty plague it as much as they do the Church.'[11]

William Schweiker uses the term 'overhumanization' to describe the combined effect of secularism and scientism, associating them with unbridled freedom and massive destructive power. 'Overhumanization', he writes, is not 'a celebration of human creativity or technological power, but, rather, an ideology and social condition in which maximizing power becomes a good in itself.'[12] One response to this unchecked exercise of human freedom and power is to regard human beings as the problem, thus rejecting human claims to have distinctive worth and responsibility within the total scheme of things. One ardent advocate of animal rights I know argues that given the way in which we humans have treated animals, we have lost the moral right to any particular privileged status in creation. I appreciate the point. Some views about the importance of humanity are arrogant to such an extent that they display scant regard for the rest of life, and the well-being of the earth. But the inference drawn by this advocate of animal rights is dangerous. Such anti-humanist tendencies are, I fear, widespread even though often well intentioned.

A book that impressed me as a theological student was C. A. Coulson's *Science and Christian Belief*.[13] From Coulson, who was then Professor of Applied Mathematics at Oxford, I learnt that scientific endeavour and Christian faith are not opponents, for both are engaged in the same endeavour to understand and interpret the whole of human experience from two different but interrelated perspectives. Since the publication of Coulson's book, and especially during the past two decades, there has been an explosion of literature on science and religion, made possible in part by the work of the Templeton Foundation. In one of them, *Belief in God in an Age of Science,* John Polkinghorne, a physicist and theologian,

---

11 Huston Smith, *Beyond the Postmodern Mind* (Wheaton, Illinois: Quest Books, 2003), p. 139.

12 William Schweiker, *Theological Ethics and Global Dynamics* (Oxford: Blackwell, 2004), p. 202.

13 C. A. Coulson, *Science and Christian Belief* (Oxford: Oxford University Press, 1955).

draws attention to five principal concerns that, for the past several decades, have come to characterize the relationship between science and theology:

> a rejection of reductionism, partly based on an appeal to science's increasing recognition of the interconnected and holistic character of much physical process; an understanding of an evolutionary universe as being compatible with a theological doctrine of *creatio continua*; a revival of a cautiously revised form of natural theology; a methodological comparison of science and theology that exhibits their common concern with the attainment of understanding through the search for motivated belief; and speculations concerning how physical process might be sufficiently open to accommodate acts of agents, both human and divine.[14]

The days in which science and religion faced each other as antagonists, leading to the supposition that you could not accept the findings of science and remain a believer in God, have long since gone. Many of the great scientists of the past and present, including those whose work seems most threatening to Christian faith, were and are believers. Though not always orthodox in their beliefs, they have recognized the limits of science. They know that science, like all intellectual endeavour, requires imagination and inspiration and, with that, a great deal of humility. And they accept, too, their responsibility to defend the interests of humanity, the well-being of humans and the earth on which we live.

All this is highly significant. For if scientific endeavour and progress was one of the key forces that led to secularization and the decline of religion in parts of the world, the persistence of religion, together with a growing correspondence between science and theology, has signalled a new awareness of human wholeness. If we want to accept the findings of science and yet remain believers we do not have to live in two worlds that are at odds with each other, as many have tried to do in

---

14 John Polkinghorne, *Belief in God in an Age of Science* (New Haven: Yale University Press, 1998), p. xi.

the past. Or reject the one in favour of the other. At the same time, this does not mean that all the problems and difficulties that have so often separated scientists and believers are now resolved. It means that we can pursue a more integrated path in search of human wholeness.

But having said that, it is important to recognize that many secular people cannot believe in God on philosophical, scientific and moral grounds, nor can they identify with the Church or other religious institutions and movements. At the same time, they share with many believers a concern for the world and its well-being. Unlike secularists who are motivated by self-interest, these secular or neo-humanists seek to live and act responsibly in the world for the sake of human well-being. They are those who, in the words of Vatican II, 'are conscious that they themselves are the artisans and authors of the culture of their community'.[15]

Secular defenders of humanity

Secular humanism has changed in various ways since the Enlightenment, and is now often referred to as neo-humanism. Neo-humanists recognize the need to move beyond the polemics of the past and co-operate with all people of goodwill and moral concern, whether secular or religious. Moreover, while claiming that reason, experience and scientific endeavour are our only resources for dealing with the challenges that face us as human beings, neo-humanists are far more aware of their limits. But above all, in contrast to the creed of secularism, they are concerned about the common good, and seek to promote values and virtues essential to democratic society and human well-being across the planet.

Few eminent neo-humanists of the twentieth century articulated this position as eloquently and persuasively as Julian Huxley, one time Professor of Zoology at the University of London, and widely regarded as a founding figure in those academic societies dedicated to spreading humanist ideas

15 Walter M. Abbott, *The Documents of Vatican II* (London-Dublin: Geoffrey Chapman, 1966), pp. 260–1.

today. He was convinced that human beings had to work out their own destiny within the framework of an 'evolutionary humanism' that links human destiny to the cosmos as a whole. Writing in the 1960s in the midst of the Cold War and the threat of nuclear war, and when new sobering statistics about the world's population explosion were becoming available, Huxley criticized Christianity for being rationally untenable, and for obfuscating the problems and preventing the attainment of a 'comprehensive vision of human destiny'.[16] He was not against religion as such, only against what he regarded as outdated theism, the religious absolutes derived from it, and religious institutions that so clung to the past that they were unable to respond to the present. Instead he proposed what he called the 'lineaments of a new religion' that would sanctify the higher manifestations of human nature, in art and love, in intellectual comprehension and aspiring adoration, and would emphasize the fuller realization of life's possibilities as a sacred trust.[17]

But Huxley despaired about humanity's ability to deal with the problems facing the future of the world, and it was this that attracted him to the writings of the Catholic palaeontologist and Jesuit theologian Pierre Teilhard de Chardin. Professor of Geology at the Catholic Institute in Paris, Teilhard was a profoundly religious and hopeful person, a humble priest and pastor, and in a certain sense, a mystic. As Huxley wrote in his introduction to Teilhard's classic, *The Phenomenon of Man*:

> Through his combination of wide scientific knowledge with deep religious feeling and a rigorous sense of values he has forced theologians to view their ideas in the new perspective of evolution, and scientists to see the spiritual implications of their knowledge. He has both clarified and unified our vision of reality. In the light of that new comprehension, it is no longer possible to maintain that science and religion

16 *The Humanist Frame*, ed. Julian Huxley (London: George Allen & Unwin, 1961), p. 40.

17 *The Humanist Frame*, p. 26.

must operate in thought-tight compartments or concern separate sectors of life: they are both relevant to the whole of human existence.[18]

I had read Teilhard in the 1960s but had never become an enthusiast. Now I can better appreciate his remarkable contribution. Despite criticisms from the Vatican at the time, he was, in the best sense of the word, a Christian apologist, dedicated to showing that scientific investigation was not a threat to Christianity but rather a resource for refining and understanding its claims. Early on, Teilhard expressed his hope that his work would 'tear away the mask of atheism' from new currents of thought, and expose them as Christian.[19] And later, in one of his classics, *Le Milieu Divin*, he sought to answer the 'great objection brought against Christianity ... and the real source of the distrust which insulates entire blocks of humanity from the influence of the Church', namely 'the suspicion that our religion makes its followers *inhuman*'.[20] All of Teilhard's work was an attempt to comprehend this 'new Christian humanism', or what it meant to be truly human from both an evolutionary and Christian perspective, in all its aspects.[21]

Given their very different backgrounds and beliefs, it may seem surprising at first glance that Huxley and Teilhard had such great respect for each other, the one an ardent Christian believer, the other decidedly not. But while Huxley recognized in Teilhard a kindred spirit who took seriously the findings of science about what it means to be human, he rejected the theistic framework of Christianity, and sought to rework many of its key beliefs in a way that would contribute to the positive evolutionary development of the cosmos. We cannot call on a

---

18 Pierre Teilhard de Chardin, *The Phenomenon of Man* (New York: Harper & Brothers, 1959), p. 26.

19 In a letter to a friend, 22 July 1916, quoted in Robert Speaight, *Teilhard de Chardin: A Biography* (London: Collins, 1968), p. 75.

20 Pierre Teilhard de Chardin, *Le Milieu Divin* (London: Collins Fontana, 1957), p. 68.

21 N. M. Wildiers, *An Introduction to Teilhard de Chardin* (London: Collins Fontana, 1968), p. 158.

'divinized father-figure' or an 'inscrutable Providence' to help us, but we can, Huxley said, call upon 'an array of potential helpers – all the possibilities of wonder and knowledge, of delight and reverence, of creative belief and moral purpose, of passionate effort and embracing love'.[22] And we need to do so because the task of developing a new and different way of responding to the world was urgent and the challenges immense. These sentiments are very different from the cynical secularism we considered previously, and even from much secular humanism of the past. But they are increasingly reflected in the position of contemporary neo-humanists.

Consider the *Humanist Manifesto 2000* produced by the International Academy of Humanism and endorsed by some of the leading contemporary scholars and intellectuals of our time. In a section on 'Ethics and Reason' the Manifesto states:

> ... *humanists recognize our responsibilities and duties to others.* This means that we ought not to treat other human beings as mere objects for our own gratification; we must consider them as persons entitled to equality of consideration. Humanists hold that 'each individual should be treated humanely'. Similarly, they accept the Golden Rule that 'we should not treat others as we would not like to be treated'. They accept the biblical injunction that we should 'accept aliens within our midst', respecting their differences with us. Given the multiplicity of creeds, we are all strangers – yet can be friends – in the broader community.[23]

One of the most significant contemporary neo-humanist voices is Mario Rodríguez Cobos, or Silo as he is also known. In a lecture given in 1994 on 'What do we understand by Universal Humanism today?' Silo declared: 'We aspire to a humanism that contributes to the improvement of life, and that stands in a common front against discrimination,

---

22 *The Humanist Frame*, p. 19.
23 *Humanist Manifesto 2000: A Call for a New Planetary Humanism*, ed. Drafted by Paul Kurtz (New York: Prometheus Books), p. 32.

fanaticism, exploitation and violence.'[24] He went on to say that this humanism had to be universal, pluralistic, unifying and creative, not simply a repeat of old forms, but 'a *new humanism* that will encompass the paradoxes of our age and aspire to resolve them'.[25] Silo then set out the qualities that he believed represent a common humanist attitude:

> (1) placement of the human being as the central value and concern; (2) affirmation of the equality of all human beings; (3) recognition of personal and cultural diversity; (4) stressing the development of new knowledge that goes beyond absolute truth; (5) affirmation of the freedom of ideas and beliefs; and (6) repudiation of all forms of violence.[26]

Whatever criticism may be levelled against these affirmations (for example, the first says nothing about the interconnected relationship between humanity and the environment), such secular neo-humanism is clearly an attractive option for people who have become disillusioned with the Church and disenchanted with the teachings of Christianity.

The journey from Christian faith to secular humanism has been travelled often since the European Enlightenment; some of its major representative figures were children of clergy and some were trained theologians. There is a whole history of what scholars refer to as 'de-conversion', that is, stories of people who once believed, but no longer do so.[27] This process still continues. Over the years, several of my friends and colleagues have resigned from the Christian ministry and given up going to church. Having started off with a strong sense of vocation, and after long years of faithful service in the Church, the decision to leave has not come suddenly or without pain. But it has come nonetheless, almost inexorably, until in the

---

24 Puledda Salvatore, *On Being Human: Interpretations of Humanism from the Renaissance to the Present* (San Diego, CA: Latitude Press, 1997), p. 146.

25 Puledda Salvatore, *On Being Human*, p. 146.

26 Puledda Salvatore, *On Being Human*, p. 147.

27 John D. Barbour, *Versions of Deconversion: Autobiography and the Loss of Faith* (Charlottesville, NC: University Press of Virginia, 1994).

end the decision to resign has been a mere formality. Perhaps just as it is usually impossible to put a time and date on when Christian commitment first began, so it is equally difficult to say precisely when the decision to de-convert is made. But whereas once they believed, now they don't; whereas once they were involved in the Church, now they are not.

For many, the journey from Christianity to secular humanism has not ended there. Like Karen Armstrong or Huxley they have sought a new or different spirituality that enabled them to be more 'truly human'. What they rejected was the 'God' represented by too many religious and Christian people. If that is what God is like, we can hear them say, I really do not want to believe any longer. How many have stopped being Christian, I wonder, because Christianity seems to have been taken over by Christian fundamentalism or imperialism, and the God it portrays? Do I really want to be identified with that God? Bad religion is infinitely worse than no religion at all. Is it not true that many secular humanists live lives that are more compassionate, more concerned about human rights, more engaged in the struggle for justice and peace, than many Christians? Would we not rather be in their company than among religious people, Christians among them, whose view of God demonizes and dehumanizes others with whom they disagree? But as one of my former Christian friends turned neo-humanist once said to me: 'You are a believer and I am not.' Yes, that is the nub of the matter, the critical difference between Christian and secular humanists. Yet there is sometimes more uniting such believers and non-believers than there is uniting believers with some kinds of religious people, or uniting such secular neo-humanists with self-centred secularists.

Christian humanists and neo-humanists share and recognize a common humanity that binds us together despite differences, and we are concerned about justice and the future of the world. So it was that in the struggle against apartheid, Christians and people of other faith traditions joined hands together with neo-humanists and communists to fight injustice and work for liberation, until the tide of protest became unstoppable. The same happened in Eastern Europe, bringing about the demise of Soviet power. In the Third Reich such co-operation was far more restricted, but no less real as a handful of confessing Christians and secular men and women formed an alliance in defence of human values. Indeed, these very values – reason, culture, humanity, freedom and tolerance – that had previously been used as slogans against Christianity suddenly came 'very near indeed to the Christian standpoint'.[28] The surprising factor in this development was that this rapprochement was not at the expense of Christian conviction, for it

> took place at a time when everything Christian was more closely hemmed in than ever before and when the cardinal principles of Christian belief were displayed in their hardest and most uncompromising form, in a form which could give greatest offence to all reason, culture, humanity and tolerance.[29]

The Christians who began to co-operate with the secular humanists were not liberal Protestants but those most committed to the Confessing Church with its categorical rejection of culture as another source of revelation. There is, in other words, no reason why committed Christians and convinced neo-humanists should regard themselves as enemies, especially if both realize, as Rahner puts it, 'that their obligations are to the future more than to the past'. What is at stake is a more humane and compassionate global future, instead of one torn apart by sectarian and ethnic conflict. So why not, Rahner says, 'try together to come to a clearer awareness of those hoped-for aspects of the future which has as yet been anticipated only dimly – justice, freedom, dignity, unity and diversity in society'?[30]

Secular humanists and Christian humanists not only share a common humanity and commitment to human well-being,

---

28 Bonhoeffer, *Ethics*, p. 55.
29 Bonhoeffer, *Ethics*, p. 55.
30 Rahner, 'Christian Humanism', p. 203.

but also try to live in depth rather than on the surface, something we now generally call 'spirituality'. The best neo-humanists I know sense the need for something more tran-scendent than the mundane, something that gives more meaning to life than science can offer. This desire, Christians believe, derives from our creation 'in the image of God'. In Augustine's celebrated words that come at the very outset of his *Confessions*: 'You have made us for yourself, and our hearts are restless until they rest in you.'[31] Secular humanism also seems to lack a sense of hope that enables one to transcend the despair about the world that those most concerned about its future often experience. Indeed, the problem with atheism as such, is its incapacity to carry the load of either human tragedy or hope. So it is important for Christian humanists to remember that we are theological, not secular humanists, lest finding common ground and fostering co-operation in the in-terests of humanity, we do not make our unique contribution. A reminder of the importance of this contribution comes from an unlikely source, Thomas Mann, the German novelist and secular humanist, who wrote in 1939 after fleeing Germany: 'Liberty, truth, true reason, human dignity – whence did we create these ideas, ideas that are the mainstay and support of our lives and without which our spiritual existence would disintegrate, if not from Christianity, which made them uni-versal law?'[32]

In some ways most of us who are committed to social jus-tice, whether neo-humanists or Christian, are a blend of the secular and the religious, something described so well by Robert Coles in his *The Secular Mind*. Recalling two conver-sations he had, one in the late 1950s with Tillich, the other some years later with Dorothy Day, founder of the Catholic Worker Movement in New York,[33] Coles noted that it is only in the midst of the secular that we experience transcendence, or moments of religious quality and significance. These trans-

---

31 Book 1, chapter 1/1.

32 Thomas Mann, 'Der Problem der Freiheit', in *Essays*, vol. 11, 1939, pp. 228–44, quoted in de Lange, 'A Particular Europe, a Universal Faith', p. 89.

33 Robert Coles, *The Secular Mind* (Princeton, NJ: Princeton University Press, 1999), pp. 3–7.

form life, give it depth, a sacred quality, meaning and hope. Concern for this world, for the material, does not mean that there is a lack of awareness of the transcendent or spiritual dimensions of reality. All of which points to what we might call a 'mature worldliness' as distinct from the immature worldliness or pious unworldliness of much religion, and the self-centred individualism that characterizes secularism.

Mature worldliness

If Kepel's book documented God's revenge against those who had prematurely announced God's death, another book entitled *God's Funeral* published nine years later in the year 2000 affirmed the 'death of God', but then in an ironic twist in its tail, spoke of an alternative vision of Christianity. Written by A. N. Wilson, a Christian turned neo-humanist, we were reminded of a legacy of Christian faith and action that still had amazing attraction in an age of religious fundamentalism and secularism. Wilson concluded his analysis with the comment:

> Just as Nietzsche's generation were declaring the death of God and Thomas Hardy was witnessing his burial, religious thinkers as varied as Simone Weil, Dietrich Bonhoeffer, Nicholas Berdayev and Teilhard de Chardin were waiting in the wings.[34]

In the same breath, Wilson referred to John Paul II, Martin Luther King Jr and Trevor Huddleston who demonstrated the potency of the Christian faith in the public arena.

There are many other names we could add to this list – some well known and famous, others less so – who have given daily expression to a vibrant and authentic expression of Christianity in responding to the challenges of modernity and a world struggling against dehumanizing forces and powers. Whatever they shared in common with secular humanists in that struggle, they remained believers. But their feet were firmly

---

34 A. N. Wilson, *God's Funeral* (London: Abacus, 2000), p. 465.

planted on this earth. They understood full well the meaning and implications of the incarnation that, in William Temple's words, made Christianity the 'most materialist' of religions. That is, being truly secular, living fully in the world, but living by faith in the God who became fully embodied in this world, for the sake of this world. This 'mature worldliness' is not, Bonhoeffer said,

> the shallow and banal this-worldliness of the enlightened, the busy, the comfortable or the lascivious, but the profound this-worldliness characterized by discipline and the constant knowledge of death and resurrection.[35]

'Being secular' understood in this way is not a denial of Christian discipleship, but an expression of free responsibility as Christians in the world.

What, then, do Christian humanists of this kind bring to the table? At the 1949 Geneva conference on 'A New Humanism' to which I referred earlier, what struck Barth most forcibly was the lack of hope that was evident in many of the participants, though more so among the liberal humanists than the Marxists. For while they were optimists with regard to human potential, they were pessimists when it came to believing that humans could fulfil their hopes for a better world. By way of contrast, Barth's own presentation on the 'humanism of God' offered a way forward whereby 'human dignity, duty and rights' could be realized.[36] This, I believe, is a critical difference, and one that is essential in combating anti-humanism. It is not romantic optimism about the human condition, but a commitment to the human project as something God-given, something to be cherished and nurtured, something that we do not give up on despite so much that would normally drive us to despair.

The rediscovery of hope as a critical theological contribution to the post-war debate in Europe was crucial to the way in which both theology and the ecumenical Church responded

---

35 Bonhoeffer, *Letters and Papers from Prison*, p. 282.
36 Barth, *God Here and Now*, pp. 6–7.

to the world situation. I remember the impact Jürgen Moltmann's *Theology of Hope*[37] made upon many of us in the
1960s as we engaged in the church struggle in South Africa,
opening up fresh perspectives on possibilities for Christian
action. Hope, not as wishful thinking, but as living and acting
in anticipation of the coming of God's reign; hope, not as res-
ignation to an unjust world, but as a refusal to accept that this
was what God wanted for humanity. Hope, firmly grounded
in the resurrection of Christ from the dead, as participation in
God's future for the world.

Shortly before the first post-apartheid democratic elections
in South Africa, I was privileged to be the only theologian
present at a think-tank of social scientists who were assessing whether or not the election could really be held, given the
levels of violence in certain parts of the country. After a day of
depressing analysis and prognosis, I eventually injected a little
theology. Hope, I suggested, is trusting in what we do not yet
see; without such hope nothing will ever change. In some respects, this understanding of hope as acting in anticipation of
change aligned us with socialists and communists who were
likewise struggling for a new world order of justice and peace.
And, indeed, some of us had been previously labelled communist for this very reason. But we were wary of totalitarian
utopias in which people are sacrificed on the altar of some
future ideal, or subsumed within the mass. The reality of God
revealed in Jesus Christ always meant that we were critical
of anything that might dehumanize people, even for the sake
of a greater good. Without that sense of transcendence that
challenges and judges us, human beings soon destroy one
another.

While neo-humanism might have some sense of the transcendence in affirming the 'other' as distinct from the self,
such transcendence remains humanly contingent. It does
not provide resources from beyond both self and other that
can check the abuse of freedom and power. Faith in God,
as affirmed by Christian humanists by contrast, signals the
recognition that we cannot live unsupported by a grace or

---

37 Jürgen Moltmann, *Theology of Hope* (London: SCM Press, 1967).

unchallenged by a commandment to love that comes from beyond ourselves. Anything less denies our full humanity and puts our common humanity and its concerns at risk. To quote again from Hammarskjöld's *Markings*: 'God does not die on the day when we cease to believe in a personal deity, but we die on the day when our lives cease to be illuminated by the steady radiance, renewed daily, of a wonder, the source of which is beyond all reason.'[38] There are many secular humanists who have come to recognize the truth of this, and some who have turned to Christianity to rediscover transcendence as the ground of hope for worldly transformation.

We are now in a position to return to the question we asked at the beginning of this chapter. Was Bonhoeffer's proposal for a 'religionless Christianity' simply wrong and misleading, giving rise to some passing and faddish experiments in doing theology, or is there some more enduring insight that is of importance for us today in seeking to be human and Christian? I believe the latter is true. What he was rejecting was not the spirituality of genuine faith and prayer, but the kind of religion that is individualistic, ego-centric and inward looking, based on a metaphysical view of the world largely discredited by science. A Christian, as Bonhoeffer put it, is not a 'religious person' (*homo religiosus*) in this sense at all, but simply a human being as Jesus was a human being.[39] True transcendence is not to be found somewhere beyond this world, but in Jesus 'the man for others' who lived 'out of the transcendent'.[40] This was important because Bonhoeffer wanted to start

> from the premise that God shouldn't be smuggled into some last secret place, but that we should frankly recognize that the world, and people, have come of age, that we shouldn't run man down in his worldliness, but confront him with God at his strongest point ...[41]

38 Dag Hammarskjöld , *Markings*, p. 64.
39 Bonhoeffer, *Letters and Papers from Prison*, p. 361.
40 Bonhoeffer, *Letters and Papers from Prison*, p. 382.
41 Bonhoeffer, *Letters and Papers from Prison*, p. 346.

5

A Believer

Put at its most stark, the choice is between seeing authentic human life as a life of participation in a supreme reality of wisdom, compassion and bliss, or as the triumph of the will to power and survival, a temporary triumph to be sure, doomed to final failure.
Keith Ward[1]

We know with a strange sort of confidence, that we draw our humanity from the God who created us. The more complex that humanity, that personhood turns out to be, the more interesting our God becomes for us ... Sara Maitland[2]

You shall not make for yourself an idol. Exodus 20.4

God is love, and those who abide in love abide in God, and God abides in them. 1 John 4.16

Christians as diverse as the fourteenth-century mystic Julian of Norwich and the Protestant Reformer John Calvin remind us that it is impossible to know ourselves without some knowledge of God, and that the reverse is also true. The way in which we understand what it means to be human says something about our understanding of God, or what is of ultimate significance for those who are non-believers. So the word 'God' means different things to different people. In what follows, I will use the word to refer to God as traditionally understood by theists whatever their specific religious tradition, aware, however, that at critical points their paths diverge. By contrast, I will use the word 'god' to refer to images of God that are, from this perspective, idols, inadequate representations of the God in whom theists believe.

'God-talk' raises many questions. Is God personal? Does God exist as a Being 'out there' who created the world and

1 Keith Ward, *God, Chance and Necessity* (Oxford: Oneworld Publications, 1996), p. 177.
2 Sara Maitland, *A Big-Enough God* (London: Mowbray, 1995), p. 73.

governs it, or is God pure *Being*, beyond space and time and therefore 'No-where' as well as 'No-thing'? Can God be both beyond us and yet immanent within us? If God does exist, what is God's character, and how do we know? Is God another word for Fate, or does God intervene in history for human good, answering prayers and performing miracles? Is God all loving and almighty, and if so how do we explain evil and suffering, and the lack of such intervention? If God is beyond human grasp, a mystery of infinite beauty and majesty, is it plausible to believe that we can 'know God' in a personal way? Is there some sense of the divine implanted in our humanity, a religious sixth sense or 'a priori' as scholars call it, that has to do with what it means to be human? If so, why is it that this sense of God is awakened in some people and not in others? Further, if God is one, as the monotheistic traditions insist, why have different ways of conceiving the divine emerged to produce varying, even conflicting faith traditions? Is only the perception of God historically and contextually shaped, or does God as God change, perhaps in response to human suffering?

Such perennial questions, some raised innocently by children, throw us into the deep end of Christian apologetics. Attempting detailed answers would take us well beyond the task at hand. But if it is true that 'to be human is to know within you – and therefore within everyone else as well – the pattern of God, a God who is beyond all boundaries and all conceiving',[3] we cannot avoid reflecting on such questions. So let me give some account of why I am a believer and what this means for me.

A sense of awe and justice

I was brought up on the slopes of Table Mountain in Cape Town and recall those long-ago nights I spent on its back table sleeping under the stars far away from the city lights that detract from that cosmic spectacle. My first recollection of reading Psalm 8 was while camping on one of its highest rocky

---

3 Mayne, *Learning to Dance*, p. 234.

outcrops during 1956, the year I entered the University of Cape Town, and not too long after my youthful conversion:

> When I look at your heavens, the work of your fingers,
>   the moon and the stars that you have established;
> what are human beings that you are mindful of them,
>   and mortals that you care for them?
> Yet you have made them a little lower than God,
>   and crowned them with glory and honour.
> You give them dominion over the works of your hand ...
>   (Psalm 8.3–6 NRSV)

Since then I have had the opportunity to hike on some of the wonderful trails of the Western Cape, to spend evenings marvelling at the Milky Way, the galaxy of which we are a tiny, yet, according to the psalmist, significant part, and the Southern Cross that locates me at the tip of Africa. Such experiences, shared by multitudes from time immemorial suggest, even though they do not prove, that there is a divine origin to the cosmos and life as we know it. They also bring our humanity into perspective. Made of stardust – carbon to be exact – we are linked to the cosmos, and despite our apparent insignificance before the vastness above and beyond us, we have the capacity to explore the mystery of the universe, as well as our place and role within it.

At the same time as I was exploring the mountains of the Cape, awakening to the grandeur of the universe and struggling to understand my fledgling faith, I was also becoming more aware of the moral order of the universe. I remember the General Election in 1948 that brought the National Party to power with its crudely formulated policy of apartheid. As my father and I listened to the election results on the radio throughout the evening, he commented time and again that the impending outcome boded ill for both the future of the country and his own future as a civil servant. At the time I did not understand that the defeated United Party led by the internationally respected statesman, Jan Smuts, was also premised on racially unjust policies. But my memory of my father's foreboding at Smuts' defeat remains with me. During the next few years I witnessed first hand, though only vaguely grasping its significance, the segregation of the buses on our home route, the removal of people of colour from their homes in the street in which we lived, and a heightening of a sense of racial awareness as we stood in line to receive identity documents. As whites, or European as we were listed, that was painless; for those who were not, it was a dehumanizing experience. Racial identity had become an idol, and those who opposed it were ostracized and penalized.

During my first year as a university student I taught Sunday School in District Six, the infamous symbol of the iniquitous Group Areas Act and, on my way home via the Parade, sometimes stopped to listen to open-air speakers from the African National Congress and Communist Party condemn the growing legislation and practices of apartheid. I began to share my father's foreboding as I heard talk of protest and revolution, and of people being arrested for opposing apartheid or going into exile rather than face detention. Even though many white people were celebrating the advent of apartheid as the entrenchment of white power, there were always some who sensed that we were entering a dark age. And I too, dimly at first, felt that something inherently wrong was unfolding, and that somehow policies that regarded people as inferior human beings could not be reconciled with belief in the God of the Bible I now faithfully read day by day. I was also vaguely aware that there were communists in our midst who did not believe in God, and that they were 'public enemy number one'. But I found it difficult to apply that label to the one family in our neighbourhood whose father had been arrested for trade union activities. As yet I had no grasp of the full magnitude of what was happening, or the political knowledge to appreciate the issues. But I would soon begin to wonder why it was that atheists were concerned about justice and human rights, and religious people in power were not.

One of the first lectures I attended as an undergraduate student was in the Department of Philosophy, the subject was Plato's *Republic*, the professor was Martin Versfeld.

An Afrikaner by birth, Versfeld had been brought up in the Dutch Reformed Church, but later, through his study of St Thomas Aquinas and St Augustine, Versfeld converted to the Catholic Church. He was a remarkable teacher who prodded us into thinking more deeply about the great issues of life and morality, about what it means to be human. Those familiar with Plato's *Republic* will know that it is an exploration of the meaning of justice or, more precisely, how a sense of justice is inculcated in us as individuals and embodied in the state. They will also know that for Plato justice was not a mere social convention, or something we pursue in order to gain reward, but intrinsically good, something that arises from within us as an essential part of being human. Justice, declares Socrates, Plato's alter-ego, 'is not a matter of external behaviour, but of the inward self and of attending to all that is, in the fullest sense, a man's proper concern'.[4]

In the same way as Psalm 8 leads us to ponder our humanity before the immensity and grandeur of the universe, so other psalms, along with the writings of the Hebrew prophets, remind us of a God of justice whose moral order provides the basis for human life. This interconnected sense of awe before the beauty of the infinite and a sense of justice when injustice becomes apparent, however imperfectly formulated in my mind and experience at that time, is affirmed in many religious traditions. It also found classic philosophical expression in the conclusion to one of the great texts of the Enlightenment, Kant's *Critique of Practical Reason*:

> Two things fill the mind with ever new increasing admiration and awe, the oftener and more steadily we reflect on them: the starry heavens above and the moral law within.[5]

Kant sought to reconstruct Christianity within the limits of reason alone. In doing so God became the universal lawgiver

---

4 Plato, *The Republic*, translated and edited by Francis MacDonald Cornford (Oxford: Clarendon Press, 1955), p. 138.

5 Kant's *Critique of Practical Reason* (London: Longmans Green, 1954), p. 260.

above all else, and morality the touchstone for determining truth and assessing faith. Although deeply nurtured by Pietism, Kant came down decisively on the side of its practical outworking, so that the fulfilment of duty and moral obligation was the source of happiness and joy. Whatever we may think of Kantian philosophy, we are surely moved by the sentiments that bring to a close his reasoned critique of rationalism. For our minds are filled 'with ever increasing admiration and awe' the more we learn about and reflect on the cosmos, the more we discover about the origin and evolution of life on our planet, and the more we learn about our own bodies, especially our brains and consciousness. Reason helps us clarify and partly explain this sensibility, but is reason capable in and of itself to explain it fully?

Our growing sense of awe before the majesty and beauty of the universe and our own bodies, would not have been possible without the evolution of the brain and the emergence of human consciousness that took more than fifteen thousand million years to develop. Without this amazing development we would have no sense of awe, no ability to choose between what is good and what is not. Science is beginning to help us understand this, but its explorations point beyond the world of material or physical reality. There is, so it seems after all, a 'mind in the machine'. 'The mystery' writes Ward, 'is how it comes about that the construction of brains, of complicated collections of purely physical particles, gives rise to something apparently non-physical: thoughts, feelings, dreams, images and intentions.'[6] Mysterious, indeed, is the evolution of a sense of beauty, of conscience, moral awareness and responsibility, and the sense of freedom to choose to participate in the ongoing creation or to destroy it.

The psalmist lived long before the rise of modern science. Although he marvelled at the universe he had little knowledge of its actual size, composition, or the earth's place within it. And even though Kant lived in a post-Copernican world in which scientific knowledge was rapidly expanding, he lived long before evolutionary biology or the exploration of space

---

6 Ward, *God, Chance and Necessity*, p. 147.

so vastly expanded our knowledge of the world. But we to-day, in considering what it means to be fully human, dare not ignore the awe-inspiring advances in science, notably in quantum physics, cosmology, evolutionary and micro-biology, that are reshaping our understanding of the universe in which we live. On the contrary, as we delight in the amazing scientific discoveries of our time, we discover the interconnectedness of all life on our planet, discerning dimensions of our humanity that expand our wonder and sense of responsibility for the world.

The same sense that moves us to wonder and worship, also makes us aware of the awesomeness of natural disasters that afflict millions of people. And the awakening of a sense of justice occurs precisely because we become conscious of the suffering caused by injustice. These sensitivities raise disturbing questions. Can the God who has created such beauty also be the author of the ugliness that afflicts the world? Can the God who creates life also be the agent of death and destruction? What kind of God allows pain and suffering, injustice and oppression to overshadow so much of the beauty that surrounds us, subverting the ends of justice in dehumanizing oppression? Many thinking people become atheists or agnostics because they cannot find an answer to these questions. It is one thing to be moved to faith by a sense of awe and justice, but any person sensitive to human suffering can equally be moved to anger and disbelief before the 'terrible power, mystery and apparent arbitrariness – in all the particular aspects of our experience'.[7] So it is that the Puritan poet John Milton begins *Paradise Lost* with an invocation to the Muses to enable him to 'justify the ways of God to men'.

My confident trust in God, awakened by conversion and confirmed by the wonder of the cosmos, was challenged early on in my ministry in Durban. A few weeks after I began my pastoral work, a five-year-old boy fell to his death out of a tree in which he was playing with his twin. This was the first funeral I conducted. I cannot remember what I said on that occasion, but I am sure it was no easy task. Later that year, a

7 Ward, *God, Chance and Necessity*, p. 153.

drunken driver ran over the six-year-old son of church members as he was crossing the street near our church. I well remember going to their home shortly after and sitting among the family members and friends who had gathered to share the parents' grief. I recall the tears and anguish, and the agonizing question: 'Why did God allow it to happen?' And the troubling response of some: 'God knows best; it was God's will.' It was not the appropriate time to suggest that it was the abuse of alcohol that was to blame, not God, or to try and answer the questions being raised. But these questions did not go away, nor are they easier to answer as the years pass. The suffering of just one person unjustly, or in the face of some inscrutable deity named Fate, moves us to question whether there can be a God, and if so, whether the nature of God can be all powerful and all loving. On a much larger scale, the Asian tsunami disaster raises this theodicy question for the twenty-first century in the same way as the Lisbon earthquake did for an earlier generation.

The problem looms large on many of the Bible's pages, but nowhere do its authors try to prove the 'existence of God'. That is assumed throughout. The problem is not whether faith in God is possible or reasonable, but whether we can trust and love God as compassionate and just, or whether we must simply resign ourselves to a God who is capricious and apparently unmoved by human pain. The psalms are full of this struggle, not between faith and unbelief, but between trust in God and anger at God's apparent absence and lack of concern. Nowhere is this more poignantly described than in the saga of Job, whose wife urges him to 'curse God and die', or on a national scale, in the prophet Jeremiah's laments that God seems blind to injustice.

There are different ways of responding to the problem of theodicy, depending on whether human suffering results from natural disasters, human violence, war and ethnic cleansing, or from widespread epidemics such as HIV and AIDS. One response has to do with the freedom God has given us to live, not as automatons but as responsible world citizens. Another response to the theodicy questions focuses on the way in which the world is created and life has evolved and continues to do so within the cosmic galaxy. What has made life possible also brings life to an end, whether through natural disaster or natural death. Tsunamis, tragic as they are, are a necessary part of the created order; this is how the universe works. The only qualification to be made, and it is an important one, is that such tragedies are often exacerbated by the extent to which nature has been abused by human exploitation, and by the failure to provide weather monitoring and warning systems that might lessen the destruction even though they cannot prevent earthquake, flood and tidal wave.

On his deathbed Werner Heisenberg, the scientist famous for his work on quantum physics, said that he had two questions to ask God: why relativity, and why turbulence? 'I really think', Heisenberg is reported to have said, 'he may have an answer to the first question.'[8] But why not the second, we may well ask? That is the question raised by 'chaos theory', the theory that seeks to account for turbulence, and reflects on the apparent randomness of so much of our experience of the world. But understanding the world as an open-ended process rather than a closed system, as something that must necessarily be thrown off balance from time to time, does not deny that there is design, pattern, rhythm, purpose and meaning. Chaos is necessary for creativity. There are countless examples of surprising events that have no apparent pattern and defy the accepted ways in which scientists have traditionally worked, but which, in hindsight, reveal purpose and meaning.

I have participated in several workshops on HIV and AIDS, and have conducted Bible studies on the book of Job as part of the programme that both those suffering from HIV or AIDS as well as their care givers evidently found helpful. Even though Job does not resolve all the problems associated with suffering and faith in God, the drama does provide a much-needed perspective if we are to grapple meaningfully with the issues. As I read the book, I constantly find myself affirming positions taken by Job's friends, the so-called 'comforters',

---

8 Recounted in James Gleick, *Chaos: The Amazing Science of the Unpredictable* (New York: Vintage, 1998), p. 121.

for although their responses to Job's plight are ultimately inadequate, they are not flippant, unthinking or uncaring but the result of careful thought and compassion reflecting the wisdom of the ages. For a long time they sit with Job in silence before daring to speak, a sign that they knew only too well the danger of the trite and pious word of comfort. But there is no consensus in the dialogue, for like Job, in the end each of us has to face our own suffering and decide whether or not to continue trusting God.

How is it, then, that people come to believe in God and, even more, continue to believe despite life-shattering experiences of God's lack of compassion or apparent absence? Like most people, I have experienced the death of loved ones and shared with others as they have journeyed through pain and dying. Like everyone else, I have also lived through some difficult times, as during the apartheid years, and there have been moments of family crisis and sadness. But my faith has not been put to the test in the way many people experience, nor did I suffer as a result of opposing apartheid in the way so many others did. Though I have counselled others in times of illness and grief, I wonder how well I would cope with cancer or the death of a child. But I find it astounding that in the most hopeless of circumstances, people have continued to believe in God, and moreover, in God's goodness; that exiles in Babylon, whose lamentations are so heart-wrenching, could still declare that 'the steadfast love of the Lord never ceases' and that God's 'mercies are new every morning' (Lamentations 3.22–3); that Bonhoeffer could write, shortly before his arrest and subsequent murder by the Gestapo:

> I believe that God can and will bring good out of evil, even out of the greatest evil. For that purpose he needs people who make the best use of everything ... I believe that God will give us all the strength we need to help us to resist in all times of distress ... I believe that God is no timeless fate, but that he waits for and answers sincere prayers and responsible actions.[9]

---

9 Bonhoeffer, *Letters and Papers from Prison*, p. 11.

Greater than we can conceive

My first year as a theological student at Rhodes University in Grahamstown ended in December 1957. My vacation job was to help plant a new congregation in Athol, a recently developed suburb north of Johannesburg. I set off from Cape Town on the train, my suitcase loaded with books to be read in preparation for the coming year. My parents told me they were proud of me as I bid them and my sister Rozelle farewell, all three startled by the parting embrace of a girl friend they had only just met on the platform. Several other memories remain vividly in my mind. One was trying to learn Hebrew, another was watching South Africa play Australia in a five-day cricket test match at the nearby Wanderer's cricket ground. This was ample reward for several abortive house visits made on foot in the hot summer sun, though many who are not cricket fans might well wonder whether there is much difference. But I was crazy about cricket, having played for the first team at SACS high school.

The rules and practices of cricket are a mystery to the uninitiated, to those who did not imbibe them with their mother's milk. And those who sit in the sweltering sun for five days to watch a test match that ends in a draw, and which at times is undoubtedly boring even to the devoted, may be regarded as mad. But to true believers, those to whom the mysteries of cricket have been revealed, it is more than a game, it is a religion with its rituals, commandments, minor and major saints, moments of sheer ecstasy and of life-threatening despair, and always the hope of better things to come which bring you back to the stadium for the next match. It is true that some people have become 'true believers', cricket devotees, later in life, but never without being introduced to the game, experiencing it for themselves at least as spectators or on TV, and having its mysteries explained. These can and often do lead to that 'aha!' exclamation when suddenly everything is revealed. This is not unlike the way we come to believe in God. As Job put it: 'I had heard of you by the hearing of the ear, but now my eyes see you.' But, however analogous, coming to faith in

God is obviously qualitatively different from being inducted into the mysteries of cricket.

Though I have used the word several times already, we must be careful not to speak of mystery too easily or quickly in order to avoid dealing adequately with atheist or agnostic criticism, or to locate God in the gaps of our present knowledge. But such hesitation does not mean that there is no mystery beyond our inevitably fallible grasp. After all, the more scientists explore the universe, the more they discover; and the more they fill the gaps, the more they recognize that their knowledge is incomplete and limited. If there are multi-verses out there, as some cosmologists now claim, then the mystery of what is not known presumably grows even greater. But we do not need to go to the stars to grasp the nature of mystery; we can find it within ourselves and our relationships. All we need do is turn to the poets, and especially the poets of love who remind us that the more we know the person we love, the more there is to be known. There is a mystery about love that pulls us deeper into its being without ever exhausting its nature. Mystery is not unknown territory; it is territory in which we know partially, yet at the same time glimpse from a distance far more that is presently beyond our grasp, waiting to be discovered – a 'cloud of unknowing', as that anonymous fourteenth-century English mystic put it, that can only be pierced by a stirring of the will and love enabled by contemplation and action.

One of the classic proofs for the existence of God, the ontological proof made famous by St Anselm of Canterbury in the twelfth century, has always appealed to me even though it cannot conclusively prove God's existence. It is found in a passage in his *Proslogium*, and is expressed in the form of a prayer:

> I do not endeavour O Lord, to penetrate your sublimity, for in no wise do I compare my understanding with that; but I long to understand in some degree your truth, which my heart believes and loves. For I do not seek to understand that I may believe, but I believe in order to understand. For this also I believe, – that unless I believed, I should not

understand. And so, O Lord, do you, who does give understanding to faith, give me, so far as you know it to be profit-
able, to understand that you are as we believe; and that you
are that which we believe. and, indeed, we believe that you
are a being than which nothing greater can be conceived.[10]

Two comments are appropriate here. The first has to do with
how Anselm understood 'faith' in his celebrated statement 'I
believe in order to understand', a comment I referred to earlier
in discussing the difference between studying theology and
religious studies. The second is this: the moment you think
you have grasped who God is, that cannot possibly be God,
for God is precisely 'a being than which nothing greater' can
be thought or imagined.

For Anselm, faith was not an intellectual exercise, as though
we can understand who God is through mental gymnastics.
And that is surely so. Faith is a matter of the heart, not literally the pump that circulates our blood, but the heart as
metaphor for our will and affections, rather than the intellect
or brain operating in isolation from them. This does not mean
that faith is absurd, or without rational foundation, but it is
experiential and experimental. Moreover, for Anselm, faith
became possible only through participation in a community
of faith. For him this meant becoming informed by the Gospel story ('You are *as we* believe'). This circular process, for
such it undoubtedly is, is not very different from the way in
which many advances in knowledge occur. Certainly progress
in the natural sciences often requires a step of faith, which
may be little more than an informed hunch, yet it is taken
from within the community of scientists, aware of what has
previously been discovered even while breaking fresh ground
and contradicting accepted theories.

But what of Anselm's second statement, that God is 'a being than which nothing greater' can be thought or imagined?

---

10 *Proslogium*, St Anselm, *Basic Writings: Proslogium, Monogium, Cur
Deus Hom and The Fool by Gaunilon*, translated by S. N. Deane (La Salle,
Illinois: Open Court, 1968), p. 7. I have modernized the translation's archaic
language.

I recall some words of Harry Emerson Fosdick, a well-known New York preacher of a previous generation, that have stuck with me over the years. 'And as the universe grew great, I dreamt for it a greater God.' It is not that we do not have some knowledge of God, but rather that our knowledge is always inadequate both by definition and in relation to our own experience. As our knowledge of the cosmos expands and as our own experience of life changes, so too must our understanding of God – and ourselves. The early European explorers set out across the Atlantic already knowing something about the ocean, its currents and islands, because of previous explorations, so they had some inkling of what might lie ahead. But it remained a mystery to be plumbed, and only as they travelled further did they begin to discover the truth of what lay beyond. The same is true today as the cosmos is explored. Despite remarkable achievements, and an expanding knowledge of what is 'out there', it simply cannot keep pace with an 'expanding universe'. So, too, must our grasp of God expand lest we are left clinging to an idol.

Science helps us understand both the universe and ourselves, but is unable to prove or disprove the existence of God. 'Absence of evidence is not evidence of absence',[11] as Sir Martin Rees, the British Astronomer Royal, puts it with reference to the existence of intelligent life beyond our planet. Atheism too is ultimately a claim that cannot be scientifically tested and verified. God is beyond abstract reasoning, beyond discovery by telescope or spaceship. Faith in God is a personal commitment but it is not blind or irrational. Because we cannot finally and conclusively prove the existence of God does not mean that God does not exist. As Keith Ward puts the matter with stark clarity: 'God is either necessary, and so God exists, or God is impossible, and so could not possibly exist. Either way, the existence of God is not more improbable than the existence of blind laws of nature.'[12] When scientists move beyond the data at their disposal and make metaphysical

11 Martin Rees, *Our Cosmic Habitat* (London: Weidenfeld and Nicolson, 2002), p. 28.

12 Ward, *God, Chance and Necessity*, p. 115.

statements they are acting as theologians, or anti-theologians, not scientists. But when theologians claim that there are gaps in scientific knowledge and that it is precisely there that God resides or becomes necessary for explaining things, we must proceed with much caution. For as scientific exploration and knowledge expands, so the gaps are explained and the possibility of God whittled away and, in principle, finally excluded. If we can only believe in God because science has limits, then we are in a sorry state. That is why the classic proofs for the existence of God may be very helpful but not necessarily conclusive.

'Proofs' for the existence of God, great and plausible as some are, cannot 'prove' that God exists. But even the notion of proving God's existence is problematic, for it suggests that God exists like any other object or person, that is, as '*a*' Being somewhere. The problem becomes more evident when we say that God also exists everywhere at the same time. For this reason, believing philosophers as well as theologians and especially mystics have tried to find a language that points beyond existence to Being. Nonetheless, if we believe in God we usually think of God as 'existing' because we lack the necessary resources to think otherwise. We think about God in terms of what we know and experience, hence words such as Father, Almighty, Redeemer, Friend or Spirit (analogous with Wind or Breath), help us to understand what we mean and so relate meaningfully to God. But such anthropomorphisms, metaphors and analogies are only inadequate attempts at speaking about God, always subject to human limitations. God is like this or that, we say; but God is not simply this or that – God is beyond this or that. The great mystics, poets and theologians of all religious traditions converge at this 'still point', and even if they describe it in different ways, they meet 'in the silence' in which the word of revelation is heard.

My first Hebrew teacher was a learned Jewish scholar who lived in a small house in Johannesburg. The rooms of the house, especially his study, were crammed with books and artefacts of Jewish history, culture and religion. I went there several times during my vacation pastoral work in that city and was, I

believe, doing reasonably well, until one day I made a terrible
mistake. While reading from the *Torah* I unwittingly uttered
the sacred name for God revealed to Moses beside the burn-
ing bush (Exodus 3.14). There are many names for God in the
Hebrew Bible, Adonai and Elohim among them, but there is
one name that is above all others, a name of such immensity
and mystery that it should never be uttered. In the original
Hebrew text there are no vowels, so the sacred name simply
reads: YHWH, usually translated 'I am who I am', though
there is uncertainty about its pronunciation. Other Hebrew
names for God bring God within our reach; they describe
God in terms we can grasp by analogy with our own experience. But YHWH refers to the God beyond our imagination,
literally so. To utter the word is unpardonable for it suggests
an arrogant familiarity with God, an ability to 'image God',
and thus a breaking of the First Commandment. In order to
convey the sacredness of this Name, many of my later Jewish
students wrote 'G-d' in their essays.

Having uttered the sacred Name in my Hebrew teacher's
study, there was nothing I could do to reverse the situation.
He was deeply disturbed by my indiscretion, not least because
he had *heard* the Name however incorrectly pronounced. He
closed the Bible, rose from his desk, left the room to wash his
hands and face, and, returning sometime later, ushered me
firmly out of the house. Few words were spoken; but those
that were made it clear that my Hebrew lessons, with him at
least, had now come to an end. He did not dare take the risk of
hearing me make the same dreadful mistake. My next teacher
at Rhodes University was a Baptist, so the danger of commit-
ting the same error of judgement was considerably lessened.
But the experience remains vivid. We Christians are often too
casual in the way in which we talk about God.

In theistic tradition, God has been and is known by many
names. This does not mean that God changes or develops,
as though God was once a God of anger and only later became compassionate. But there are images of God that have
been used to sanction domination, discrimination and dehumanization, and others that speak of God as the God of

love, mercy and justice. This 'naming of God' is an essential part of the 'grand narrative' of a faith community, one from which the community derives its identity, as for example in the development of the Christian doctrine of the triune God. It is also invariably related to the social and political forces that have shaped the particular historical contexts in which a faith community has developed. As David Nicholls reminds us, 'successive concepts and images of God have been related to political rhetoric', and 'have to some degree echoed, or at times heralded changes in the social structure and dynamics – in the economic, political and cultural life – of given communities'.[13]

Even if we do not believe, the images of the God we reject are constructed, at least in part, by the cultural contexts in which we live, and by our own experience. None of this implies that all images are of equal merit, or equally reflect what many of us would regard as the core of biblical tradition. Many people who have rejected belief in God have an image of God that often bears little resemblance to God as understood by the great theistic faith communities. There are many idols, images of God that are inadequate, distorting and perverting what the great traditions of faith hold true. Theologians of all traditions are often the best iconoclasts, the breakers of false images, knowing only too well how easily their own religion can become idolatrous.

Largely because the Christian story emphasizes the love of God and has traditionally given preference to the term 'Father', we have often assumed a familiarity with God that too easily reduces our understanding of God to that of a 'household god' with whom we occasionally chat. When we do so we lose a sense of God's transcendent holiness that is so fundamental to Judaism, Islam and also Christian tradition. But there are other ways in which we use the name 'God' far too casually, not least when we use it to justify our own agendas. Nowhere is this more apparent than when nations believe that God is

---

13 David Nicholls, *Deity and Domination Vol. 1: Images of God and the State in the Nineteenth and Twentieth Centuries* (London: Routledge, 1989), pp. 2f.

their 'god', and therefore on their side when it comes to conflict and war. In such cases the 'naming of God' is nationalized. This is part of what is meant by 'taking the name of God in vain', that is, emptying it of its proper content.

During my term of office as President of the United Congregational Church in 1980, I was invited by the Chaplain-General along with other church leaders to observe what was happening in the war on the Namibian-Angolan border. As an opponent of the war and a supporter of conscientious objectors, I felt decidedly out of place talking to South African army officers. But I did start a casual discussion one evening in the officers' mess about the morality of the war, in the course of which one officer insisted that God was on the side of the South African army. The reason given was that none of 'his men' was killed during a particular engagement with 'the enemy'. I asked him whether his view would change if some were killed next time, or if 'the enemy' forces happened to be victorious. His mumbled reply said it all: 'I have never thought about that.' But it is precisely this unthinking language about God that becomes so dangerous, justifying national and other agendas that are highly questionable. This was one reason why Barth insisted on the 'wholly Otherness' of God. In doing so he challenged those Christians in Germany who supported the Kaiser's declaration of war in 1914 and who had no difficulty in uncritically affirming the slogan 'Gott mit uns' inscribed on the belt buckles of the soldiers.

The reduction of God to a national idol is only one way in which we transgress the First Commandment. There are several other ways that come to mind, for idols are not hand-carved figures or figurines that make God angry or jealous. When the Hebrew prophets decry those who carve bits of wood into idols, they are not giving them any divine power; they are speaking out against human stupidity, incredulity and superstition. Idolatry is condemned because it dehumanizes, defacing the true image of God. Contemporary idols are no different; they are modern-day equivalents of past idolatries. I will never forget visiting the Woolworth's building in New York, that famous landmark in downtown Manhattan, near the then recently devastated site of the International Trade Center. On entering the bank's ground floor (you could go no further without authorization), I had the impression that I was in the nave of a gothic cathedral. And, indeed, the Woolworth architects had been sent to Europe to study the cathedrals in order to design a building that would be the high temple of capitalism. I find it very significant that one of the few times that the New Testament speaks about idolatry is in terms of human greed (Colossians 3.5). There can be little doubt that greed, the core of what we previously described as secularism, like war, devours both its own children and that of others. That is why Christian ethics has traditionally condemned financial policies that promote greed and corruption, entrenching cycles of poverty rather than promoting the common good.

Another idol, brought to awareness by feminism, is patriarchy understood as an ideology of domination. The protest launched against the sole use of Father to describe God has met with both resistance and acceptance within the churches. But it is a necessary, indeed, vital reminder of the danger of human metaphors when applied to God. Uncritically used, the language of fatherhood, as Anne Carr puts it, reduces the reality of God 'in a single male measure', and the protest against it 'is a powerful grace for theology and for the church in our time'.[14] This, she goes on to say,

> challenges a pervasive idolatry that has crept into Christian thought and practice and at the same time provides new awareness, for women and the whole church, of God as the fully transcendent mystery who encompasses *all* of creation, *all* of our lives in universal presence.[15]

The widespread abuse of and violence against women cannot be attributed simply to patriarchal language, whether in the Church or in other faith communities, but such language is

---

14 Anne Carr, *Transforming Grace: Christian Tradition and Women's Experience* (San Francisco: Harper & Row, 1990), p. 134.

15 Carr, *Transforming Grace*, p. 134.

symptomatic of the problem. Wittingly or not it contributes to a climate of gender discrimination in Church and society. And because such patriarchalism is identified with God, the abuse of women is given divine sanction, adding immensely to a much broader cultural problem.[16] Quite rightly, feminist scholars argue that patriarchy has not only contributed to the dehumanization of women, but also to the degradation of nature, both evident in so-called 'macho cultures'.

The problem of 'naming God', and therefore the danger of idolatry, is related to the danger of 'naming the other' instead of allowing 'the other' to name herself or himself. For this, too, leads to a 'de-facing' of the 'image of God', recalling our discussion of stereotyping and dehumanizing rhetoric, as in racism or in describing 'the enemy'. It applies also to the debate about gay rights. Both Catholic and Protestant conservative representatives who have spoken on this issue have too often indulged in what one Catholic scholar calls 'symbolic genocide'.[17] By that he means using language about homosexuals that is degrading, and often results in vicious and violent actions against gay people. That this is often the language of the world's dictators, but decidedly not that of its Mandelas and Tutus, should give us good reason to reflect that it should not be the language of Christians. Our daughter, Jeanelle, a medical doctor, is gay, and her journey towards the recognition of her sexual orientation is one that Isobel and I know well. It is not something that any of us would have chosen; but 'coming out' has, for Jeanelle, led to a personal maturity and flourishing that I am convinced would not have happened otherwise. The anti-gay rhetoric and actions of Christians makes me both sad and angry because of the idolatrous way in which the name of Christ is used, and because it makes people like my daughter feel excluded from the faith in which they have been nurtured and found meaning. 'God is God', and every attempt to try and box God into some national,

---

16 I have learnt much from feminist theologians in South Africa on these issues. See, inter alia, Denise Ackermann, *After the Locusts: Letters from the Landscape of Faith* (Grand Rapids: Eerdmans, 2003).

17 Edward J. Ingebretsen, 'Post-Colonial Gothic Dramas: Roman Catholicism and the Homosexual', *Political Theology* 6 no. 2, April (2005), p. 248.

ecclesiastical, mental, sexual or other container, that demonizes the other thus creating God in our own image, is idolatrous. It de-faces the 'image of God'.

Rumours of divine purpose

George Ellis, Emeritus Professor of Applied Mathematics at the University of Cape Town, and a cosmologist of international note, presented a paper on the 'argument from design', or the cosmological proof for the existence of God, at a theological meeting some years ago that surprised many of us. Schooled in the theology of Barth, we were sceptical of the claims made by 'Natural Theology', whether in preparing the ground for faith through reasoned argument, or positing a religious a priori on which faith could flourish. But as Ellis responded to our questions, it soon became apparent that he was offering a new approach to the subject, one that might well indicate a rapprochement between science and theology in support of faith in God. This awakened, on my part, a renewed interest in science and religion.

This 'new natural theology', which is not a rival but a companion to scientific explanation, does not talk about proofs of God's existence, but is, as Polkinghorne puts it, 'content with the more modest role of offering theistic belief as an insightful account of what is going on'. It appeals 'to cosmic rationality and the anthropic [that is, designed for human well-being] form of the laws of nature'.[18] It is not a matter of finding God 'in the gaps', but of trying to make sense of the world and the cosmos beyond as we know it, and as it makes life possible. Such an approach turns things around.

We are not now looking to the physical world for hints of God's existence but to God's existence as an aid for understanding why things have developed in the physical world in the manner that they have.[19]

---

18 John Polkinghorne, *Belief in God in an Age of Science* (New Haven: Yale University Press, 1998), p. 10.

19 Polkinghorne, *Belief in God in an Age of Science*, p. 13.

What are these rumours of divine purpose that speak of cosmic intelligibility and anthropic design?

First, there are those qualities 'of elegance, economy and naturalness' that scientists take for granted in pursuing their exploration of the universe. Second, there is the reality of the moral order, indicating that this is a value-laden world. 'I believe' writes Polkinghorne, 'that it is of the highest significance that we live in a moral world, that we have moral knowledge which tells us that love and truth are better than hatred and lies.'[20] Third, there is aesthetic value, whether discerned in mathematical beauty, so fundamental to the scientific enterprise, or in the mystery of music that defies scientific explanation. And fourth, Polkinghorne refers to human hopefulness in the face of death. That is, the sense that there is ultimate meaning and purpose, that there is a point to the creation and evolution of the universe, the way things are, rather than a nihilistic meaninglessness, which reduces our lives to a 'tale told by an idiot'. 'The human paradox', Polkinghorne tells us, 'is that we perceive so many signs of value and significance conveyed to us in our encounter with reality, yet all meaning is threatened by the apparent finality of death.' He continues:

> If the universe is truly a cosmos, or the world is really intelligible through and through, then this life by itself cannot be the whole of the story.[21]

Few Christian theologians today would challenge the basic evolutionary hypothesis that life as we know it has evolved over past aeons. This does not mean an uncritical acceptance of Darwin's theory of 'natural selection', even though the hypothesis is undoubtedly partly correct in explaining the evolution of life.[22] The dividing line between evolutionary naturalists such as Huxley, and Christian theists like Teilhard, has to do with the way in which evolution operates. Is it by blind chance, or is it a process that is best understood in terms

---

20 Polkinghorne, *Belief in God in an Age of Science*, p. 17.
21 Polkinghorne, *Belief in God in an Age of Science*, p. 23.
22 See the discussion of 'natural selection' in Ward, *God, Chance and Necessity*, pp. 60–95, 112–26.

of what Christians have traditionally referred to as divine providence, implying hope and meaning, purpose and direction? This is very different from the deistic notion of a God who creates the universe and then lets it run its own course, like the proverbial clockmaker. It is different because God is involved in every moment of the ongoing creative/evolutionary process; it is one of great beauty and elegance, designed and guided by supreme wisdom and power.

Christians believe creation was 'ex nihilo' (out of nothing) but it is equally 'creatio continua', an amazing work in progress that requires threatening interruptions *in order to* open up fresh possibilities for life. The truth is, new creative initiatives are stifled unless something happens to break open the encrusted legacies that prevent renewal. This does not mean that discontinuity replaces all continuity, that paradigm shifts do not take the tried and tested into the new dispensation, or that chaos precludes purpose. Creation 'out of nothing' means that God is the source of everything that exists; but the next stage in the ongoing process is necessarily creation out of chaos, the 'formless void and darkness' of the Genesis narrative (1.1). Paul speaks about the 'birth pangs' of the new creation (Romans 8.22), and the vision of a 'new heaven and earth' in the Book of Revelation comes after flood, famine, war and death. Creation as evolutionary process is 'open ended', constantly experiencing turbulence, but leading in the direction of cosmic fulfilment, even when human freedom threatens its destruction.

The argument for the existence of God from design, reasonable as it is, remains premised on faith. But the more I reflect on the amazing character of the universe and the intricate complexity of the evolution of life, the more I am convinced that it is the work of a cosmic Mind rather than chance. Indeed, to 'grasp the idea of God is to grasp an idea of the only reality that could form a completely adequate explanation of the existence of the universe, for God is the only reality which, in being supremely intelligible or comprehensible to itself, explains itself'.[23] I do not deny that others may come to a very

---

23 Ward, *God, Chance and Necessity*, p. 59.

different conclusion, believing that the cosmos happened by chance, and that the evolutionary process depends on the roll of dice. But such views, while fundamental to secular humanism in the past, are increasingly challenged by some scientists, and are themselves, in the end, statements of faith.

What is scientifically beyond doubt, Ellis insists, is that 'the Universe provides a hospitable environment for humanity'.[24] Moreover, the fine-tuning of the cosmos that makes human life possible and sustainable is not confined to one aspect of its structure, but 'refers to the total inter-related organization of the laws of nature and the boundary conditions for those laws'.[25] This is at the heart of what is meant by the Anthropic Principle, an extension of the argument from design. A strong reading of this principle as offered by Ellis is 'that it is necessary that intelligent life exists in the Universe'; indeed, 'the presence of life is required in order that a universe model makes sense'.[26] Equally important for Ellis, a Quaker by conviction, is that this sense of the cosmos is inseparable from the view that it is ultimately also just. The Anthropic Principle cannot simply be confined to physics or chemistry, but must extend 'to the full nature of our existence'. It must 'include our fears and hopes, love and caring, value judgments, ethical choices and moral responsibility, as well as pain and suffering, whose reality I take to be at least as indisputable as any other area of experience'.[27]

This linking of cosmology and ethics confirms my own early experience of an awakening sense of awe before the majesty of the universe and of the demands of justice in the face of oppression. But it has also led me in more recent times to a deeper appreciation of the aesthetic dimension to reality and its relationship to justice. This prompted the writing of my book *Christianity, Art and Transformation* in which I reflected, among other things, on the redemptive and ethical

24 George Ellis, *Before the Beginning: Cosmology Explained* (London: Boyars/Bowerdean, 1993), p. 92.
25 Ellis, *Before the Beginning*, p. 92.
26 Ellis, *Before the Beginning*, p. 93.
27 Ellis, *Before the Beginning*, p. 127.

significance of the 'beauty of God'.[28] More recent reflection on evolution, inspired by Teilhard, has helped me to take a further step towards what John Haught calls an 'aesthetic-evolutionary' perspective. This provides a firm basis in evolution for ethics consisting as it does 'in the view that the cosmos is a restless aim toward ever more intense configurations of beauty'.[29] There is a 'deep and ageless evolutionary straining toward an intensification of beauty' which provides us with 'our own sense of meaning and morality'. Haught continues:

> An awareness that our own conduct can contribute at least something to the ongoing creation and expansion of cosmic beauty can give our moral lives what they have often lacked, a sense of being connected meaningfully and creatively to what is going on in the universe at large.[30]

Beauty and the moral universe together provide a key to understanding why it is that I and many others believe in an infinite and unique beauty that we name God.

Of all the theologians of the twentieth century, it was the Catholic theologian Hans Urs von Balthasar who was largely responsible for the recovery of the aesthetic as fundamental to Christian theology and faith. Instead of trying to bring secular humanists to faith in God on the basis of reason, the Christian apologist should help them to *see* things differently. 'God's art in the midst of history is irreproachable', he wrote in his magnum opus, *The Glory of the Lord*, '... the masterpiece of the divine fantasy, which puts all human fantasy to naught.'[31] Building in part on Balthasar, Orthodox theologian David Hart writes of 'an overwhelming givenness in the beautiful', something 'discovered in astonishment, in an awareness of something fortuitous, adventitious, essentially indescribable', something 'known only in the moment of response, from

28 John W. de Gruchy, *Christianity, Art and Transformation* (Cambridge: Cambridge University Press, 2001).

29 John F. Haught, *God After Darwin: A Theology of Evolution* (Boulder, Colorado: Westview, 2000), p. 128.

30 Haught, *God After Darwin*, p. 133.

31 Hans Urs von Balthasar, *The Glory of the Lord: A Theological Aesthetics*, Vol. 1: *Seeing the Form* (Edinburgh: T&T Clark, 1982), p. 172.

the position of one already addressed and able now only to reply'.[32] If one's experience of God's redemptive grace can be described, as it was by C. S. Lewis as 'being surprised by joy', it can equally, and perhaps even more be described as being overwhelmed by beauty.

Beauty is surely part of God's character, something apparent in creation and, to the eyes of faith, in redemption. Such beauty can be expressed very simply or extravagantly, in the symmetry of 'the Vitruvian Man' made in the perfect 'image of God', in the precision of mathematics, in the embrace of the Piéta with all its pathos, and the *Shona* sculpture of the maternal womb in which our humanity is formed. But it also has to incorporate the strange beauty of the Man of Nazareth on the cross, the ultimate sign of God's love. How are we to understand this beauty that attracts us, overwhelms us and redeems us? Can it be that beauty is, at one and the same time, as majestic as the starry sky above and the setting sun on the distant horizon, and as disturbing and strange as a human being dying a violent death as a common criminal for the sake of peace on earth? In responding to this question we are drawn irrevocably beyond the limits of reason into the realm of Christian faith, parting company with theists of other faiths.

God's love story: a strange beauty

The small old town of Verenna lies on the shore of Lake Como, nestling beneath the pre-Alpine mountains of Northern Italy, across the water from Bellagio. It is a magical place with its colourful houses built on top of each other on steep slopes, its cobbled streets and alleys, its small harbour with a variety of craft at rest, and cafés along the water's edge. There are two ancient church buildings in the piazza, both containing frescoes that date back at least to the fifteenth century. San Giovanni Batista, founded in the tenth century, is a small, rectangular building and is the more important of the

---

32 Hart David Bentley, *The Beauty of the Infinite* (Grand Rapids: Eerdmans, 2003), p. 17.

two churches. San Giorgio, founded in the twelfth century, is much larger but gracious in its very different architecture. What attracted me most about San Giorgio, however, was neither its frescoes nor its architecture but a notice board at its entrance that welcomed visitors with these words:

> Beauty lives here, come in!
> But first, order your thoughts,
> Prepare yourself to meet her.

The words intrigued me, not least because they were so unexpected. Normally you are welcomed, if you are, by words which remind you to be properly dressed and keep as quiet as possible. Sometimes you are also reminded that it costs much to maintain the buildings, and photographs are not permitted. But not at San Giorgio; visitors like myself are invited in to meet Beauty.

What do these intriguing words mean? What did the priest or parish council have in mind in making such an invitation? The words are ambiguous. An obvious reading might simply have to do with experiencing the beauty of the place, a space made sacred over many years by the prayers of the faithful. Another might have particular reference to the presence of Christ in the reserved sacrament, symbolized by the red sanctuary light glowing near the altar. Yet another reading is that we would encounter the Virgin Mary in all her beauty, hence the need to prepare ourselves 'to meet her'. As a Protestant, this possibility would not have dawned on me were it not for the fact that I have increasingly recognized, with many others, the need to transcend anti-Catholic polemics of the past in order to discover the profound truth in Marian tradition. The humanity and personhood of Jesus cannot be understood apart from his relationship to his mother, Mary; Christology begins in the womb even though faith begins at the empty tomb.[33] But the reading of the invitation outside

---

33 On this, and much else, I am indebted to my former student, personal assistant, and now colleague, Lyn Holness. See Lynette J. Holness, 'Christology from Within: A Critical Retrieval of the Humanity of Christ, with Particular Reference to the Role of Mary' (PhD diss., University of Cape Town, 2001).

San Giorgio that encompassed all of these possibilities was that those who entered should prepare for a possible encounter with the Beauty of God.

I shared these thoughts with a Jewish friend who was with me at the time I visited San Giorgio in the European summer of 2004. She did not know what to make of these words, even though the beauty of the church, its frescoes and architecture, impressed her. But pointing to the large crucifix that hung above the entrance to the sanctuary, she told me how much that image disturbed her. What I accepted as at the heart of Christian faith had, for her, severely distracted from the beauty of the place. The sight of the crucifix brought back memories of the persecution of Jews through the centuries under the banner of the crucified. The cross meant something very different to her than it did to me, and her comment reminded me of the sad truth that what, for Christians, is a sign of redemption has become, for others, a sign of persecution. It is a scandal and stumbling block, as Paul declared (1 Corinthians 1.18–25) but in a way not anticipated by the apostle.

As a result of centuries of crusades and wars, pogroms, the Holocaust, racism and oppression, justified by Christians as the will of God and pursued under the banner of the cross, Christians have crucified Jesus afresh. What was originally a violent death motivated by love for the sake of redemption and peace has too often become a justification of violence against a perceived enemy. In an awful ironic twist, the cross has become a symbol of Christian arrogance beneath which the armies of Christendom's emperors from Constantine onwards have conquered others. And if my Jewish friend found the crucifix offensive for these reasons, many secular humanists regard the claims we Christians make about its redemptive significance as irrational. What could be more stupid, defying all credulity, than the claim that God became a human being, and was put to death as a criminal? No one expressed this more stridently than the nineteenth-century philosopher Friedrich Nietzsche. Christianity had eliminated everything 'strong, brave, masterful, proud ... from the concept of God', he wrote. God had become 'the poor people's

God, the sinner's God', the God who exalted weakness and ugliness, rather than strength and beauty.[34]

Christians should not disparage the body, human strength and bravery, or the aesthetic dimensions of life. But Nietzsche is right, if not wholly so. The Christian God is 'the poor people's God, the sinner's God'. The Christian icon of the truly human is not primarily embodied in the bronzed athletes of the ancient Greek or modern Olympics, nor in the lives of the rich, the powerful and famous, and the beautiful people that grace the catwalk, nor typified by the humanist 'man of letters'; it is embodied in Jesus the crucified Jew who gave his life for others. He has been given 'the name that is above every other name' (Philippians 2.9). 'The God of Jesus Christ', Bonhoeffer wrote shortly before his death, 'has nothing to do with what God, as we imagine him, could do or ought to do. If we are to learn from what God promises and what he fulfils, we must persevere in quiet meditation upon the life, sayings, deeds, sufferings and death of Jesus.'[35] When we do so, we begin to understand what Paul intended when he wrote to the fractious Christians in Philippi:

Let each of you look not to your own interests, but to the interests of others.
Let the same mind be in you that was in Christ Jesus,
who though he was in the form of God,
did not regard equality with God
as something to be exploited,
but emptied (*kenosis*) himself,
taking the form of a slave,
being born in human likeness.
And being found in human form,
he humbled himself
and became obedient to the point of death –
even death on a cross. (Philippians 2.5–8)

---

34 Friedrich Nietzsche, *Twilight of the Idols: The Anti-Christ* (Penguin: London, 1968), p. 127.
35 Bonhoeffer, *Letters and Papers from Prison*, p. 391.

This passage, which was probably a very early Christian hymn, links faith and ethics. This is the good news of the incarnation. Not that God became a human being in power to rule as Lord, but that God became a human being in love in order to serve and redeem. In this act of divine self-emptying (*kenosis*) and accommodation to our human limitations, the language of lordship is radically overturned into the language of service and suffering on behalf of others. This does not imply a surrender of power, but its recovery as a source of human transformation.

Despite the reservation that some feminist theologians have about the term 'Lord' to describe Jesus, I have always felt strongly that no other term is adequate. Not only does it have strong biblical foundations that contrasted the authority of Jesus with that of Caesar, but it was also the confession through the centuries of Christians who stood firm against unjust regimes. This was certainly so in the struggle against apartheid. Rather than describe Jesus' authority in other terms, we should allow Jesus as Lord to judge all forms of power that are oppressive and dehumanizing. To say 'Jesus is Lord' is to challenge all unjust power relations with a radically different understanding of power, the power of the cross.

We have reached the point at which the Christian story diverges from its Abrahamic partners, Judaism and Islam. It is not because Christians alone believe in God as 'Father', for that language is deeply rooted in the Hebrew Bible, as in the psalms for example. Nor is it because the other Abrahamic faiths do not believe that God loves the world. But it is because Christians understand God through the gospel narrative of the life, death and resurrection of Jesus of Nazareth. This does not mean that Christians believe in a different God, as though there is another in whom to believe, other than the God of Abraham and the prophets. But Christians believe in the same God differently. The God who is One, Holy and Almighty is the God who loves the world fully and freely in Jesus Christ in order to redeem humanity. For Christian believers,

Jesus is the 'human face' of God or, in the words of the Nicene Creed: 'fully God and fully human'.

The claim that Jesus was 'truly God' was understandably blasphemous to devout Jews, but the claim that the 'Son of God' was 'fully human' was inconceivable to the Hellenistic Gnostics of the early centuries of Christianity. Gnosticism regarded physical matter, the material world and human body, as un-spiritual. While God was spiritually present in Jesus, Christian Gnostics argued, God could certainly not be incarnate in 'the flesh'. Jesus' physical body was simply a cloak that made it seem as if he was a human being – a view called 'docetism' from the Greek word 'to seem'. Docetic views keep creeping back into Christianity, exalting Jesus' divinity at the expense of his humanity. So the spiritual is separated from the material in a way that denigrates the latter, confuses sinful nature ('the world, the *flesh* and the devil') with embodiment and sexuality, and turns the message of God's reign into one of saving disembodied souls from this world for the next. Such dualism was firmly rejected in the New Testament on the grounds of the incarnation. 'By this you know the Spirit of God: every spirit that confesses that Jesus Christ has come in the flesh is from God' (1 John 4.2–3). The astounding claim at the heart of the Christian story is that 'the Word became flesh and dwelt among us' (John 1.14).

Jesus was a Jew, who lived at a particular time and place, not some divine being clothed in human garments, a *Supermensch* or Romantic hero of mythology but not of history. The New Testament Gospels, as distinct from the Gnostic ones, affirm Jesus' humanity in unambiguous terms: he weeps, thirsts, hungers, suffers, gets tired, angry, and enjoys the company of friends, not least women. The true *Mensch* is Jesus the carpenter's son, the child born to the peasant girl, Miriam. In other words, he was a real person with his own identity that came to fruition through his development as a young boy, adolescent, and man of flesh and blood who eventually 'suffered under Pontius Pilate, was crucified, died and was buried'. He was, that is, not an ideal human being, but a particular person who as the 'truly human being' was confessed by Christians as 'truly God'.[36] 'God', Bonhoeffer writes, 'does not seek the most perfect human being with whom to be united, but takes on human nature as it is. Jesus Christ is not the transfiguration of noble humanity, but the Yes of God to real human beings ...'[37]

As young converts we were encouraged to learn passages of the Bible by heart. The first text that I learnt was one that, through overuse and misuse, now often sounds trite. Yet nothing expresses the gospel story better, or deserves our consideration more than John's great statement of faith: 'For God so loved the world that he gave his only Son, so that everyone who believes in him may not perish but may have eternal life' (John 3.16). The core of biblical revelation is the story of God's love. God creates the universe and its rich diversity of life out of love; God calls a people into being through a love that sets them free to be a light to the world, and continually restores them as they fail in their task; God loves this world to such an extent that God enters fully into its life in order to redeem humanity and make all things new. So Bonhoeffer invites us to 'behold God become human, the unfathomable mystery of the love of God for the world'. 'God', he continues, 'loves the world.'

> Not an ideal human, but human beings as they are; not an ideal world, but the real world. What we find repulsive in their opposition to God, what we shrink back from with pain and hostility, namely real human beings, the real world, this is for God the ground of unfathomable love.[38]

The Bible calls this kind of love 'grace', a love which takes the initiative in creating, embracing, forgiving, redeeming

36 See Walter Wink, *The Human Being: Jesus and the Enigma of the Son of the Man* (Philadelphia: Fortress, 2003). Unfortunately, I only became aware of Wink's volume after completing my manuscript. His description of Jesus as the 'Son of the Man', which occurs over 80 times through the sources, corresponds to my description of Jesus as the 'truly human being', thus adding considerable New Testament backing to my discussion.

37 Bonhoeffer, *Ethics*, p. 85.

38 Bonhoeffer, *Ethics*, p. 84.

and giving life to humankind. From this perspective, God's purposes are eminently secular, for it is the 'world' that God loves, not a religious part of the world. Moreover, God's love for the world is inclusive, for 'everyone' is invited to experience God's grace and the fullness of life that comes as a result. The way to such life is faith, not faith as a purely cerebral act, but faith as trust, commitment and participation in God's love story. That is what it means to 'believe in God'.

It may seem incongruous to jump from the simple yet profound beauty of John 3.16 to the doctrine of the Trinity, yet nothing better prepares the ground for the development of that doctrine than the assertion that God is love, and loves the world so much. That is why, despite the inadequacies of language, and the inevitable need for metaphors to express what is meant, the doctrine of the Trinity is so central to Christian tradition. While many have found its mathematical expression perplexing if not absurd, the doctrine is the most distinct, the most central of all else in the Christian creed, distinguishing Christian believers from other theists. Even though the word 'trinity' as such does not occur in the New Testament, the experience of God as 'Father, Son and Spirit' is etched into its pages, and revealed at key points in the Jesus story. Long before the Councils of the early Church formulated the doctrine to counter views that undermined faith and experience, Christians prayed, lived and worshipped in ways and words that expressed this trinitarian faith. The One God Christians experience in the history of Jesus Christ and the presence of the Spirit, is what God is in God's self. The doctrine of the Trinity is an attempt to understand God's love story and our own response to that story, to put the beauty of God's creative and redemptive drama into words that cannot express what is beyond explanation.

Perhaps the most misunderstood aspect of the doctrine derives from the use of the word 'person'. It is problematic because of the individualistic way in which we now understand it. But as I earlier indicated, 'person' (or *persona*, the Latin word used in the creeds) does not mean individual, as though God could be three individuals. The word refers to the relational character of God, God's interpersonal nature. God is not an impersonal force or Absolute Monad, but God is love; that is, God subsists in a relationship that embraces difference in unity, a beautiful relationship. To say that God is triune is to say that God is personal in the sense of always being in relation, both within the Godhead and in relation to the world. It is to say with the New Testament that 'God is love'.

> Beloved, let us love one another, because love is from God; everyone who loves is born of God and knows God. Whoever does not love does not know God, for God is love. God's love was revealed among us in this way: God sent his only Son into the world so that we might live through him. In this is love, not that we loved God but that he loved us and sent his Son to be the atoning sacrifice for our sins. Beloved, since God loved us so much, we also ought to love one another. No one has ever seen God; if we love one another, God lives in us and his love is perfected in us. By this we know that we abide in him and he in us, because he has given us of his Spirit. And we have seen and so testify that the Father has sent his Son as the Saviour of the world. (1 John 4.7–14)

These words express perhaps better than any others what we Christians mean, or should do, when we say we believe in and therefore know God. We believe, because God first loved us in Jesus Christ, and enables us to do so in the strength of the Spirit. But the test of that faith, the proof of our believing, whether, in fact, we 'know God', is whether we too love others in the way God loves us.

Biblical 'knowing' has to do with intimacy. To know *about* someone is different from 'knowing' someone. I do not claim to 'know God' intimately as the mystics do. But faith in God does imply a personal relationship, for that is what we mean when we talk about 'trusting' God. But 'knowing God' also means 'doing justice, loving mercy, and walking humbly with God', as the prophet Micah exclaimed (6.8). To claim to know

God but not to seek justice and live with compassion is surely evidence that people do not know God, whatever they might say to the contrary. And it may well be that those who say that they do not know God, or even that they cannot believe in God, but who 'do justice and love mercy', actually do know God better than some of us who may claim that knowledge. Whether or not they would want to be known as 'cryptic believers' or 'anonymous Christians' is another matter.

The issues we have discussed throughout this chapter, not least at the end, thus prompt the question: well, then, what is a Christian? What does it mean not only to be a believer, but a Christian believer? In what sense is Jesus Christ normative for being truly human? How are we to understand Rowan Williams' assertion that '*Christ* is a word that has come to mark out the shape of the potential future of all human beings [and all creation], while remaining at the same time the designation of a specific person'?[39] In short, the question that Bonhoeffer so frequently posed must be our question as well: 'Who is Jesus Christ, for us, today?' My (our) answer to that question will indicate what I (we) mean by 'being Christian'.

---

39 Rowan Williams, *On Christian Theology* (Oxford: Blackwell, 2000), p. 171.

6

A Christian

*When the Son of God was incarnate and made man, he recapitulated
in himself the long line of the human race ... so that what we had lost
in Adam, that is, the being in the image and likeness of God, that we
should regain in Christ Jesus.* Irenaeus[1]

*To be a Christian does not mean to be religious in a particular way,
to make something of oneself (a sinner, a penitent, or a saint) on the
basis of some method or other, but to be a human being (Menschsein)
... the human being that Christ creates in us.* Bonhoeffer[2]

*Being a Christian cannot mean ceasing to be human. But neither
can being human mean ceasing to be Christian.* Hans Küng[3]

*You are the salt of the earth; but if salt has lost its taste,
how can its saltiness be restored?* Matthew 5.13

The nineteenth-century Danish philosopher Søren Kierkegaard is reported to have said that there has only ever been
one Christian, and he was Jewish. Kierkegaard was protesting the nominal Christianity of his day as represented by the
state church in Denmark. In doing so he was defining 'being Christian' in terms of following Jesus, or being a disciple.
That is undoubtedly fundamental to being a Christian, and
presumably no Christian denomination would think otherwise. But many would challenge whether it is an adequate
definition.

With the exception of a few Christian communities, being
baptized is regarded an essential part of being a Christian,
for it is the rite of entry into the Christian community. But
there is a range of conviction about baptism that separates,

---

1 Irenaeus, *Adversus haereses*, III, xviii. From the translation in *Documents
of the Christian Church*, ed. Henry Bettenson (London: Oxford University
Press, 1954), p. 42.

2 Bonhoeffer, *Letters and Papers from Prison*, p. 361.

3 Hans Küng, *On Being a Christian*, p. 601.

for example, those in the Catholic church from those in the Baptist. And whereas baptism is associated by some as the sacrament of re-birth 'by water and the Spirit', 'being born again' for evangelicals comes as a result of personal commitment to Jesus Christ as saviour. Then again, some traditions would put a stronger emphasis than others on adherence to the creeds or a confession of faith, whether it is the very early confession that 'Jesus is Lord', the Nicene Creed of the fourth century, or the confessions of the Reformation. Defining what it means to be a Christian, in other words, involves different ways of understanding behaviour (discipleship and ethics), belonging (membership of the Church), and personal commitment and belief (confession). This accounts in part for the varieties of Christianity and churches. Nonetheless, Kierkegaard's distinction between 'nominal' and 'real' Christianity is a necessary one, reminding all traditions that the first Christians were named as such because of their identification as disciples of Jesus the Jewish Messiah, the Christ.

Jesus the Christ

Virtually all we know about Jesus derives from the Gospel stories in the New Testament. But the Gospels are neither biography nor straightforward historical accounts; they are sermons, theological tracts, written from the perspective of Christian faith in Jesus as the Christ, the one whom God raised from the dead. For this reason it is difficult to separate the pre-Easter Jesus of history from the post-Easter Christ of faith, the Jesus the disciples knew in the flesh, and the Christ they knew through the Spirit. This does not mean that we have no reasonably solid information about Jesus' life and teaching.[4] There is, in fact, considerable consensus among biblical scholars about what we can and do know, though we must always keep in mind that the New Testament was written from the perspective of faith in the story we call gospel.

---

4 See Marcus Borg, 'From Galilean Jew to the Face of God', in *Jesus at 2000*, ed. Marcus Borg (Boulder, Colorado: Westview Press, 1997), pp. 7–20.

The consensus is: Jesus was a Jew in first-century Palestine who was regarded by many of his contemporaries as a remarkable teacher and healer in the tradition of both rabbinic and charismatic Judaism. His teaching focused on the reign (or kingdom) of God, and much of what he said aligned him with the eighth-century prophets of Israel and the Wisdom traditions of the Hebrew scriptures. He had a passion for justice and regarded social righteousness as the foundation of true peace. He had great compassion for the underdogs in society, the poor and the victims of injustice; he welcomed women and children into his circle and gave them a status often denied; and he embraced people from beyond the boundaries of strict Judaism. One of the most striking things about Jesus was the way in which he continually crossed over cultural, religious and ethnic barriers in reaching out to others, especially those in need, to bring them into his disciple community. While Jesus had a deep respect for the Law or *Torah*, he always interpreted the Commandments as given by God for human well-being. People mattered far more than rules of exclusion, or those that added burdens too difficult to carry.[5]

Jesus' approach to people was shaped not just by his love and compassion for them, but also by his vision of God's purpose to restore humanity to its fullness. In reaching out to embrace those often excluded – a hated tax-gatherer, harlot, leper, child, despised Roman centurion, or Samaritan – Jesus anticipated what God had in mind for humanity as a whole when all things are made new. It was this vision of God's reign, an eschatological vision of the coming kingdom at the 'end of the age', that found expression in many of his parables and miracles. Jesus taught his disciples to live in anticipation of this coming reign of God, notably but not only in his Sermon on the Mount (Matthew 5—7). He encouraged them to seek justice and be peacemakers, to love others irrespective of their background; to forgive others far beyond what might normally be expected; to serve one another rather than claiming some preferred status, and so put God's reign first in their

---

5 William Loader, *Jesus and the Fundamentalisms of His Day* (Grand Rapids: Eerdmans, 2001), pp. 12–30.

lives. The Beatitudes, described by the martyred Archbishop of San Salvador, Oscar Romero, as a 'subversive witness ... which have turned everything upside down',[6] was the charter of true discipleship.

Jesus was arrested and judged by the Jewish authorities on charges of blasphemy as a Messianic pretender. He was condemned to death by the Roman authorities on the grounds that he was a threat to society, fomenting rebellion and claiming an authority that challenged that of Caesar. Although some of his actions and words could be construed in these ways, the charges were vacuous. Jesus did not claim divine status, nor did he plan to overthrow the Roman authorities; he witnessed to the reign of God, and therefore to the demands of God's righteousness. In doing so he made it clear that God's reign was not to be confused with a form of religion and politics that dehumanized others, but with the well-being of all people, especially the common people oppressed by Roman rule and by corrupt religious leaders. Challenging the love of power that unjustly subjugated others, with the power of God's love and justice that liberated them, Jesus was perceived as a threat by those in authority. He was arrested then executed as a common criminal on a cross that was erected on a rubbish dump outside the walls of Jerusalem.

Christians believe that God raised Jesus to life as the 'first fruits' of the coming of God's reign. The evidence for the resurrection is widely contested, but for Christians, however they understand the event, it is the basis on which all else depends. In the risen Christ, God has inaugurated a 'new age' in which God's judgement and salvation have already begun. This transformed the meaning of discipleship. Now it was no longer a matter of following Jesus as teacher and rabbi, but obeying him as Lord and believing in him as saviour of the world. No one has helped me understand this transition better than Bonhoeffer, notably in his classic study *Discipleship* (previously translated as *The Cost of Discipleship*)[7] in

---

6 Oscar Romero, *The Violence of Love* (London: Collins, 1989), p. 58.

7 Dietrich Bonhoeffer, *Discipleship*, Dietrich Bonhoeffer Works, vol. 4 (Minneapolis: Fortress, 2001).

which he relates discipleship and obedience to Jesus as Lord, to justification by faith in Jesus as saviour. In his memorable words: 'Only he who believes, obeys, and only he who obeys, believes.'[8] But how are we to understand this in relation to what we previously decribed as a 'mature worldliness'?

The cost of discipleship

My introduction to Bonhoeffer's *Discipleship* came when I joined a study group as a theological student. I recall the impact it made upon me at the time. But, like many others I later had difficulty in reconciling it with the 'other Bonhoeffer' of his *Ethics*, written during his involvement in the resistance against Hitler, and especially his prison letters. This difficulty was reinforced by his own expressed reservations there about what he had written in *Discipleship*. I find it helpful to reflect on the continuity and change in Bonhoeffer's thinking in trying to understand the connection between being a Christian and 'being human', between being a disciple and becoming conformed to the image of Jesus Christ, the icon of the truly human, living fully in the world.

In a letter to Elizabeth Zinn, a distant cousin, written in 1936, Bonhoeffer described how, in his words 'he became a Christian' after years of studying theology and preaching. It was during his year of study (1931–2) at Union Theological Seminary in New York when 'the Bible, and in particular the Sermon on the Mount, freed' him to become a Christian. This, he declared, was 'a great liberation'.[9] His students in Berlin during the next few years recognized a new, more personal commitment to Jesus Christ, especially when he spoke passionately on the Sermon on the Mount. This, he told them, was the basis on which all Christians should live their lives. In particular, he spoke of the urgent demand for Christians to take Jesus' teaching about peace making seriously, and

---

8 As translated in the first English edition of *The Cost of Discipleship* (London: SCM Press, 1959), p. 54.

9 Quoted in Eberhard Bethge, *Dietrich Bonhoeffer: A Biography* (Minneapolis: Fortress Press, 2000), p. 205.

encouraged them to be conscientious objectors, a message that was extremely unpopular at the time within Germany and the Evangelical Church.

During our year in Chicago, Isobel and I visited Reba Place, a Mennonite community on the north side of the city. In the course of the weekend I was invited to talk about my studies on Bonhoeffer's theology. During the ensuing discussion I was hard pressed to explain how the author of *Discipleship* could have participated in the conspiracy to assassinate Hitler. For the first time in my life I had come face to face with deeply committed Christian pacifists. Later I was privileged to know John Howard Yoder, a distinguished Mennonite scholar whose book *The Politics of Jesus*, published in 1972, influenced many Christians including myself.[10] And then, during a sabbatical in the Fall of 1977 at Bethel College, North Newton, Kansas, we were enriched as a family through a more extended exposure to the Mennonite tradition with its strong pacifist convictions. It was there that I gave the Menno Simons lectures that were eventually published as *The Church Struggle in South Africa*.

Originating in the more radical wing of the Swiss Reformation, or what is loosely referred to as the Anabaptist movement, the Mennonites suffered persecution for their faith at the hands of both the Catholic and the established Protestant Churches. Rejecting the Constantinian model of Christianity which made it the religion of empire and state, and therefore reduced discipleship to nominal membership of the Church, the Anabaptists recovered the costliness of following Jesus through personal commitment and living out the Sermon on the Mount. Thus, among their distinctive convictions was a deep suspicion of patriotism that placed the kingdoms of this world above the reign of God, turning the cross into a symbol of crusade and conquest instead of suffering servanthood and redemptive love. This was particularly expressed through their refusal to do military service, in the same way as Christians had done during the first centuries of Church history in

---

10 See the concluding chapter of the first and second editions of de Gruchy, *The Church Struggle in South Africa* (Grand Rapids: Eerdmans, 1979).

obedience to Jesus' teaching in the Sermon on the Mount. Both our sons, Steve and Anton, were influenced by their exposure to this tradition, refusing to do military service when eventually conscripted into the South African army. Not all conscientious objectors in South Africa were pacifist by conviction; some refused to do military service on the grounds that they could not defend apartheid. Likewise, many of us who were pacifist found it difficult to oppose unequivocally the armed liberation struggle that had begun, after many years of non-violent resistance, when Nelson Mandela and others saw the necessity to embark on this course of action.

It is debatable whether Bonhoeffer was ever a 'principled pacifist', even during the period in which he wrote *Discipleship,* but if he was, he was obviously no longer one by the time he became engaged in the resistance and the plot against Hitler's life. This did not mean that he was not a deeply committed 'peace maker'; peace making was, for him, essential to being a Christian. In the contemporary climate of violence, wars on terror, and the idolatrous waste of resources on developing and building weapons of destruction, I believe he would insist, as he did before, that Christian discipleship demands that of us. And certainly it is a travesty of the truth to use Bonhoeffer to justify war or violent revolution, as though his last-ditch attempt to rid the world of Hitler can be used as justification for wholesale slaughter.

By the time Bonhoeffer was imprisoned, he had some reservations about what he had written in *Discipleship.* As he wrote from prison in July 1944:

> I remember a conversation that I had in America thirteen years ago with a young French pastor [Lasserre]. We were asking ourselves quite simply what we wanted to do with our lives. He said he would like to become a saint ... At the time I was very impressed, but I disagreed with him, and said, in effect, that I should like to learn to have faith. For a long time I didn't realize the depth of the contrast. I thought I could acquire faith by trying to live a holy life, or something like it. I suppose I wrote *Discipleship* at the

end of that path. Today I can see the dangers of that book, though I still stand by what I wrote.[11]

What was it in *Discipleship* that Bonhoeffer regarded as its dangers, and what did he still regard as important as his life drew to its untimely end? Undoubtedly he was concerned that *Discipleship* would be understood in a way that was too pietistic and religious. That is why he goes on to say 'that it is only by living completely in this world that one learns to have faith', that is, being truly secular. For that reason, he continues, one 'must completely abandon any attempt to make something of oneself, whether it be a saint, or a converted sinner, or a churchman (a so-called priestly type!) ...'[12]

Bonhoeffer's reticence about making oneself into a saint was partly due to the fact that saints are not self-made, they are 'righteous' because they have been made so by Christ. That is why all members of the Church are called 'saints' in the New Testament.[13] But Bonhoeffer was also unhappy about thinking of sainthood as something distinct from being truly and fully human, as Jesus was. This does not mean that he was rejecting the need for 'holiness', but rather that he was shifting its focus from an unworldly piety, to what he called 'mature worldliness'. This means living fully in the world, but as those who are becoming conformed to the incarnate, crucified and risen Christ. In other words, to be a Christian does not mean primarily living by a set of rules or principles, but being formed by the gospel story. This enables us to discern the will of God within the ambiguities of each situation we face, aware that we do so imperfectly and always dependent on God's grace and in need of forgiveness. On this basis Bonhoeffer wrote his 'ethic of free responsibility' which meant that in some situations (for example, the resistance) Christians would have to make decisions that were not 'pure and undefiled', but necessary if they were to be responsible. They could only do so if they their lives were shaped by the gospel.

---

11 Bonhoeffer, *Letters and Papers from Prison*, p. 369.
12 Bonhoeffer, *Letters and Papers from Prison*, p. 369.
13 Bonhoeffer, *Discipleship*, pp. 253–5.

What, then, did Bonhoeffer continue to affirm in *Disciple-ship*? I have no doubt that he would have continued to describe discipleship in terms of following Christ in faith and obedience, and that he would have understood this in terms of personal commitment.[14] I also have no doubt that he would not have retracted anything about the costliness of grace and following Christ. An 'ethic of free responsibility' did not make being a Christian less costly; it could make it more costly. He knew this from first-hand experience, and he sensed he was about to discover the full cost involved. No one who has read the opening chapter on 'Costly Grace', so powerfully contrasted with 'cheap grace', will ever forget it. This contrast, perhaps more than anything else in Bonhoeffer's writings, provided the language we, in South Africa, have so often used to distinguish between the costly reconciliation of restored justice, and cheap reconciliation without justice.

In commenting on the Gospel story of the rich young ruler who came to Jesus in search of 'eternal life', Bonhoeffer contrasts the young man's position with that of ours who claim to be Christian but bask in the cheap grace of forgiveness without repentance and change:

> This is the difference between us and the rich young man. In his sadness, he is not able to calm himself by saying to himself, 'In spite of Jesus' word, I want to remain rich, but I will become inwardly free from my riches and comfort my inadequacy with the forgiveness of sins and be in communion with Jesus by faith.' Instead, he went away sadly and, in rejecting obedience, lost his chance to have faith.[15]

Jesus says a great deal about the dangers of wealth, and how difficult it is to serve God and money. I confess that too often I have preached about 'solidarity with the poor', but not followed that through in practice. As I have intimated previously, as a white South African I have been privileged, even in opposing apartheid, and know only too well the techniques

---

14 Bonhoeffer, *Discipleship*, p. 59.
15 Bonhoeffer, *Discipleship*, p. 78.

to deal with the feeling of guilt that invariably ensues. This is not some false guilt in the Freudian sense; it is real because it reflects the material state of things in our local and global village. Privilege is all about unequal access to available resources. So, if we are concerned about the common good of humanity, as well as the good of those poor living cheek by jowl with us, then those of us who are privileged in the world have to find ways whereby we can share our resources better. It is not a question of philanthropy; it is a matter of justice and ensuring genuine peace in the world. Such justice demands more than individual charity, important as this may be; it requires reparation. Making reparation for past injustices is not just politically expedient; it is a spiritual obligation that has very practical outcomes. This is a global challenge that goes to the heart of the relationship between the so-called developed and developing worlds.

No amount of theologizing can water down Jesus' call to costly discipleship. 'If any want to become my followers,' he said, 'let them deny themselves and take up their cross daily and follow me. For those who want to save their life will lose it, and those who lose their life for my sake will save it' (Luke 9.23–4). These words are deeply etched in the Gospels, and they recur time and again in the classics of Christian spirituality. They stand in vivid contrast to the gospel of prosperity and that of ego-satisfaction. But they are not intended to break down our humanity or destroy our personalities. Already in the Gospel story we find solace that helps us cope with the call to costly obedience. Those who heard Jesus asked him: 'Then who can be saved?', to which Jesus replied, 'What is impossible for mortals is possible for God' (Luke 18.26). The challenge in being a Christian is how to live fully in the world by grace alone, yet not abusing grace by making it an excuse for disobedience. Jesus is the Lord we are called to obey. But he is also the saviour in whom we believe. The evangelistic rhetoric that led to my conversion was that of salvation. But what precisely does this mean? The answer, I suggest, has to do with a further question posed long ago by Anselm: 'Why did God become a human being?'

Why did God become a human being?

In 1973, during my final weeks on the staff of the South African Council of Churches, I was one of several hundred participants in the Congress on Mission and Evangelism held in Durban under the auspices of the SACC and African Enterprise, an evangelical organization engaged in evangelism on the continent. The event, which was attended for a while by Billy Graham, drew together a wide range of Christians, from Catholics to Pentecostals, from ecumenicals to evangelicals and charismatics. It included both those who were involved in the struggle against apartheid and those who were more supportive of it – though the Dutch Reformed Church officially refused to participate. For me, one of the most moving and challenging moments in the ten-day event came when Manas Buthelezi, a Lutheran theologian and leading exponent of the 'black theology' movement in South Africa, presented 'Six theses on evangelism in the South African context'. His third thesis was:

> For the sake of the survival of the Christian faith it is urgently necessary that the black man must step in to save the situation. He should now cease playing the passive role of the white man's victim. It is now time for the black man to evangelise and humanise the white man.[16]

I have often returned to these words, and have increasingly recognized their prophetic insight and power. What struck me at the time, and even more forcefully now, is the way in which Buthelezi juxtaposed evangelization and humanization. 'But surely,' some may well retort, 'evangelism is about "saving souls", not humanizing white people!'

Christian tradition, drawing on the images, metaphors and rhetoric of the Bible, has developed various 'theories' of the atonement to answer the question of how God saves us. But like proofs for the existence of God, all of them are expres-

---

16 The complete text is in de Gruchy, *The Church Struggle in South Africa*, pp. 156–7.

sions of faith seeking understanding rather than convictions that can be conclusively proven. In an earlier book *Reconcili-ation: Restoring Justice*, I discussed some of these theories, focusing especially on the Pauline doctrine of reconciliation.[17] I did so because it is especially pertinent to Christian wit-ness in South Africa and elsewhere today where estrangement between racial and religious groups has to be overcome if there is to be genuine peace. Reconciliation with God is not the same as, but it is related to the restoration of justice in the world, and although the theological doctrine cannot be reduced to politics, it is therefore of considerable social rele-vance. If that were not the case, then the Christian doctrine of reconciliation or redemption, indeed the gospel of Christ, would have little earthly-historical significance. Salvation understood in terms of reconciliation has to do with over-coming alienation between God and ourselves in a way that is inseparable from restoring human relationships and therefore human well-being. And if to be truly human means living in a right relationship with others, understanding salvation in this way is of central importance.

For centuries, however, salvation has generally (if not sole-ly) meant saving sinners from damnation in hell, and enabling them to reach heaven, whether directly or through purgatory. I suspect that this is still how the vast majority of Christ-ians understand salvation and therefore why Jesus became a human being. Can we still believe this? Could a Christian humanist possibly think in these terms? After all, how often has the threat of hell been used to dehumanize people, or the promise of heaven been held out as a sop to the oppressed and the poor?

Contrary to what some might think when they superficially compare the Old and New Testaments, there is more about hell and God's judgement in the latter than the former. There is no easy way round Jesus' parables on sheep and goats, or rich Dives and poor Lazarus and their respective ends. But even more so, the reality of hell is embedded in the story of

17 de Gruchy, *Reconciliation: Restoring Justice* (London: SCM Press, 2002).

the crucifixion. As Jesus' cry of dereliction from the cross so poignantly portrays, he experienced alienation from God in his agonizing death and 'descent into hell'.[18] Whether in the visions of the seer in the book of Revelation, Michelangelo's portrayal of the last judgement in the Sistine Chapel, or Dante's account in the *Divine Comedy*, blissful images of paradise, and grotesque images of hell, are part of the traditional Christian world-view. How, then, are we to understand this?

Dante's *Divine Comedy* is not about the furniture of heaven and hell, but a powerful critique of the misuse of power and the importance of virtue, and the purgatorial struggle to make reparation for past misdeeds. In the same way, the 'spirituals' sung by those enslaved in the Deep South of the United States often expressed longing for justice and peace in the world now, even though their words projected that longing into the hereafter. However much the language was about a heaven that awaited them, and the hell that awaited those who oppressed them, it was code-language about present hopes and struggles in this world. The truth being expressed is that God is a God of justice, that there is a moral order that we transgress to our peril. So it is reasonable to believe that those who oppress others will get their just deserts even if not in this life, and that the downtrodden will be blessed. How else, it may be argued, are we able to address the problem of the unrepentant tyrant (or concentration camp commandant) who has oppressed the poor and, in the process, enjoyed the good things of life to the full and who, as Jesus put it, 'have their reward now'? The basis of judgement, according to Jesus' parable in Matthew 25, is whether we truly respect God's image in others, or dehumanize them.

During the summer of 1964, Isobel and I lived for several weeks in the beautiful town of Stockbridge in the Berkshire hills of western Massachusetts. I was the supply pastor of the First Congregational Church, a church with a distinguished history stretching back to the early colonial period. Its second pastor was the famous puritan divine, Jonathan Edwards, a key figure in the Great Awakening, and later President of

---

18 Karl Barth, *Church Dogmatics* III/2 (Edinburgh: T&T Clark, 1960) pp. 602–3.

Princeton University. One Sunday I decided to use shock tactics to gain the attention of the congregation at the start of my sermon. I announced that I was going to preach on 'sinners in the hands of an angry God', the title of one of Edwards' famous sermons. I must confess that I did not have the courage to repeat what he had said, but the congregation did become attentive. What I did say was that while judgement and salvation are real, when we speak about heaven and hell we are inevitably speaking in allegories, along the lines of Charles Williams' *Descent into Hell* or C. S. Lewis' *The Great Divorce*.[19] Heaven, or living in the presence of God, is open to all who desire God; hell, which is about alienation from God, is of our own making. Paradise may well be an eternal shopping mall for some; for me that would be sheer hell.

Having created us humans with the freedom of choice, God does not coerce us into choosing heaven any more than he desires that we end up in hell. So choosing between the ways of life and death, as the prophets put it, remains an imperative. But there is a difference between recognizing that our choices affect our destiny, and deciding on behalf of God that someone's wrong choices place him or her irrevocably beyond God's love. We should, in any case, stop trying, as Lewis wrote, 'to see the final state of things ... what cannot be answered to mortal ears'.[20] To believe that God has devised and maintained a prison torture chamber infinite in extent and reminiscent of the worst concentration camp for those who step out of line demeans God and destroys the integrity of the gospel. Can the God revealed in Jesus Christ, and those who have spent their lives trying to 'save the lost', be 'eternally blest' while those they failed to convert are being tormented eternally in hell? The idea is bizarre. It is even more theologically obscene to think that a believing Christian who is the commandant of a concentration camp will go to heaven, and those Jews, gypsies and homosexuals whom he incarcerated and killed will end up in hell. Is Ghandi, a Hindu, to be

---

19 Charles Williams, *Descent Into Hell* (Grand Rapids: Eerdmans, 1949); C. S. Lewis, *The Great Divorce* (New York: Macmillan, 1946).
20 Lewis, *The Great Divorce*, p. 128.

excluded, and a member of the Ku Klux Klan who, in the name of a 'white Christ' bombed a black church, killing children, to be welcomed by St Peter with open arms?

Holy Saturday, the day after Good Friday, reminds us that Christ 'descended into hell' in order to liberate its captives; that is the extent of God's grace. The terrifying 'No' of God's judgement on the cross on all that is wrong, is the final word on sin, but not on the sinner; the cross is above all else God's gracious 'Yes' to humanity, the good news of forgiveness, wholeness, that is, salvation. Julian of Norwich counselled Christians not to delve into the mystery of God's eternal plans, but recorded Jesus' words to her in a vision that while 'sin is necessary', 'all will be well, all will be well, and every kind of thing will be well'.[21] But let us return to our question: did God become a human being simply so that we can escape hell and get to heaven in some life hereafter? Is this what his teaching about the kingdom of God (or heaven) is all about? Or has it more to do with this life, with undoubted implications and consequences for the next?

For Jesus, as for Judaism at the time, the coming of God's reign had to do with the establishment of God's *shalom* or peaceable kingdom on earth. It was not primarily about life after death, but about the establishment of justice and peace here and now. In his parables, Jesus teaches us how to become participants in this coming kingdom by entering it *now*. In his healing miracles, Jesus demonstrates that in the coming kingdom humanity will be made whole, restored to its fullness, by healing people *now*. In John's Gospel this present experience of God's reign is described in the words 'eternal life', words that refer literally to 'life in the new age', the age inaugurated through Jesus' resurrection. This is the 'abundant life' described in Jesus' parable of the Good Shepherd, life in its fullness. And while it is a quality of life over which death itself has no power, it is not simply 'everlasting', as though time has any meaning in eternity. So in answer to the question 'Why did God become human?' the gospel answer is: in order

21 From the Thirteenth Revelation, Julian of Norwich, *Showings*, in *The Classics of Western Spirituality* (New York: Paulist Press, 1978), p. 225.

to inaugurate God's reign of justice and peace so that we may have life in all its fullness. 'I am come,' Jesus says, 'that you may have life, and have it abundantly' (John 10.10). Or, as St Irenaeus put it: 'The glory of God is humanity fully alive.'[22]

Humanity fully alive

I have long found Irenaeus' insights among the most helpful in thinking about the process of salvation. Converted to Christ in Asia Minor in the latter half of the second century Irenaeus became the bishop of Lyons in Gaul, where he was martyred. A biblical theologian and apologist of considerable stature, his understanding of human sin pre-dates that of Augustine's doctrine of the Fall. At the risk of over-simplification, he argued that humanity was not made perfect at creation, but innocent and immature.[23] The story of Adam and Eve is the story of every human being, the grand narrative of which all our stories are a part, though our own personal stamp marks each. Subject to hurtful passions, men and women, ungrateful for what they are as human beings, disobey God by trying to be gods.

Irenaeus' insights relate well to an evolutionary perspective on the growth of consciousness as a result of making bad choices. From this perspective

> original sin means that each one of us is born into a still unfinished, imperfect universe where there already exist strong pressures – many of them inherited culturally over countless generations – for us to acquiesce in an indifference to God's creative cosmic aim of maximizing beauty. Original sin consists of all the forces that lead us away from participation in this most essential and vitalizing pursuit.[24]

We are all contaminated by this human failure, not as a result of some genetic flaw, but as a result of our 'entering a

---

22 Irenaeus, *Adversus Haereses*, 4.20.6.

23 See the selection on Irenaeus' understanding of the Atonement taken from his *Adversus Haereses* in Henry Bettenson, *The Early Christian Fathers* (Oxford: Oxford University Press, 1969), pp. 78–83.

24 Haught, *God After Darwin*, p. 138.

world in which the banality and ugliness of evil are tolerated so easily'.[25] This is what it means to be 'in Adam'. Unless we recognize and deal with this 'shadow side' to our lives and personalities we won't be able to journey towards human maturity and wholeness.

By contrast, redemption or salvation, as Irenaeus understood it, came about as a result of the reversal of this downward spiral in the story of humanity through the life, death and resurrection of Jesus Christ. In the story of the incarnation, Jesus born of Mary overcame Adam and Eve's disobedience through obedience. Irenaeus described this process in two different ways. The first was 'deification'. God became a human being in Jesus Christ in order to make us truly divine; that is, to restore God's image in us. While few biblical texts speak directly of deification,[26] this understanding of salvation is deeply rooted in the writings of the early Church fathers and is central to Eastern Orthodoxy.[27] It refers to a growth in holiness or 'mystical union' with God, in which humans come to share in the attributes of God, such as love, self-giving and compassion. Deification is the work of the Spirit changing human nature to reflect the divine nature. As venerable as this description of the process of salvation is, I hesitate to use it. To say someone is 'divine' today often means something quite different from holiness. A person who claims 'divine' status is invariably a tyrant, a gangster, a pop star or a boxer. I cannot but think that true saints, martyrs and prophets would find it pretentious. Jesus, who had every right to claim such a status, refused even to be called good (Luke 18.19).

The other concept used by Irenaeus to describe the process of salvation was 'recapitulation', a term borrowed from the letter to the Ephesians (1.10). Understood in this way, redemption is the restoration or fulfilment of our humanity as

25 Haught, *God After Darwin*, p. 139.

26 The references to divinization are few, but see 2 Peter 1.4, Romans 2.7.

27 See Vladimir Lossky, *The Mystical Theology of the Eastern Church* (Crestwood, NY: St Vladimir's Seminary Press, 1976); Jaroslav Pelikan, *The Spirit of Eastern Christendom (600–1700)*, The Christian Tradition: A History of the Development of Doctrine, vol. 2 (Chicago: Chicago University Press, 1974), pp. 10–11.

all things are brought to completion in C hrist. Reflecting on the doctrine of recapitulation, Tillich wrote:

> Adam is fulfilled in Christ; this means that Christ is the essential man, the man Adam was to become but did not actually become. Adam was not in a state of fulfilment from the beginning; he lived in childish innocence. Here we have a profound doctrine of what I call a transcendent humanism, a humanism which says that Christ is the fulfilment of essential man, of the Adamic nature ... we can become fully human through participation in this full humanity which has appeared in Christ.[28]

Interpreted in this way, we can say that God became fully human in Christ, not in order to make us divine, but to make us truly human. In effect, and properly understood, this process of humanization is not ultimately different from deification because they both refer to the restoration of the 'image of God' and our transformation by the Spirit. Yet humanization, a word widely used in ecumenical circles in the 1960s and by Buthelezi in connection with evangelism, does seem to be a better, more modest and appropriate way to describe salvation. Not only does it tie in better with what I have said about 'mature worldliness' in conformity to the life, death and resurrection of Jesus, but it also reminds us of what I wrote at the beginning about human well-being and the recovery of innocence.

But there is another aspect to Irenaeus' theology that I find helpful, even if speculative, that takes us further along these lines. His understanding of recapitulation is given credence by advances in micro-biology in the recognition that the 'DNA of any person contains, as well, the DNA history of not only humanity as a whole but of life in general'.[29] John Robinson

---

28 Paul Tillich, *A History of Christian Thought* (London: SCM Press, 1968), p. 45.

29 Theodore W. Jennings Jr, 'Theological Anthropology and the Human Genome Project', in *Adam, Eve, and the Genome: The Human Genome Project and Theology*, ed. Susan Brooks Thistlethwaite (Minneapolis: Fortress Press, 2003), p. 105.

put this with startling clarity when, in *The Human Face of God*, he wrote:

> Jesus must have been linked in his biological tissue to the origin of life on this planet and behind that to the whole inorganic process of reaching back to the star dust and the hydrogen atom ... as any other living thing ... theologically this has indeed always been asserted by saying that the Incarnation was prepared from the foundation of the world.[30]

What was lost 'in Adam' is retrieved 'in Christ'; redemption is not the salvation of the soul, but rather the recapitulation of the totality of human life along with the whole of creation. We recall the words of Paul in his letter to the Romans (8.22) about 'the whole creation' which 'has been groaning in travail together until now' along with the rest of us, awaiting redemption in Christ. All of this, whether from a theological or biological perspective, indicates a deep connection between human beings and the rest of creation, within an evolutionary/historical and cosmological framework, as well as that of the history of redemption. Bonhoeffer called recapitulation a 'magnificent conception, full of promise'.[31] It means, in effect, 'that nothing is lost, that everything is taken up into Christ, although it is transformed, made transparent, clear and free from all selfish desire'.[32]

In a remarkable vision based on his scientific endeavours but going well beyond them and echoing Paul's teaching on the 'cosmic Christ' (Colossians 1.15–20), Teilhard spoke of evolution as an ongoing process moving towards Christ as the 'Omega Point' of all creation. Starting with evolutionary theory that roots humanity in the earth, connecting us to all other forms of life, Teilhard ends with a vision of all life, including human life, finding its goal or end in the cosmic

---

30 John A. T. Robinson, *The Human Face of God* (London: SCM Press, 1973), p. 54.

31 Bonhoeffer, *Letters and Papers from Prison*, p. 170.

32 Bonhoeffer, *Letters and Papers from Prison*, p. 170.

Christ in and through whom all things are finally brought to fulfilment. From this perspective, to be human has to do both with our connectedness to the earth, and our sharing in a common journey and destiny with 'Adam' and 'Christ'. Or, as Paul put it in his letter to the Romans: 'As in Adam all die; in Christ shall all be made alive' (5.12–21). The thrust of evolution, in other words, is towards human fulfilment, by which is meant arriving at the point where human beings 'can share, consciously and fully, in the creative activity of God'.[33] Understood in this way, Christian redemption is both the sanctification and humanization of all endeavour, and thus the basis for a new Christian humanism rooted in the earth and expressed in human activity from the humblest to the most sublime.[34]

It may well be, as Jürgen Moltmann pointed out, that Teilhard failed to recognize the ambiguities in evolution, and therefore 'paid no attention to evolution's victims'.[35] Though impressed by his courage during the First World War, I was dumbfounded by his uncritical patriotism and the optimistic spirit in which he accepted the appallingly inhuman conditions in the trenches and the death of comrades, including two of his brothers.[36] Can this really be justified on the basis of evolutionary progress? I do not think so. Yet as Charles Raven put it, 'Teilhard's full-scale interpretation of cosmic evolution in terms of the universal Christ disposes at once of the versions of creation and fall that depose God from his world and assign to man the power to frustrate God's purpose ...' In Teilhard's vision, the old heretical dualisms of 'matter and mind, body and spirit, God and the devil are plainly transcended'.[37] This is not unlike Bonhoeffer's own understanding that in Christ, the separation of the world and of God is overcome. 'There is no part of the world,' Bonhoeffer wrote,

33 Ward, *God, Chance and Necessity*, pp. 162–3.
34 See Pierre Teilhard de Chardin, *The Future of Man* (New York: Harper & Row, 1964), pp. 33–4.
35 Quoted in Celia E. Deane-Drummond, *Biology and Theology Today: Exploring the Boundaries* (London: SCM Press, 2001), p. 22.
36 Speaight, *Teilhard de Chardin*, pp. 57–74.
37 Raven, *Teilhard de Chardin: Scientist and Seer*, p. 177.

'no matter how lost, no matter how godless, that has not been accepted by God in Jesus Christ and reconciled to God.'[38]

In the same passage in which he wrote of the cosmic Christ, Paul declares that he preached the gospel 'in order to bring each one into God's presence *as a mature individual in union with Christ*' (Colossians 1.28 TEV). The words translated in the last phrase refer to human completeness, the outcome of God's saving grace. So there is, as Buthelezi told the Congress in Durban, a clear connection between evangelism and humanization. What this means for you and me is not something we can fully grasp, any more than we can finally say with certainty precisely who we are at any stage along the journey of life. But we can say that accepting the good news of salvation and following Jesus as disciples means becoming conformed to the one who has become human and that this 'is what being human really means'.[39] And, we can add, the Christ who is formed in us always enhances us as persons, making us not into someone else, but more truly ourselves. Such conformation does not simply happen; it is a life-long process. With Rowan Williams we 'must wait without the expectation of a tidy personality profile ever being provided, but in the hope that Christ's knowing of me will give me whatever wholeness I am capable of receiving'.[40] Such waiting is not inactive, but a way of living that is open to the action of the Spirit through whom Christ is formed in us, making us more truly human.

Christian spirituality is about the means of grace that make this possible. It is a spirituality that arises out of the biblical grand narrative, especially that of the gospel which constantly reminds us of the one who, though truly God, became fully human so that our humanity may be restored. Christian spirituality therefore has to do with living lives of compassion, mercy and justice in the world that reflect the teaching of Jesus as expressed in the Sermon on the Mount and embodied in his ministry of service and self-giving on the cross. While costly, such spirituality is not dehumanizing but liberating, a

---

38 Bonhoeffer, *Ethics*, pp. 66–7.
39 Bonhoeffer, *Ethics*, p. 94.
40 Rowan Williams, *Christ on Trial* (Grand Rapids: Eerdmans, 2000), p. 36.

spirituality of grace that sets us free to be more fully human as persons on a journey to greater wholeness. This becomes a reality for us as we participate in that story through prayer, reading and reflection on the Scriptures, sharing together in the eucharistic meal, and embodying the story in our daily lives. The Christian life, then, is one in which we journey with Christ in a way that meshes our own story with that of his, a cosmic love story yet one rooted in the history and particularity of Jesus of Nazareth and, we must now say, with the community of those who have sought, in faith and obedience, to believe in him as saviour and obey him as Lord. For belief and behaviour without belonging is incomplete.

A new humanity: agent of human wholeness

Being a Christian implies being part of the Christian community or Church. But let me acknowledge at the outset the gap between what the Church professes to be, and what it often is. So it is unsurprising that some people give up on being Christian precisely because of their experience of the Church. For them, the Church is a symbol of bad religion, incapable of opposing injustice, far too wrapped up in its own affairs, lacking vision and a spirituality that addresses their need. The litany of ecclesial failure is a long one, and has been discussed in much detail through the centuries starting in the pages of the New Testament itself where time and again lofty images of the Church coexist with descriptions of tension, immorality, animosity and division. Every movement for Church renewal, and I have participated in my fair share, is an indication that things are not as they ought to be. Indeed, having spent much of my energy within the Church in the cause of Christian unity, I am dismayed by the way in which so much ecumenical achievement of the third quarter of the twentieth century has been squandered in more recent times.

The gap between claim and reality led Augustine to distinguish between the Church visible and invisible. This distinction is not one found in the New Testament and, in any case, it has proved to be unhelpful suggesting as it does that the true

Church is not embodied in the world, comprised of human beings with all our strengths and weaknesses. This is simply another form of docetism, insisting on the divine structure of the Church without recognizing its human character. But the Church is comprised of people of flesh and blood with all that this implies, and it exists in a world where social and political forces continually challenge and undermine its professed values. Moreover, it is comprised of a very diverse range of women and men, drawn from every race and class, with different needs and expectations, and at different stages in their life's journey. As a social and not just a spiritual entity this also means that it cannot avoid being an institution of some kind. Just as a body requires a skeleton to prevent it collapsing in a heap, so the Church requires proper management, leadership, funding and the seemingly endless meetings needed to ensure its maintenance. It cannot be otherwise. The New Testament fully acknowledges this, but nevertheless also speaks of the Church in ways that point beyond its human foibles to its divine character. There are many images of the Church in the New Testament that do this.[41] The portrait painted there is that despite its failures, the Church is the body of Christ, the community of the Holy Spirit, the embodiment of a new, reconciled humanity.

As a student, I was struck by John Robinson's comment that it 'is almost impossible to exaggerate the materialism and crudity of Paul's doctrine of the church as literally now the resurrection *body* of Christ'.[42] The Church as the embodiment of Christ in the world is a mind-boggling concept, one that is particularly rich but equally open to abuse. A wrong inference has led to the assumption that as 'the body of Christ' the Church is perfect, infallible, not subject to error or liable to make mistakes. But the Church is not 'the kingdom of God'; it exists to bear witness to God's reign as revealed in Jesus Christ. Moreover, for the Church to claim a divine status that Jesus himself refused to claim, and to impose that on others, is nothing short

---

41 See Paul S. Minear, *Images of the Church in the New Testament* (Philadelphia: Westminster, 1960).

42 John Robinson, *The Body* (London: SCM Press, 1957), p. 51.

of idolatry. Christ did not regard his 'equality with God as something to be exploited' (Philippians 2.6), but emptied himself and became the suffering servant. If Christ is the head of the body, then the body should reflect who Christ is.

Nonetheless, to confess that the Church is 'the body of Christ' does express the essence of the Church in a way few other images do, especially if we understand it as a dynamic process in which Christ is present and takes form in a community of persons in a way that intrinsically links the Church to humanity as a whole. In Bonhoeffer's words:

> So the church is not a religious community of those who revere Christ, but Christ who has taken form among human beings. The church may be called the body of Christ because in the body of Jesus Christ *human being per se*, and therefore all human beings, have really been taken on. The church now bears the form that in truth is meant for all people. The image according to which it is being formed is the image of humanity. What takes place in the church happens vicariously and representatively as a model for all human beings.[43]

From this perspective, the Church is far more than a conglomerate of like-minded individuals voluntarily joined together for some common purpose, like some club or society. As distinct from describing the Church as a social institution, its description as the 'body of Christ' is one of faith. Nonetheless, it is something tangible, something that can and is experienced and embodied – something we often experienced during the Church struggle against apartheid. Believers, Paul tells us, 'are members one of another', they are baptized together into the 'body of Christ', so that if one suffers, all suffer, if one rejoices all rejoice. In sharing bread and wine in the eucharistic meal, the many are one body for 'all partake of the one bread' (1 Corinthians 10.17). In modern parlance, we are talking here of a network of relations, or the weaving of connections that help to bring about wholeness both to the

---

43 Bonhoeffer, *Ethics*, p. 96.

persons involved, and to the wider society. As I shall shortly tell, this is not just theory but true to my experience of the Church as it is to others.

This profoundly relational understanding of the Church in which all members play a role, in which truth is spoken in love, and in which all are brought to maturity in Christ as human beings, is fundamental to its nature and purpose. As Christ is the icon of true humanity, so the Church as the 'body of Christ' is called to be the icon of the 'new humanity', a community in which human relationships are healed and people made whole. The *Shona* sculpture depicts well this circle of embrace, inclusion and wholeness, a maternal image that reminds us that theologians from Augustine to Calvin spoke of the Church as 'our mother', and that in the Catholic tradition, Mary is understood as a model of the Church.

It is not accidental that the third article of the Apostles' Creed includes in one breath belief in the Holy Spirit and in the Church: 'I believe in the Holy Spirit, the holy catholic Church.' Ever since Pentecost, these two articles belong together. As the risen Christ is the 'first-fruits' of the new age of God's reign, the Church is the first-fruits of the Spirit in bringing God's new humanity into being. As such, the Church is charismatic in that its life is dependent on the Spirit, on the gifts that the Spirit gives to the community for the building of the body, and on the power of the Spirit in fulfilling its mission in the world. But does this understanding of the Church bear any relation to historical reality? Is there any evidence that it is, in fact, a sign of the 'new humanity', an inclusive community rather than an exclusive sect or club?

The Church does have standards of discipleship that are often costly, as Jesus himself taught, so there is an important sense in which it is exclusive. But too often the standards used in practice are not those of discipleship but those shaped by prejudice, culture, ethnicity, nationality, and far too often by a very narrow, legalistic and literal reading of Scripture. In Jesus' wonderful image: we strain out gnats and swallow camels (Matthew 23.24)! How often during the apartheid years churches excluded people for the wrong reasons, and failed to discipline members who supported and reinforced apartheid. Conscientious objectors to military service were frowned upon, but church members engaged in nefarious work for the security police were made elders; ministers who condemned apartheid were often sidelined, and those who kept silent in the face of injustice were welcomed into the pulpit; and, of course, people of the wrong racial group were kept outside the fold. Segregation was not just a political policy and social reality; it permeated the lives of too many congregations. I fear, today, that homophobia and xenophobia are playing the same dehumanizing role in the life of many churches. That is why it is important to recall the origins of the Church as the sign of God's 'new humanity'. What, according to the New Testament, did God intend in calling this very fallible community of persons into being? Was it to create a religious community of some kind? Or did it have a world-historical significance in terms of which we need to understand God's salvific purpose?

Christianity began as a Jewish messianic sect, and the first Christian believers had no expectation that their movement would embrace people from other ethnic backgrounds. But Pentecost drove the first somewhat fearful followers of Jesus from behind its closed doors into the world with a message that embraced people of every known land and tongue. The full implications of this only became apparent as a result of what it sometimes called the Gentile Pentecost (Acts 9—10) when the infant Church, much against its all-too-human inclination, began to embrace non-Jews, that is, people from other ethnic backgrounds. In the process the Church moved decisively beyond the boundaries of Judaism to become a socially inclusive movement. This historical development was described in the New Testament in terms of Christ breaking down walls of hostility that separated Jew and Gentile and, in his body, creating a new humanity (Ephesians 2.1–10).

We know only too well that within a few decades church and synagogue acrimoniously parted company, thereby contradicting this vision of a new humanity; we also know that time and again throughout history the Church has been divided along ethnic and national lines, and so denied its founding Pentecostal vision. Nowhere was this more so than in apartheid South Africa where churches were too often divided along racial lines reflecting their captivity to social norms and political pressure. Both political and church segregation were justified by some on the basis of the story of the Tower of Babel (Genesis 9), understood to mean that God was not in favour of the unity of humanity, but wanted all cultural and language groups to live and worship separately. This was not only a bad reading of that narrative, it was also a rejection of the meaning of Pentecost, namely, that in Christ, God willed to bring all people from every nation together through the power of the Spirit – in other words, in a way that was humanly speaking an impossibility.

This Pentecostal vision provided the theological basis for declaring apartheid a heresy, and gave direction to those who struggled against segregation and racism in the Church.[44] Church unity, as we understood it, was not primarily the uniting of divided denominations, but the overcoming of alienation between people hostile to each other, whether on the basis of ethnicity, class or gender (see Galatians 3.28). And that must surely still be the case. The Church does not exist to promote its own institutional interests but the gospel of Christ's peace that reconciles those divided by enmities, both ancient and modern. The Church struggle against apartheid was fundamentally a struggle to affirm the reality of the new humanity that the Church is called to be, and therefore to challenge social and political forces that contradicted this gospel of reconciliation.

The realization of the new humanity as understood in the New Testament is always something in the future; it is a vision of what God intends, and in that sense utopian, beyond present achievement. Yet the Church is called to be a sign of that future already now in the present, and therefore to embody the new humanity as an increasingly inclusive com-

44 David Bosch, 'Nothing but a Heresy', in *Apartheid is a Heresy*, ed. John de Gruchy and Charles Villa-Vicencio (Cape Town: David Philip, 1983), pp. 24–38.

munity. Drawing on a statement from Vatican II, Duncan
Forrester speaks of the Church as called to be 'an exemplifica-
tion of a kind of egalitarian community which is intended to
encompass all humankind, and of which the church is also an
instrument, helping to bring such inclusive community into
existence as well as providing a preliminary manifestation of
it'. This implies, as Forrester goes on to say, overcoming old
hostilities as well as new ones in establishing communities of
reconciliation 'in which human beings may flourish together
in love and peace'.[45] Understood in this way, far from making
unwarranted claims, or ones that lead to triumphalist domination, the claim that the Church embodies the new humanity
is a challenge to the Church to move beyond sectarian narrowness and become a sign of what God wills for the whole of
humankind. In doing so it challenges the dehumanizing processes currently at work in globalization, and becomes an
anticipatory sign of a true globalism of justice and peace, a
globalism in which people who are different from each other
find themselves at home together, a celebration of God's
jubilee.

There are at least two dimensions to the Church's calling
to embody or represent God's new humanity as an agent of
human wholeness and instrument of humanization. The first
has to do with the critical or prophetic role of the Church in
society. In this respect, the Church is called to challenge all
forces and processes that are dehumanizing and depersonalizing, and especially those that are blatantly crimes against
humanity. In doing so, the Church has to be critical of its
own life, and the causes it supports. Key concerns here are
human rights and dignity, economic justice, the protection
of the environment, the struggle against hunger, poverty, disease, a lack of education, and the reduction of violence in the
world. Reflecting on these concerns, we soon discern the connection between them and the agenda of the biblical prophets
and Jesus, and of the Church through the centuries when it
has been faithful to its calling to oppose dehumanization and
serve the common good.

---

45 Duncan Forrester, *On Human Worth* (London: SCM Press, 2001), p. 195.

The second fundamental aspect has to do with its pastoral, evangelistic and nurturing roles. Over against other social institutions that dehumanize and depersonalize, the Church should be an institution in which people are enabled to be truly human, truly themselves, in Christ. This has ramifications for the structures of the Church and the way they are managed, for they are sometimes as depersonalizing as those of other institutions. It also has implications for its liturgical life, spiritual formation and inclusive ministry to all people, especially those in need or those pushed onto the boundaries of society. The model for this is surely the ministry of Jesus, his nurturing of the disciple community, his ministry of healing and wholeness, and his embracing of the 'outsider'. As a community patterned on the ministry of Jesus, the Church itself becomes a humanizing model for society, rather than simply reflecting its dehumanizing and depersonalizing tendencies. Although the Church has often re-discovered its role in this regard from progressive movements in society, it is called to be in the vanguard, not the rearguard of humanization. The Church of Pentecost must necessarily be open to the future, not closed in on itself or entombed in the past, recognizing that the Spirit is always at work bringing into being fresh life, new hope and unexpected possibilities. Only in this way does the Church discover resources and develop capacity for the challenges of the present.

But are these just words or are there concrete examples to which we can point that exemplify the Church as an agent of a new humanity? I can only speak of what I know, but I am certain my experience is not a solitary one. For more than 30 years Isobel and I have been members of the Rondebosch United Church (RUC). Traditionally a white, suburban, middle-class, reasonably politically liberal church established in 1901, RUC was, until the 1970s, the spiritual home of professional people, university students and established families. But increasingly, during the 1970s and 1980s, under the leadership of Douglas Bax, a pastor of courage and theological acumen, it began to identify more directly with the struggle against apartheid. On two occasions during the States of Emergency,

I vividly recall, the church building was surrounded by armed soldiers and police, to enforce an order that no public meetings were to be held there. Undaunted, Bax walked past the soldiers and ripped the proclamation from the front door of the church. The church had become known as a 'communist church' because it provided a home for conscientious objectors, and allowed the United Democratic Front (a surrogate for the liberation movement) to use its premises for meetings.

At the risk of idealizing a far from perfect Christian congregation, but in order to portray a picture and thus provide a concrete example of a church trying to be inclusive, let me say that in the post-apartheid period, the RUC has continued to give its support to people often shunned or ostracized by society or other churches. Gay people are made welcome, street children are trained to play marimbas and included in Sunday worship, domestic workers from nearby homes and schools have been welcomed into membership, and French- and Swahili-speaking refugees from violence in Burundi, Rwanda and the Congo have found a home. Members now engage in ministry at Pollsmoor Prison, home to many members of the gangs that plague the townships. Its present pastor, Robert Steiner, has developed a special ministry to those who are too often forced onto the edges of society. But what is equally remarkable is the extent to which the older, white membership has remained part of the life and fellowship of the church, sometimes unsettled by the experience, but invariably enriched, fulfilling Buthelezi's hope that evangelization by those formerly excluded would lead to the humanization of those who have been privileged. This pattern is repeating itself to some extent across the country in congregations of many different denominations, providing evidence of the Church being a community in which the gospel of reconciliation makes us more truly human.

What I have described in this chapter about what it means to be a Christian is far from exhaustive as my intention has been to show the connections between being human and being Christian rather than expound more generally on what Christianity is all about. Much more could be said, for example, about other doctrines, ministry and mission, the importance of hospitality, and about worship and spirituality. These are clearly not addenda to Christian faith and life, but of its essence, even if in these pages I have inferred or referred to them in passing rather than discussing them at length. Indeed, I not only learnt the importance of worship and spirituality early on in my Christian journey, but discovered their relevance even more so during the struggle against apartheid.[46] And, today, as I will tell, I live in a Christian community sustained by daily prayer and eucharistic celebration. But the time has now come to say some more about the character of Christian humanism as an attempt to engage culture, whether contemporary or classical, African or European.

---

46 See, for example, my essay on 'Christian Spirituality and Social Transformation' in my book *Cry Justice!* (London: Collins, 1986) pp. 23–46.

7

A Christian Humanist

*... what we should honour passes without a word and what we
should strive for with all our might is regarded with contempt.
Hence gold is more valued than learning, ancient lineage more than
virtue, the gifts of the body more than the endowments of the mind;
ceremonies are put before true piety, the rules of men before the
teaching of Christ, the mask is preferred to the truth, the shadow
to the reality, the counterfeit to the genuine, the fleeting to the
substantial, the momentary to the eternal ...* Erasmus[1]

*The job of the Christian is to try and give an example of sanity,
independence, human integrity, good sense, as well as Christian
love and wisdom, against all establishments and mass movements
and all current fashions ...* Thomas Merton[2]

*Wisdom is better than weapons of war,
but one bungler destroys much good.* Ecclesiastes 9.18

In seeking to give more content to the description of Christian
humanism in a way that is in continuity with its origins and yet
contemporary in its character, a way that is honed by historical experience and therefore critical of its own legacy, I wish
to explore four related themes. The first, a love of learning,
reflects the origins of Christian humanism in the scholarship
of the Renaissance that broke the stranglehold of a decaying
scholasticism, and led to both social and church renewal, as
well as to remarkable scientific achievements. The next three
themes derive from the classical trilogy of truth, goodness and
beauty, they express the vision of human wholeness that characterized the best of Renaissance humanism and must equally

---

1 From the letter of Erasmus to Urban Regius, Basel, 24 February 1516, in
Desiderius Erasmus, *Erasmus: Documents of Modern HIstory*, ed. Richard L.
DeMolen (London: Edward Arnold, 1973), p. 84.

2 Thomas Merton to Daniel Berrigan, 10 October 1967, in Merton, *The
Hidden Ground of Love: Letters on Religious Experience and Social Concerns*
(London: Collins, 1985), p. 98.

inform contemporary Christian humanism. And they must do so in a way that is both consonant with Christian conviction and open to dialogue and co-operation with people of other faiths as well as with secular humanists. What I propose, then, is to offer some suggestions as to how this may be expressed in relation to some of the issues and concerns that I have raised in previous chapters, in the hope that this stimulates further reflection – and action.

A love of learning: seeking wisdom

There is an essay in John Coetzee's Nobel Prize-winning novel *Elizabeth Costello* about a Catholic nun who has been awarded an honorary doctorate in the humanities from a major university in South Africa. The award was made because of her compassionate service to the poor and especially to those suffering from HIV and AIDS in rural KwaZulu-Natal. In her acceptance speech, Sister Bridget was outspoken in her criticism of the academic community as remote from reality, disengaged from the immense suffering that surrounds us in the world. It so happened that her sister, Elizabeth Costello, from Australia, a decidedly secular woman and a noted author, had been invited to the graduation ceremony. The academics around the post-graduation celebration dinner table found her a much more congenial guest than Sister Bridget from whose critical speech they were still reeling. At least they could engage her in meaningful discussion about literature and the humanities and thereby avoid thinking too much about human suffering and the sharp rebuke they had received.

Following the graduation, the secular sister joined her religious sibling for a vacation at the monastery in KwaZulu-Natal. It was there, during this brief sojourn, that she encountered an old arthritic African carver of crucifixes. He had carved the huge crucifix that hung over the sanctuary in the monastery chapel, and he spent every day carving replicas for visitors and churches. Elizabeth was indignant that such artistic talent should be wasted on sculpting crucifixes, symbols of suffering, rather than being allowed to craft other artefacts that expressed more of the beauty of life. She remonstrated with her sister for allowing this to happen, asking why the monastery allowed it.

Why a Christ dying in contortions rather than a living Christ? A man in his prime, in his early thirties; what do you have against showing him alive, in all his living beauty? And, while I am about it, what do you have against the Greeks? The Greeks would never have made statues and paintings of a man in the extremes of agony, deformed, ugly, and then knelt before those statues and worshipped them. If you wonder why the humanists whom you wish us to sneer at looked beyond Christianity and the contempt that Christianity exhibits for the human body and therefore for man himself, surely that ought to give you a clue.[3]

I can fully appreciate the indignation of Elizabeth Costello. It is the same feeling many of us have after seeing television pictures of human suffering *ad nauseam*. Surely there is more to life than this voyeuristic, overwhelming concentration on people dying with AIDS, starving children with extended bellies, the crippled victims of landmines. Or a man dying in agony on the cross so graphically portrayed by Mel Gibson's movie *The Passion*. Surely we should focus on the resurrection, on joy, on beauty, on life in all its fullness. If we are to speak at all about a Christian *humanism*, then surely this is what it should be about. Yes, indeed, that is so. But Coetzee's Sister Bridget represents the Christian conviction, one shared by all who have struggled with suffering – from Job to Dostoevsky, from Julian of Norwich to Simone Weil – and countless others who have suffered for the sake of justice, that there is no cheap and easy way to the peace that passes human understanding. *Christian* humanism insists that this is so. And that is why Coetzee's juxtaposing of Bridget and Elizabeth is so profound and relevant.

---

3 John Coetzee, *Elizabeth Costello: Eight Lessons* (London: Secker & Warburg, 2003), pp. 138–40.

I first heard Coetzee's essay read by him at a seminar on 'The Future of the Humanities in Africa' in the Graduate School in Humanities at the University of Cape Town in 2001. As I understand the story he told through the mouth of Sister Bridget, Coetzee is saying that the humanities have lost their way, confining themselves to the rarefied and elitist environment of the university where the cut and thrust of intellectual debate, stimulated by the latest innovation, has lost touch with what it actually means to be human. The future of the humanities in Africa and, by extension, across the world, thus depends on whether or not they are able to deal compassionately and redemptively with the problem of human suffering.

It was perhaps serendipitous that Coetzee's reading came at a time when I was beginning to think more concertedly about the relationship between the legacy of Renaissance humanism and Christianity, and about my role as a theologian in the Graduate School in Humanities of which I became the first director in 2000. The Faculty of Humanities had only recently been established, bringing together the former Faculties of Arts, Social Science, and Education, as well as the Schools of Fine and Performing Arts. As I had become more involved at the interface between theology, politics and aesthetics over the past decade, the Graduate School provided an ideal context within which to pursue my interests on the borders of theology and other academic disciplines. It also raised fresh questions about their relationship, and opened up new intellectual vistas. Out of this mix came the idea for rethinking Christian humanism as a way of critically engaging the legacy of both Renaissance and secular humanism. But the clue for doing so was discovered in the interaction between the sisters Bridget and Elizabeth and their reception at the graduation ceremony and celebrations.

Sister Bridget's graduation speech attacking the academy reminds me of Erasmus' *Praise of Folly* in which he excoriates the 'wisdom of the wise' and exalts that of the simple. It also highlights the perennial tension between classical culture and Christianity, between the Renaissance and the Reformation, between the academy and the Church. Sometimes the tension has erupted into open warfare, at other times it has been more creative, benefiting both sides. For the Christian humanist it is important to recognize this difference and to keep it creative. But keeping it creative cannot be at the expense of denying what Christians believe to be true. The Christian's primary responsibility is to be faithful to Jesus Christ. No one put this more bluntly than Kierkegaard in his comparison of a genius and an apostle. 'As a genius,' he wrote, 'St Paul cannot be compared to either Plato or Shakespeare,' for as 'a coiner of beautiful similes he comes pretty low down in the scale' and 'as a stylist his name is quite obscure.'[4] The genius has innate gifts and abilities that express themselves in creative newness; the apostle is called to proclaim the gospel on the basis of an authority given to him from above. Like a prophet, the apostle does not seek to please his hearers, but to communicate the truth he has received. For humanism to be *Christian* it cannot by-pass St Paul's confession of Christ crucified as 'the wisdom of God', for it would have nothing distinctive to contribute to the humanist project. But for it to be *humanist* it cannot ignore the truth wherever it is to be found, for all truth ultimately reflects the beauty and goodness of God. As such, the Christian humanist understanding of wisdom is akin to the practical wisdom reflected in the Wisdom theology of the Hebrew Bible. A wisdom that exalts in and cares for creation, discerns God's presence in the natural order and the rhythms and requirements of daily life, treasures the legacies of past lived experiences that give significance to the present, and gives priority to moral action above theoretical formulation.[5]

In his study of the influence of Christian humanists during the Reformation, Harris Harbison writes of the 'conscious tension between love of learning and devotion to Christ' as 'a sign of health and vitality in the Christian tradition rather than the reverse'.[6] Most of the leading Reformers were

---

4 Søren Kierkegaard, 'On the Difference Between a Genius and an Apostle', in *The Present Age* (London: Oxford University Press, 1940), p. 140.

5 Brueggemann, *Theology of the Old Testament*, pp. 680–82.

6 Harbison, *The Christian Scholar in the Age of the Reformation*, p. 166.

scholars skilled in rhetoric, philosophy and the classics, and well versed in Hebrew and Greek, thus able to translate the biblical text into the vernacular and interpret its meaning. This led, over the ensuing centuries, both to the rebirth of education along classical humanist lines and to the recognition within the major Church traditions that priests and pastors needed exposure to the humanities as preparation for their study of theology. This legacy is sometimes sacrificed today for financial reasons or the lack of other resources and opportunity, but often because of a resistance to the idea that it is necessary and helpful.

There is a deep anti-intellectualism in the history of Christianity, as though good scholarship and holiness are inevitable enemies, and that being ignorant fosters spiritual wisdom. This bothers me today as it bothered me when I took my first steps away from fundamentalism. For one thing it suggests that the Church does not need well- and broadly educated leaders. This does not mean one cannot be a good Christian pastor or preacher unless one is first a good academic. There have been countless saints and martyrs who were unschooled, like the first apostles, just as today throughout Africa there are pastors and preachers, and carvers of crucifixes, whose education is at best elementary, but whose wisdom is often profound. But this does not alter the fact that the Church suffers when its leadership is inadequately educated both in the theological disciplines and those that broaden and deepen our understanding of the world in which we live.

Of course, this anti-intellectualism may be a genuine reaction to an academic elitism that rides roughshod over the wisdom of experience, especially the experience of suffering, of poverty, of struggling against oppression, or of exclusion from privilege. This, it seems to me, is precisely the critique of Sister Bridget – the humanities had lost their way. And, I would add, because their value no longer seems self-evident to many, it feeds the anti-intellectualism of those who would sunder Christianity from the love of learning. Yet all those who deeply care about the humanities today are aware of its shortcomings, bothered by the fragmentation of their disciplines, and the distractions of novelty as distinct from genuine intellectual exploration, and, in my experience, are finding ways to meet these challenges. The legacy of the humanities and their potential contribution for today is too important to be squandered.

However, the danger to the humanities more generally lies outside their domain rather than within. They are under immense political pressure in the interests of science and technology, and are thus often at risk for financial reasons. Erasmus' observation that 'gold is more valued than learning' is as true today as when he penned those words. Learning and scholarship is too often reduced to a commercial commodity. Far too many people go to university and college to obtain the knowledge and skills they need to make money, without much interest in being educated. Many funding agencies are more interested in supporting research projects that will improve market performance than they are in research driven by intellectual curiosity in the interests of knowledge and truth. And university administrators as well as academics are forced to develop strategies that speed up outcomes and outputs rather than those that produce wise and well informed human beings. This raises serious questions about cultural priorities and the values that determine the educational formation of coming generations.

The humanities are meant to be the custodians and therefore advocates of what it means 'to be human'. A proper education in the humanities should stimulate critical thought, and help form people of wisdom and insight, moral value and commitment, aesthetic appreciation and judgement, historical memory and understanding, and creativity. For technological advance, commerce and social development (urban planning, housing and so forth) to be human and humanizing, leaders are required whose moral, rational and aesthetic instincts have been sharpened both by experience and by exposure to the rich resources of cultural tradition. We need to recognize, as did many Renaissance humanists, that the love of learning is not simply for its own sake, but for the transformation of society in ways that make human flourishing possible. Moral issues relating to technological and bio-medical progress, the meaning, inter-connectedness and value of life within the cosmos as a whole, and the struggle for peace in a world increasingly torn apart, are key issues for social and human well-being. So, too, are those to do with human consciousness and the quest for a spirituality adequate to the challenges of a post-modern world.

It should go without saying that the development of capacity in technology is vital for the future, so advocacy of the humanities is not intended to down-play the need for education in the natural sciences, especially in so-called developing countries. Indeed, the humanist vision cannot be realized independently of or in competition with science. Certainly Renaissance humanists did not think of the humanities and the natural sciences as disciplines separated into self-contained, discreet academic enterprises, however important academic disciplines in and of themselves have become. Their love of learning and search for wisdom transcended such barriers. Long before the term 'interdisciplinary' was invented, they were engaged in pursuing knowledge on the boundaries of what was already known. The simple reason was that human well-being is organically related to the well-being of the world in its entirety, and should therefore be the concern of the natural sciences, just as the built environment in which we live should be a concern of the humanities. The truth is, all disciplines, whether they belong to the physical or biological sciences, the social or behavioural sciences, or the humanities in all their variety, are concerned about human well-being and activity embodied in nature in different, yet interlocking ways. The embodied human, in other words, is a major intersection where all scholarly disciplines converge.

Christian humanists cherish the love of learning both for the sake of the Church's ministry in the world, and because of its importance for human well-being, for the simple reason that the two belong together. The leadership of the Church and its mission in the world is not simply a clerical affair. For centuries the Church has established schools and universities precisely because it has recognized the importance of education both for society and personal well-being. One of the great iniquities of apartheid was that it led to the demise of the vast majority of church schools in South Africa that had, in previous times, produced many African leaders, and replaced them with a system of Bantu Education that was designed to keep people in menial positions. The present lack of skills in South Africa is in large measure a result of this disastrous policy. So it is of paramount importance that Christians regard education highly, and become committed to teaching as a vocation – and to do so motivated by a love of learning that leads to wisdom and nurtures human wholeness.

Christian humanists, along with humanists of other faiths, have a particular responsibility within the contemporary academy, where secular humanism (not to speak of secularism and scientism) is often espoused uncritically as the only criterion of wisdom. This does not mean trying to return to a time when Christianity dominated education in many places, an unlikely scenario today; nor does it mean setting aside the necessarily rigorous norms of academic enquiry in which positions have to be rationally articulated and defended. But it does mean that Christians should engage in their scholarship in such a way that their Christian commitment influences the values they promote and in the perspectives they bring to their task. No one has argued this position better in recent times than George Marsden in *The Outrageous Idea of Christian Scholarship* where he writes: 'One of the great tasks of Christian scholarship is to recover some dimensions of Christian teaching that have been alienated from their theological roots.' 'This task', he goes on to say, 'is particularly urgent in an era when secular morality is adrift and traditional Christianity itself is too often beholden to the politics of self-interest and simplistic solutions.'[7] The problem is most evident around the question of relativism and truth.

Respecting difference: standing for truth

If a love of learning was one of the virtues of Renaissance humanism, another was tolerance for the opinions of others.

---

7 George M. Marsden, *The Outrageous Idea of Christian Scholarship* (New York: Oxford University Press, 1997), p. 93.

So there is some irony in the fact that Renaissance humanism and scholarship was the midwife of the Protestant Reformation. The mainstream of the Reformation was adamant in its insistence on the sole authority of Scripture, the centrality of Christ alone as God's revelation, and the sinfulness of human nature; the Catholic counter was equally adamant in stating its position without compromise. Such dogmatic claims did not sit comfortably with the broader vision of most humanist scholars in their love of the classics, and their affirmation of human goodness and potential.

The controversy between Luther and Erasmus, the quintessential Christian humanist, on the freedom and bondage of the will, epitomizes this tension. Marked, as Roland Bainton suggests, by 'misunderstanding on the part of Erasmus and exaggeration on the part of Luther'[8] it highlighted the problems faced by all who take seriously the paradoxes of the gospel. But it also highlighted another problem, namely what it means to stand for the truth. 'You and your peace-loving theology,' Luther declared to Erasmus, 'you don't care about the truth.' But Erasmus did care about the truth, for 'what happens to truth when men are embroiled in a war of religion?'[9] In his *Complaint of Peace*, Erasmus speaks powerfully:

How can you say *Our Father* if you plunge steel into the guts of your brother? Christ compared himself to a hen; Christians behave like hawks. Christ was a shepherd of sheep; Christians tear each other like wolves ...[10]

Despite the efforts of many on both sides, Erasmus chief among them, tolerance soon became a casualty in the cause of Reformation, as did Erasmus himself. Those who espoused the humanist project were confined within the boundaries of whatever confessional and institutional framework they found themselves. There was no place for a non-

---

8 Roland H. Bainton, *Erasmus of Christendom* (London: Collins, 1969), p. 228.

9 Quoted in Bainton, *Erasmus of Christendom*, p. 235.

10 Quoted in Bainton, *Erasmus of Christendom*, p. 155.

sectarian, ecumenical Christianity within the new climate of Reformation and post-Reformation struggles.

Tolerance of the opinion of others, or better, respect for difference, is seldom a virtue in the thrust and counter-thrust of theological controversy when the issues are those of life and death, and where each side claims a monopoly on the truth – as both the Confessing Church in Germany, and those engaged in the struggle against apartheid discovered. It was necessary to name apartheid as sinful, a heresy, a crime against humanity, even though for many the word heresy sounded self-righteous and judgemental, conjuring up visions of inquisition and witch-hunt. So, too, in Germany it was necessary to confess Christ over against Nazi idolatry, as was done in the famous Barmen Declaration of 1934, drafted largely by Barth. But can we reconcile such dogmatic claims to represent the truth with humanism, something that most, if not all of those at the Barmen synod would have found inconceivable? It is one thing for a more liberal Christianity to be acceptable to humanists, but what about such confessing Christianity?

Many years later, on the occasion of the fiftieth anniversary of Barmen, Eberhard Bethge remarked that the Declaration was far more than 'a verbal happening, it was linked with the cries and actions of and for dehumanized groups of men', in such a way that 'dogmatics and humanism were bound together'.[11] This involved both confessors and their compatriots in great personal risk in a common endeavour to rid Germany of tyranny, to defend its victims and to restore justice. On that same occasion, Franz Hildebrandt, Bonhoeffer's earlier friend, who was deeply committed to Luther and the gospel of the Reformation, likewise insisted that the 'church is called to make common cause with the humanists for the sake of peace and of the rights of man'.[12] The opponents of the Confessing Church in Germany were not secular humanists or

---

11 Eberhard Bethge, 'Self-Interpretation and Uncertain Reception in the Church Struggle', in *The German Church Struggle and the Holocaust*, ed. Franklin H. Littell and Hubert G. Locke (Detroit: Wayne State University Press, 1974), p. 183.

12 Franz Hildebrandt, 'Barmen: What to Learn and What not to Learn', in *The Barmen Confession*, ed. Locke, p. 300.

communists, but Christians who had capitulated to Nazism; just as in South Africa, those charged with the heresy of apartheid were not people outside the Church, but insiders – those who, in the name of Christ, perpetrated what was contrary to the gospel. In other words, a true confession of Christ is not for the sake of demonstrating doctrinal purity, to show whether or not you are 'sound', but for the sake of the well-being of the world. To surrender the truth of the gospel, to deny Christ, meant denying humanity, denying the victims of Nazism and apartheid. To affirm the truth of the gospel, by contrast, meant affirming humanity, expressing solidarity with the victims of injustice, and affirming the good and great in culture, and thus standing with those secular humanists who stood for the same values.

While respect for other people as human beings, irrespective of their views, is always necessary, an uncritical tolerance for their opinions is not always a virtue. Tolerance can become an excuse for ignoring what is reprehensible, overlooking what is hurtful to others, and thus reinforcing what is evil. We cannot be tolerant of racism, sexism and exploitation: we must be tolerant towards people, recognizing their weaknesses and sins, as we acknowledge our own. As Martin Prozesky puts it: 'tolerance can be a firm feature in our lives without loss of moral strength. But its strength will be the fruit of human concern, not of coercion or domination.'[13]

Nonetheless, standing for the truth does sound arrogant in a post-modern age where the idea of any absolute truth has given way to relativism. Is there not an alternative between these two poles? It is noteworthy that opposition to relativism is not only strongly opposed by more conservative Christians, but also by others who are more liberal. Many years ago Tillich expressed his uneasiness 'about the victory of relativism in all realms of thought and life',[14] and declared his unwillingness 'to surrender to absolute relativism' not

---

13 Martin Prozesky, *Frontiers of Conscience* (Johannesburg: Equinym, 2003), p. 61.

14 Paul Tillich, *My Search for Absolutes* (New York: Simon and Schuster, 1967), p. 64.

because he was 'authoritarian or reactionary, but for definite reasons both theoretical and pragmatic'.[15] Absolute relativism, he argued, is a contradiction, for it makes the relative absolute, turning it into an ideology. What is important is to distinguish between absolutes that are evident in moral claims such as 'Love your neighbour' or 'Do justly and love mercy', and the various attempts that have been made over the centuries to say what such moral imperatives mean within diverse contexts. That is, to recognize that there is a difference between the claim that there is truth, goodness and beauty, and the ways in which we apprehend and articulate truth, embody goodness and perceive beauty.

The Christian humanist is not a relativist, but is conscious of how easy it is for what is relative to be given an absolute status contrary to what we know about God revealed in Jesus Christ. Jesus had problems with 'the traditions of men' because, for example, they made Sabbath regulations absolute in a way that undermined the commandment itself, namely God's concern for human beings, animals and the earth. The Protestant Reformers were wary of 'church tradition' because of the same danger: tradition was important but not equal with the teaching of Scripture. They also insisted that within Scripture itself it was necessary to distinguish between what Calvin called 'adiaphora' or matters of indifference or relative unimportance, and those that were of absolute significance. The dietary, ritual and purity laws in Leviticus are not obligatory on Christians, and the insistence that women should wear head-covering, which was once regarded as 'absolute', is no longer. To justify the belief that God is a God of war, on the basis of some texts in Joshua, so that the absolute inerrancy of the Bible is maintained, is to worship the Bible, not the God of Jesus Christ. It is bibliolatry. But the convictions that God is all loving and just, and revealed in Jesus Christ, are, for Christians, absolute. The trouble is, we keep on turning relatives into absolutes and absolutes into relatives. And we generally do so not out of a concern for truth, but out of self-interest, fear or ignorance, and in order to shore up the authority on

---

15 Tillich, *My Search for Absolutes*, p. 65.

which we are dependent. But that reveals a lack of faith rather than a concern for truth. Perhaps the greatest legacy of the Christian humanist scholars of the Renaissance handed down to us was their critical scholarship of the biblical text, not denying its authority, but in the interests of liberating its core message from the strictures of a closed dogmatism.

Genuine faith in the God of the Bible is not impervious to doubt, as the Bible itself makes clear, any more than standing by one's convictions requires that we are intolerant of the convictions of others however much we may disagree. 'The test of faith', writes Rabbi Sacks, 'is whether I can make space for difference.' The inability to do this characterizes all fundamentalisms whether religious or secular, all closed ideologies whether of the right or the left. Making 'space for difference' is not compromising one's own convictions, but respecting other people. So Sacks continues: 'Can I recognize God's image in someone who is not in my image, whose language, faith, ideals, are different from my own. If I cannot, then I have made God in my image instead of allowing him to remake me in his.'[16] In other words, becoming more truly human is learning to respect the image of God in others. This is not simply tolerating them for the sake of peace; it is a confession of faith in God. People of all faiths, along with secular and Christian humanists, can be true to their convictions and join hands in defending values they share in common that promote human flourishing and the well-being of the environment. They can also stand together as critical patriots and partners in the struggle for justice and peace.

Critical patriotism: struggling for justice and peace

During the years I worked for the SACC I had several opportunities to travel to other parts of Africa – something denied most South Africans at the time unless they were in exile. The first of my visits was late in 1968 when I attended the General Assembly of the All African Conference of Churches (AACC) in Abidjan, Ivory Coast. At that meeting I was elected as an

---

16 Jonathan Sacks, *The Dignity of Difference*, p. 201.

alternate member to its General Council which, in turn, led to my next visit to West Africa, this time to Monrovia, the capital of Liberia. I vividly recall arriving at the airport. Although I had an official letter of invitation to attend the Council meeting, I did not have a visa. When I presented my South African passport, the duty officer was unimpressed, and ordered me to wait on one side while he consulted with other officials. I could judge from their expressions that I was not welcome. But just then I noticed someone beckoning me from a side door. It was Canon Burgess Carr, General Secretary of the AACC, who had anticipated the problem and had come to get me through the barrier. I was literally snatched away from under the nose of the officials, and was soon on my way to the meeting. Ironically, during the course of the Council meeting we were all dinner guests of the then President of Liberia who, on hearing that there was a South African present, invited me to join him at his table. Later, on leaving the country, I came face to face with the same passport control officer who had confronted me on my arrival. He recognized me, but refused to stamp my passport with the normal exit stamp saying, 'As you have nothing in your passport to say you arrived, I cannot say you have left. In fact, it is clear you have never been here!' He might well have said, 'You don't exist.'

Experiences like that, and there were others, made me painfully aware that South Africans, especially white ones, were not welcome in the rest of Africa, and for good reason. Nonetheless, my journeys into post-colonial Africa at a time when our country had become notorious across the world reminded me that, as a white South African, I could never be free as long as apartheid remained. I was always conscious that I was an outsider, a citizen of a pariah state. When the delegates of other nations attended receptions at their embassies to celebrate their national identities, I had nothing to celebrate, no embassy to visit, no flag I could honour or anthem I wished to sing. It was not always so.

As a Boy Scout in the early 1950s I was taught to honour 'Die Stem' (the national anthem) and, as we were then still part of the British Commonwealth, to sing 'God Save the King.' I was also taught to respect our national flag. Such patriotism was normative, an unquestioned part of being a white South African. The time came, however, when it became emotionally impossible for many of us to sing 'Die Stem' and, as we were no longer in the Commonwealth, the British national anthem was not an option even if we were inclined that way. And seeing that we had never been as good as Americans in saluting the flag, even at football matches, that was not an issue. In any case, the flag under which my father and other relations had served in the Second World War had become a symbol of the apartheid state. Patriotism meant obedience to a regime that was perpetrating injustice. Love for country meant a concern for the short-term interests of white security. And we soon discovered, as one scandal followed another, that those who claimed to be the most ardent patriots often turned out to be the most corrupt opportunists. Patriotism had become, as Samuel Johnson once observed, 'the last refuge of scoundrels'.

Most people have a genuine love for their country, but not many have a critical love. Patriotism too often implies an un-thinking loyalty, 'My country, right or wrong', but that is false love. Patriotism is also too often motivated by sectional or even individual self-interest, rather than a commitment to the people who comprise the nation as a whole, and to global society irrespective of nationality and difference. Christian nationalism, which regards the nation as 'chosen by God' and therefore a nation with a special divine calling, is particularly problematic and contrary to the spirit of Christian humanism. Such Christian nationalism, deeply embedded in the notion of Christendom, has been prevalent in parts of Eastern Europe where Orthodoxy is often indistinguishable from national identity, in the United States with its notion of 'manifest destiny' going back to the New England Puritans, a conviction perpetuated today by fundamentalists and others, and in South Africa, where Afrikaner Christian nationalism was aligned with apartheid. Many more examples could be mentioned.

Beyers Naudé helped many of us in South Africa to discover the true meaning of patriotism from a specifically Christian standpoint. He had impeccable credentials as a former member of the Broederbond and a Dutch Reformed minister and moderator. His father, also a dominee, had been an unofficial chaplain to the Boer forces, and was one of the *bittereinders* who refused to surrender.[17] Nobody could accuse his son, Beyers, of being suspect, like expatriate bishops or missionaries, or of not understanding Afrikaner history or the racial complexities of the country. But his ardent patriotism was eventually challenged and reshaped both by the gospel and by a growing awareness of the iniquities of apartheid. Like Bonhoeffer, whose example so powerfully influenced him, Naudé became a prophet and a pastor to all the people of South Africa. As a prophet, he spoke the truth and stood for justice irrespective of the cost; as a pastor he worked for healing and reconciliation. In doing this, he always demonstrated a loyalty to Afrikanerdom, though vilified as a traitor, even as he increasingly identified with the victims of apartheid, accepting their fate as his own.

Naudé could so easily have left South Africa. The honour he did not receive at home was his for the taking in Europe and North America. Some people simply had to go into exile. Naudé understood this and supported them in their choice. But that was not his decision. He believed that as a Christian he had to remain with his people – and by that he meant not just the Afrikaner community and Dutch Reformed church, but the people of South Africa as a whole. In fact, it was Naudé's willingness to express solidarity with those who were oppressed, and to do so in a remarkably un-paternalistic way, which ultimately enabled him to contribute so significantly to the liberation of whites. In the process he was able to break open the narrow patriotism of ethnic loyalty and help create the inclusive patriotism of a new South Africa in the making.

How reminiscent this is of Bonhoeffer. His, too, was the highest form of patriotism, not an uncritical acceptance of one's country whether right or wrong, but a willingness to die for its redemption in the service of those who were despised,

---

17 Peter Randall, ed., *Not Without Honour: Tribute to Beyers Naudé* (Johannesburg: Ravan Press, 1982), pp. 2 f.

rejected and persecuted. Only in this way, Bonhoeffer believed, was it possible to preserve what was best in Germany's history and culture; only in this way was it possible to save it from demonic madness, purge its guilt and restore its dignity; only in this way could the integrity of the Church's witness to the gospel be restored. None of this came easy to Bonhoeffer. Twice he sought refuge in exile, first in London in 1933 shortly after Hitler came to power, and then again in New York in 1939 just before the outbreak of war. But on neither occasion could he remain cut off from the people and the land he loved, or from doing something on behalf of its victims. In a celebrated letter to Reinhold Niebuhr, a professor at Union Theological Seminary in New York, he irrevocably identified himself with Germany's fate and sealed his own:

> I have come to the conclusion that I have made a mistake in coming to America. I must live through this difficult period of our national history with the Christian people of Germany. I will have no right to participate in the reconstruction of Christian life in Germany after the war if I do not share the trials of this time with my people ... Christians in Germany will face the terrible alternative of either willing the defeat of their nation in order that Christian civilization may survive, or willing the victory of their nation and thereby destroying our civilization.[18]

At the Second International Bonhoeffer Society Congress, held in Geneva in 1976 shortly after the Soweto Uprising, I was asked to read these words to the congregation as part of the closing service. It was a deeply emotional experience for me, and one that I barely managed to do. These words have always haunted me, especially when, during the apartheid era, I was tempted to leave South Africa.

South Africans of British origin, especially those of a previous generation like my parents, have often found it difficult to identify fully with South Africa. This sense of ambivalence

---

18 The passage is based on Niebuhr's recall of the original, which was lost. Dietrich Bonhoeffer, *The Way to Freedom* (London: Collins, 1966), p. 246.

intensified during the apartheid era as Afrikaner nationalism tightened its grip on all aspects of life. I, like many of my peers, never felt as our parents did that we belonged in some way to Britain, but were equally uncertain about belonging to apartheid South Africa. For that reason, and out of a fear for the future, many left to build their homes elsewhere. Those who could go but stayed, again like myself, and not least those who became conscientious objectors, did so because we had a sense of loyalty to South Africa in a much broader sense, and longed for the day when we could be proud of our country as other people were of theirs. That is why, for us, the inauguration of Nelson Mandela as President on 10 May 1994 was such a cathartic event.

Four hours of mesmerizing drama watched by millions seemed to expunge the bitter memories of the years devoured by the locusts. Not that those memories of the past were now buried. How can one forget the suffering and pain of those who struggled and died in combating racism? Yet as the inaugural hours went by, so for once everything seemed sparkling fresh and pure. Something remarkable happened. Disparate groups divided by centuries of racism, hatred, fear and everything we associate with apartheid, suddenly felt as though they were being melted down and remoulded as one nation. At long last truth, human rights, justice, the human struggle for dignity were victorious. We were proud when the new, colouful flag was unfurled because it represented the achievement of moral struggle, and the birth of a new nation as yet untainted by the failures which time would bring. We now had national symbols of which we could be proud precisely because they had the potential to unite rather than divide; and, in that brief liturgical space, they did unite.

As patriots of the new South Africa we gladly salute and respect the flag and sing the anthem, and such actions help foster a common sense of identity and purpose. But like all national symbols, they, too, can turn sour and become the servants of national idolatry. For this reason we need to be constantly reminded that at best they represent penultimate loyalties – in themselves they are not bearers of the truth, they cannot achieve justice, equity or freedom. The building of a national culture of which we can be justly proud requires far more than symbols of nationhood, however worthy and appropriate. It requires a vision of a new humanity, something expressed in the historic Freedom Charter in South Africa, and the vision of those who speak of a new, critical humanism. And it continues to require courageous prophets who, even now in our post-apartheid society, are prepared to be unpopular in reminding us of the demands of justice, equity and freedom – prophets who speak the truth out of love for the nation and its peoples to whom they are committed. They will not be surprised if they experience rejection. But they are the best patriots because they know better than most what a country really needs, what true peace and reconciliation require; and above all else, they know about the righteousness that exalts a nation.

Being a Christian humanist, a true patriot, requires that I exercise critical judgement as a responsible citizen of my own country, but also of the world, for in the end the two are inseparable. This mean recognizing faults and failures, and acknowledging guilt when that is appropriate and needed. Such 'honest patriotism', as Donald Shriver has so eloquently shown, is not easy and is often regarded as treasonable, for it demands that we pay attention to the suffering of others, often caused by the country we love and therefore in our own name. But it is what is demanded of us if we wish to be Christian and human, as well as American, British, German, Nigerian or South African. 'Though we cannot plumb the depths of all the unjust suffering among our neighbors past and present,' Shriver concludes, 'we can grow in comprehending more of it.'[19] And in doing so, we can express solidarity with others simply because we share a common humanity, and as humanists, whether Christian or otherwise, a concern for human well-being.

No one has symbolized genuine love for his nation and what it means to be a global citizen than Nelson Mandela who, for

---

19 Donald W. Shriver Jr, *Honest Patriots: Loving a Country Enough to Remember Its Misdeeds* (New York: Oxford, 2005), p. 267.

multitudes, has become the icon not only of the struggle for justice, but also of the reconciliation of former enemies. His aim was not to liberate South Africa at the expense of some, but to set it free for all. Likewise, his aim was not to make South Africa strong at the expense of other nations, but as a beacon of hope for all. There are few better models of love of country and a commitment to global justice and peace from a Christian humanist perspective.

Creativity of the Spirit: cherishing beauty

The purpose of human evolution is, in the words of Ward, '*growth* in creativity, sensitivity and community ...'[20] And in a profoundly moving passage in his foreword to *The Phenomenon of Man*, Teilhard de Chardin wrote of the need for a new and deeper vision of what it means to be human in order to 'increase our capacity to live'. His interest was not simply scientific or apologetic, but the enhancing of human life. For this reason he saw the need for us to 'focus our eyes correctly' with the aid of science. 'For man to discover man and to take his measure,' he wrote, 'a whole series of "senses" are necessary, whose gradual acquisition ... covers and punctuates the whole history of the struggles of the mind.'[21] With the awakening of these 'senses' we begin to see ourselves entirely related to the rest of humanity, to life as a whole and to the universe. We begin to appreciate the splendour and elegance, coherence and complexity that lies before and within us. The Cornish sculptor Barbara Hepworth, whose 'Single Form' in memory of Dag Hammarskjöld stands in front of the United Nations building in New York, expressed this when she wrote:

> I think the very nature of art is affirmative, and in being so it reflects the laws and evolution of the universe – both in the power and rhythm of growth and structure as well as the infinitude of ideas which reveal themselves when one is

---

20 Ward, *God, Chance and Necessity*, p. 164.
21 Pierre Teilhard de Chardin, *The Phenomenon of Man* (New York: Harper & Brothers, 1959), pp. 33–4.

in accord with the cosmos and the personality is then free to develop.[22]

Thinking again of Leonardo's 'The Vitruvian Man' I wonder whether what he had in mind was the perfect, self-sufficient human being of post-Enlightenment secularity, or the perfect human being made 'in the image of God'. At one level Renaissance humanism was a recovery of classical paganism, but it was also a critique of bad religion in the interests of a better one, one that valued rather than repressed human dignity, beauty and potentiality. Much of the creative energy and output of the Renaissance painters and sculptors, many of them priests and monks, was dedicated to 'the glory of God' and for the purpose of representing the gospel story in the precincts of monastery and church, and sometimes the market square. The Renaissance humanists were not 'aesthetes' in the secularist sense of 'art for art's sake', where beauty is wrenched from truth and goodness; their aesthetic sensibility was for the sake of human well-being and wholeness, excesses and exceptions notwithstanding. So is there a way whereby we can overcome the perceived dichotomy between 'The Vitruvian Man' and the 'crucified Christ', between Sister Bridget's critique of the humanities as irrelevant to human suffering, and Sister Elizabeth's bothers about the waste of artistic talent in carving crucifixes?

I have searched, largely in vain, in the Bible for references to what might be regarded as the gift or *charisma* of creativity; I have also looked in many classic texts on Christian spirituality with the same result. There must be references that I failed to find. But I do know that traditionally the Church has frowned on creativity, for it suggests going beyond the boundaries of the orthodox and acceptable, trying to emulate God, the one and only creator of all that exists. What is esteemed is faithfulness, not creativity. The danger of creativity is that of hubris or human pride, the glorification of humanity at the expense of the creator. Especially, but not only with regard

22 Barbara Hepworth, *A Pictorial Autobiography* (London: The Tate Gallery, 1985), p. 24.

to the visual arts, Christianity has traditionally trod an uneasy path between the Scylla of idolatry and the Charibdis of iconoclasm. In the Western Church the pendulum has swung between artistic creativity bordering on the idolatrous and heretical, and iconoclastic zeal that has sometimes destroyed great works of art. In the Eastern Orthodox tradition, the problem was resolved during the Iconoclastic controversy, a watershed event in the history of Christendom, which ensured the future of icons within Orthodoxy as windows that made the eternal visible in time. The argument that carried the day was that through the incarnation God had become visible and embodied, thus opening the way for iconic representation of the divine Word. But icons are not regarded as works of art in the sense of being produced by creative innovation and genius, quite the contrary. They are the outcome of spiritual disciplines that follow strict dogmatic rules within the context of liturgical worship.

Yet what if, as Irenaeus put it, 'the glory of God is humanity fulfilled', and what if 'being made in the image of God', who is creator, means that God intends us to be co-creators in making this world more humane and beautiful? What if honouring human creativity is a way of honouring God who enables us to be creative? What if creativity is not something to be frowned on, but something to be encouraged as a gift of the Spirit? What if creativity has to do with what I earlier referred to as a 'second naïveté', a recovery of childlike innocence described in those wonderful words of Sara Maitland already quoted, in which we find 'the world beautiful, magical, wild beyond dreams, dancing its complex patterns of truth, weaving its multicoloured threads of discourse so that all things can be true and we can once more be ravished by the beauty of God'?[23] Is it not true that while creativity might not be referred to as such in the biblical text, it permeates the Scriptures from the first day of creation in which the Spirit brought form out of chaos to the beginning of the new age depicted with such artistry in the book of Revelation? This should not surprise us who believe in God the Creative Spirit whose beauty

---

23 Maitland, *A Big-Enough God*, p. 189.

is displayed all around us. And is it not true that Christians have been numbered among the greatest of the poets, artists, dramatists, authors and scientists through the ages? So let me now extol the value of creativity as a gift of the Spirit and an essential part of the Christian humanist creed, and in doing so emphasize the need to cherish beauty and to recover aesthetic sensibility as part of the Christian vision of being human. This gift of creativity is not as important as faith, hope and love, but it is surely as important as many other gifts of the Spirit, and is acknowledged as such in the Bible (Exodus 31.1–5). From a Christian humanist perspective creativity, as a gift of the Spirit, is not given for self-satisfaction but for human well-being, whether personal or social.

Christian tradition, starting in the Old Testament, always distinguishes between God the Spirit (Holy Spirit) and the human 'spirit', the 'breath of life' that makes and keeps us alive and human. Yet, in so far as creation is understood also as the activity of the Spirit bringing order out of chaos, the Spirit connects humans with the rest of creation, and especially with all that has life, giving all of life a sacred quality. There is a further distinction that is important for the Christian understanding of the Holy Spirit, namely the relationship between the Spirit and Jesus the Christ. The Holy Spirit is not some alien god, or impersonal force, but has character and personality, as God the Spirit who creates and redeems. The Spirit is, as both St John and St Paul remind us, the one who enables us to live 'in Christ', so what the Spirit does is always in conformity with the 'mind of Christ' and the gospel of the incarnation. Put differently, the gifts of the Spirit enable us to become more truly human in the image of the incarnate one. For Christians the Holy Spirit is God's gracious presence in our lives enabling us to become more truly human, more truly ourselves. And for that very reason the Spirit also enables human creativity, making humans in some sense co-creators with God, playing a special role within creation, and expressing the beauty of creation in artistic celebration. Or, we might say, the Spirit awakens within us both aesthetic sensibility and a desire for beauty.

In thinking about this. I have been struck by one of the lesser known passages in Bonhoeffer's prison letters where he expressed the hope that it would be possible 'to regain the idea of the church as providing an understanding of the area of freedom (art, education [*Bildung*] friendship, play), so that Kierkegaard's "aesthetic existence" would not be banished from the church's sphere, but would be re-established within it'.[24] This, Bonhoeffer believed, was 'eminently Christian'. Tragically, as he also observed, for many people today, human beings are 'just a part of the world of things, because the experience of the human simply eludes them'.[25] Meditating on the Old Testament in particular led Bonhoeffer to a strong affirmation of the body and the earth, and to his celebration of human freedom, *hilaritas* and the polyphony of life. These themes, which burst forth so passionately in the *Letters and Papers from Prison*, find their theological formulation in what it means to be a *Mensch* and a Christian in a 'world come of age'.

In expressing his desire for the recovery of aesthetic existence in the life of the Church, Bonhoeffer was countering the critique of Nietzsche and many secular humanists who have followed in his footsteps, in rejecting Christianity because of its lack of appreciation for the aesthetic, for the body, and for human creativity. Like Nietzsche, they have regarded Christianity as something that eschews human creativity, the body and the aesthetic. But this denial is a travesty of Christianity, even though it has been a dominant tradition in the course of its history, regarding humanity as worthless, the body as a sensual snare, and the aesthetic as a means of seduction. Of course, like all that is created, and therefore good, these can and do become debased, but to regard as unclean that which God has given for human enjoyment, fulfilment and well-being is a sign of unbelief, not faith. In this regard, I am constantly attracted to Bonhoeffer's counsel, based on

---

24 Bonhoeffer, *Letters and Papers from Prison*, p. 193. See my discussion in John W. de Gruchy, *Christianity, Art, and Transformation* (Cambridge: Cambridge University Press, 2001), pp. 240-1, 147-58.

25 Bonhoeffer, *Letters and Papers from Prison*, p. 386.

an analogy from the music of J. S. Bach, that if we hold fast to Christ as the centre of life, the *cantus firmus*, we can be greatly enriched by the polyphony that gives life its wholeness.[26] Without the *cantus firmus* our lives lack coherence and disintegrate into fragments; with it we can enjoy to the full all that is given to us by God as human beings.

Fortunately, in the course of the twentieth century there was a remarkable resurgence of aesthetic sensibility in the life of the Church, corresponding to an equally remarkable interest in the arts.[27] Already at the turn of that century P. T. Forsyth, whose works I read avidly as a student, insisted that art speaks to the soul and can save religion from becoming closed and hardened. Faith without a sense of beauty, or religion severed from imagination and over-engrossed with public and practical affairs, Forsyth wrote, leaves us with 'a drought in our own souls'.[28] It no longer evokes a sense of wonder. Art, in fact, is 'not a luxury' but 'a necessity of human nature'. For this reason, no 'religion can be a true religion if it does not encourage great art'[29] – and, we might add, if it does not cherish beauty, whether the beauty of the creation or the cross, the beauty of love, whether that of God or humans.

Balthasar, whose writings I turned to in exploring art and theological aesthetics, embodied a deep commitment to Christian faith and to the spirit of classical culture and Renaissance humanism. Regarding the representation of the gods of classical culture as 'unique images and unveilings of Being' that within 'finite contours ... validly encompass and embody the fullness of the universe', he wrote: 'A Michelangelo, a Goethe, a Keats must still have seen such gods with their inner eye ... And we must ask ourselves whether the inability of the modern heart to encounter gods – with the resultant withering up of human religions – is altogether to Christian-

---

26 See his letter to Eberhard Bethge, 20 May 1944 Bonhoeffer, *Letters and Papers from Prison*, p. 303.

27 See, for example, John Dillenberger, *A Theology of Artistic Sensibilities: The Visual Arts and the Church* (London: SCM Press, 1986).

28 P. T. Forsyth, *Religion in Recent Art* (London: Hodder & Stoughton, 1905), p. 7.

29 Forsyth, *Religion in Recent Art*, p. 145.

ity's advantage.'[30] Like Forsyth, Balthasar would undoubtedly have chosen Christ rather than Apollo or Dionysius, if that
was the only choice, but he recognized that there was a point
of connection between the Holy Spirit and the poetic spirit
of the muses. It all has to do with the awakening of aesthetic
sensibility, the ability to appreciate the world in which we live
from a different perspective than the purely utilitarian and
secularist.

Exploring what this means for theology and the Church
today in dialogue with the humanities and especially artists
provides new perspectives and insights concerning the meaning and significance of the incarnation, the sacramental character of reality, as well as the agonies and ecstasies of human
life. For embodiment is not simply about the material but also
about its relation to transcendence; it is about the creative
spirit that shapes and gives life and form to the material as
is evident in all great sculpture. Theologically speaking, we
celebrate the body against a false dualism of soul versus body;
yet we also refuse to make it a fetish and thereby the creative
and redemptive Spirit that gives life to the body. And while
a dose of genuine asceticism is perhaps a necessary antidote
to the over-indulgent lifestyles of those of us who are afflu-
ent, we really need to be educating our desires in ways that
serve the kingdom, not in ways that denigrate the body,
repress our sexuality and result in equally unhealthy attitudes
and practices. As Timothy Gorringe argues so persuasively:
'Desire needs education and Christianity is an alternative education of desire ... It is not about denying the body, but about
channelling its energies creatively.'[31]

There are many people in all societies whose poverty keeps
them in bondage to ugly environments that crush their creativity just as they crush their bodies, and whose lack of resources
and education prevents them from developing an appreciation
for art. At the same time, through discovering their creative
abilities, people are enabled to rise above their circumstances

---

30 von Balthasar, *The Glory of the Lord: Vol. 1*, p. 500.
31 T. J. Gorringe, *The Education of Desire* (London: SCM Press, 2001), pp.
92–3.

and contribute not only to their own well-being but also to the healing of their communities, helping to restore dignity and humanity. I know this is true, for example, where art has enabled people living with HIV and AIDS to recover a sense of dignity and hope.

Artistic creativity and aesthetic sensibility are, I believe, among ways whereby the power of God is unleashed, awakening both a thirst for justice and a hunger for beauty. Artists help awaken our awareness to the present reality in all its pain and hope, thereby enabling transforming vision. Such artists are not necessarily the professionals, but those of our own communities who can discern beyond the surface to the depths of being-in-the-world; indeed, to discern the Spirit at work in our midst. And just as there are important points of contact between Christian and secular humanists, so there should be a common bond between all who believe 'in justice and truth, mercy and love, in art and poetry and music' for these are indestructible.[32]

My sketch of the contours of Christian humanism can undoubtedly be developed further. But hopefully sufficient has been said to suggest how the term may be recovered today. What is more important, however, is to stress my intention in doing what I have done. My aim has not been to proclaim 'Christian humanism' as though it was the only or even the most adequate term to express all dimensions of Christian faith, but to offer it as one that I have increasingly found eminently useful to convey what I confess by way of contrast with other expressions of Christianity and humanism. Above all, it speaks to me of what Barth, in a remarkable essay, called 'God's humanism';[33] that is, of the God who became a human being in order that we might become fully human ourselves.

32 G. K. A. Bell, *Christianity and World Order* (Harmondsworth, England: Penguin, 1940), pp. 146f.

33 Karl Barth, *The Humanity of God* (London: Collins, 1960), p. 37.

8

Epilogue

God,
you were before us at our life's beginning;
be so again at our journey's end.
You were beside us at our soul's shaping;
be so again at our life's finishing.[1]

There is something beyond history.
There is something that passes the threshold of matter and time.
There is something called the transcendent,
the eschatological,
the beyond,
the final goal.
Oscar Romero[2]

For everything there is a season, and a time for
every matter under heaven. Ecclesiastes 3.1

For now we see in a mirror, dimly, but then we shall see
face to face. Now I know only in part; then I will know fully,
even as I have been fully known. 1 Corinthians 13.12

On retirement Isobel and I joined the Volmoed Community in the Hemel en Aarde Valley near Hermanus, 120 kilometres east of Cape Town along the Indian Ocean coast. The valley, with the Onrus river running through, and vineyards and olive groves nestling beneath the surrounding hills and mountains was appropriately named, as its beauty suggests the meeting of heaven and earth. But this should not hide from us the tragic history of the valley. In the nineteenth century it was inhabited by lepers, prior to the establishment of the leper colony on Robben Island, and in more recent times its has been the home to farm labourers, many of them poor with all

---

1 *Book of Common Order of the Church of Scotland* (Edinburgh: St Andrew Press, 1994), p. 553.
2 Romero, *The Violence of Love*, p. 162.

the attendant problems that poverty creates. Alcoholism and drug abuse, TB and a lack of education are among the issues facing those who seek to improve the standard of living today. The name Volmoed, given to the farm on which we now live in community, means 'full of courage'. It is appropriate as a symbol of all those who have struggled against the odds to keep their humanity intact, and of those who have sought to serve others in need. Among these latter were the Moravian missionaries who came over the mountains from Genadendal in the eighteenth and nineteenth centuries en route to deserved rest at the coast. They established a school and farm, and also served the lepers as best they could. As always, Moravian piety was practical in character.

The Volmoed Community, established on the farm in 1986 to promote reconciliation and healing, was the vision of several people, some who had only recently become Christians, and were involved in an Anglican parish in Cape Town. Their passion was to establish an ecumenical place of hospitality where people of all races could meet, discover each other as human beings reconciled in Christ, and, in those dark days of political strife with all its personal traumas, find healing and renewal. Most of those who first came to Volmoed were from the coloured townships on the Cape Flats, people who were not only the victims of apartheid but also living in the midst of violent turmoil. At the beginning, there was virtually no infrastructure on the farm, no electricity or piped water, and only one old farmhouse. Since then the Volmoed Community has developed into a retreat and conference centre that attracts people from around the country and beyond. At the heart of the Community are several buildings: the office, the guest chalets, the service building with its kitchen and dining room, workshops, art studios, a potters' shed, and the simple but splendid chapel. Each of these, built by the Community and funded by the generosity of prayer partners and friends, conveys the ethos of the Community. Every morning members of the Community, often joined by visitors, gather for prayer in the chapel, sharing in the eucharist once a week. It is a rare privilege to begin one's 'retirement' in such a community, to enjoy a different rhythm to life at a stage when its seasons are shortening.

Seasons of life

As a schoolboy, I learnt about Shakespeare's 'seven ages of man'. Then in Chicago I learnt from Erik Erikson about the life cycles that characterize our human journey, and later from the Hindu *Upanishads* about the four stages of life that are the ideal from birth to maturity and wisdom. So I have long been aware that life has a rhythm; that there are passages through which we pass that need to be appropriately negotiated, starting with birth and ending with death. At each stage along the way the challenges are different, but how we meet them at each juncture shapes the way in which we will, in all probability, respond to the next. The story of our lives is a story of phases and passages, some more significant than others, but all contributing to the whole. The challenge is how, along with that Christian humanist, martyr and friend of Erasmus, Thomas More, we can become people 'for all seasons'.

There have been many moments in my life that have determined its course. One of these, as I have told, was my adolescent conversion. But, important as it was, that was not the only one. Such moments are significant in themselves, yet become more so as we reflect on them, perhaps with some regrets, hopefully with some gratitude, accepting them as part of who we are. This enables us to grow into maturity as we face the diminishing choices of old age and the reality of death. All of this is part of being human, and learning to become more truly so. For the Christian, each stage also involves a fresh discovery of the relevance of the gospel.

I am fully aware that not everyone has the privilege of experiencing the 'three score years and ten' that the Bible refers to as the full complement of human life. The past century has witnessed the death of many prophets and social activists who, in standing for truth and justice, have suffered martyrdom. For many, life is cut short soon after birth, or in the prime of life, through disease or accident, and for many others, retirement, instead of ushering in years of a more relaxed period, and one of activity free from institutional constraints, can suddenly mark the end. Or it may be dogged by crippling, debilitating illness, frightening loss of memory and inability to recognize others. For many people, especially those who are poor, the normal life span is often truncated, and the possibility of retirement is not an option. With limited resources, the prospects of growing old are undoubtedly much more fearsome. Even as I write these words, the news tells me that the latest statistics on HIV and AIDS in southern Africa are far worse than previously believed. Today, as every Tuesday, we prayed in chapel for its victims and their caregivers, as we pray daily for people in need around the world.

Personally speaking, I am not sure how well I would cope with the realities that many others – indeed, the majority of the world's population – have to endure throughout their lives, let alone as life comes to a close. I can only speak from within the framework of my own, privileged position – recognizing that it could change, and change dramatically at any moment. Indeed, two weeks before we left our home of thirty-one years in Cape Town and moved to Volmoed, Isobel was diagnosed with Parkinson's Disease, a reminder of the fragility of life and the unexpected ways in which this is brought home to us.

But for both Isobel and I, the privilege of spending these early retirement years in the Volmoed Community provides a deeply satisfying and fulfilling rhythm to life that brings much of our journey into fresh perspective. The daily round of prayer, study, writing and teaching, furniture making and art that we pursue, reminds us of the Benedictine balance that has become so attractive to many people in search of a wholesome spirituality for today. I have also been able to continue as a research associate at the University of Cape Town and teach on occasion at the University of Stellenbosch. Looking back, I am convinced that achieving this balance is really what life is meant to be, even though it eludes so many, not simply because of an inability or unwillingness to grasp hold of it, but because of a lack of opportunity to do so. On the other hand, it is not something that is handed to us on a platter

– the building bricks have to be laid, bit-by-bit over the days of our lives. All things being equal, not to have 'prepared' for the final stages of life will, I am convinced, affect their quality. Instead of discovering time as something rhythmic, time becomes something to be dreaded both because it is passing too quickly and because it is not passing quickly enough.

Jim Forest, former General Secretary of the International Fellowship of Reconciliation, reminds us of the British comedy film *Last Holiday*. George Bird, a cautious civil servant, dreads life, is dull and unattractive to women. Persistent headaches send him to a doctor. But as a result of bureaucratic bungling his diagnosis is confused with someone else's. All he needs is an aspirin, but he is told that he has only six weeks to live. This startling information transforms his life. He immediately stops work and embarks on a perpetual holiday, doing things he never dreamt of, spending all his money, and in the process becoming attractive to women. Suddenly important people, bankers, politicians, CEOs, seek his advice, sensing that he has 'a mysterious quality, a detachment and freedom that make him a figure to be reckoned with'. But all too soon, on one of his errands of mercy, he is killed in a motorcar accident. The doctor's prediction came true after all. But the recognition of his impending death had set Bird free to live life more fully than he had ever done. 'Bird's death sentence has been his liberation.'[3]

This is the season of life when one does not have to plan and prepare for a vocation and career, establish a family, and much else beside. Now, more than ever, is the time to recognize that life is not just about future options, choices and plans, but about living each day as a gift. This should set us free for being more spontaneous, more open rather than less so, to what is happening in the world around us, more willing to grasp the moment as though it were the last. Above all else, becoming more intentional about our relationships, our family and friends, healing wounds, offering and receiving forgiveness, recollecting moments that have made life memorable,

---

3 Jim Forest, *The Ladder of the Beatitudes* (Maryknoll, NY: Orbis, 1999), pp. 155–6.

and celebrating life with each other as much as we can – even
though, sadly we are often separated by distance from those
we love most. All of this is about being more truly human. But
there is one further option available to those who have been
privileged during the course of their lives: sharing gifts and
talents that we may have in a way that might not have been
possible before.

My father was a skilled amateur craftsman. He built our
first family house and made all the furniture. I will never forget the sad day when, in his old age, he finally gave away all
his tools, many of them now in my possession. An essential
part of his life had come to an end. Every spare moment, as I
recall, he had spent in his workshop either shaping wood or
turning metal. But he did pass on some of his knowledge and
skill. At an early age he taught me to use a plane, a chisel and a
saw, and while I was in junior school he bought a second-hand
wood-turning lathe so that I could learn that craft. My interests shifted elsewhere as those early years passed, but he had
awakened something in me that never disappeared. In recent
times it has returned a hundredfold as I have re-discovered the
joys of woodturning and furniture making, crafts that now
consume many of my retirement hours. I know the day will
come for me also when I will no longer be able to cut, plane
and turn wood – or write books. But for the moment, to work
with one's hands, to observe the intricate patterns of wood,
to smell the resin and to create something, makes me feel
particularly human.

But there is more to this than simply personal satisfaction.
My father imparted knowledge and skills that have enriched
my life, but also showed me the importance of doing this. As
a university professor and church pastor I have spent much of
my life in teaching others, and I still do. But I am now more
conscious of the fact that those who have developed knowledge, skills, and hopefully wisdom over the years, have a
special responsibility to hand them on to the next generation,
and especially to those who have been deprived of opportunities of learning. It has therefore been a great privilege to be
engaged in a mentoring programme at the University of Cape

Town designed to help junior faculty members with their research. And also to lecture in the University of the Third Age (U3A, that is, 'retirement') where retired academics and professionals share their knowledge and expertise with others. As Jesus said, 'to those who have been given much, much shall be required' (Luke 12.48). Perhaps the meaning of retirement for those who 'have been given much' and who still have the physical and mental capacity to do so, is to share with others what they have received. There is wisdom in the ancient adage that 'all we can take with us at the end of life is what we have given away'. This, too, is what being human is about.

End of story: a new beginning

We were in Chicago when President John Kennedy was assassinated in November 1963. With millions of others we witnessed his final moments that came with a shocking suddenness and then, over the next days, watched and wept as the funeral events dominated the TV screen. Likewise we joined multitudes in mourning the sudden and tragic death of Princess Diana. But I cannot recall any other recent occasion when the actual process of dying became such a public event until the final weeks and days of John Paul II. As I watched those events unfold, and heard the great words of the Christian funeral liturgy being intoned, I wondered about how all of this was being perceived by secular humanists around the world – or even in St Peter's Square. What do they make of the words and the convictions, the symbols and signs we Christians use at times like these? Indeed, as I watch murder mysteries on TV, especially those set in the villages of England, with their inevitable burial scenes in an old church graveyard, I wonder what viewers make of the words, as dust is scattered on the coffin: 'in sure and certain hope of the resurrection of the body and the life everlasting'. Such ponderings are also part of our being human.

But it is not only the reactions and thoughts of secular unbelievers that I wonder about; I also ponder these time-honoured and solemn words for myself, and those I love – words I have often used as I have buried the dead, and as I have tried to comfort those who mourn. Do *I* believe them myself? And if so, how do I understand them? Of course, belief in the 'resurrection of the body' is an article of faith, so once again we are faced with a mystery that remains beyond our rational grasp. We see 'through a glass darkly' as St Paul aptly described it. But we can reflect on its possible meaning in the hope that we will in due course see things more clearly, 'face to face' as it were.

Earlier I indicated that 'eternal life' in the New Testament, especially in the Gospel according to St John, refers to a quality of life rather than to endless quantity; it is life lived under the reign of God, in the 'kingdom of heaven' here and now. Such life is as much about relationships as anything else, and it has an indestructible quality about it. Part of what we are saying in proclaiming the 'resurrection of the body' is that we are part of a web of human life, for Christians, 'the body of Christ', that has been raised to newness of life. The New Testament says little about the 'immortality of the soul'; it says a great deal about the 'resurrection of the body'. Whereas immortality puts the emphasis on the individual as a soul who departs life, often implying some kind of depersonalizing as the soul is reunited with cosmic Being, the 'resurrection of the body' suggests something organic, it has to do with the inter-connectedness of life of which death is an inevitable and indispensable part. This might not give much comfort to those who wonder about the whereabouts of loved ones who have died, or about their own destiny, but it may well provide a fresh perspective from which we can look at the reality of death and 'the life everlasting'.

The 'resurrection of the body' is not to be understood in a crude, literal sense; it refers to the reconstitution of our personhood in relation to others in ways that we cannot even begin to imagine. As we have previously noted, within the 'body' personality is not lost in the mass, but enriched through relationships. Who I am is not sacrificed but enhanced through being related to God and to others in the risen 'body of Christ'. Michael Mayne, whose comments were helpful earlier in the Prologue, is helpful here too: 'I have lived and I shall die trusting that God will *re-member* me; that I shall be put together again.'[4] He goes on to say:

> While we can know nothing of what lies beyond death, there are all kinds of clues in our sense of incompleteness, a hunger for that which in this life just eludes our grasp, the need to glimpse in the confusion of our lives a purpose and a meaning. And they all point to home, a place where there is an end to all searching; and where there is no need to explain, for everything is known.[5]

If the incarnation provides the basis for Christian humanism by overcoming the dualism between the sacred and secular, reconciling God and humanity and asserting human dignity, and if the cross roots such humanism in the reality of a suffering world and the struggle for justice, it is through the resurrection that the power of death is broken and human hope fulfilled. It is, Bonhoeffer writes, the 'risen Christ who bears the new humanity in himself, the final glorious "yes" which God addresses to the new human being'.[6]

As far as we know, from an eye-witness to that horrendous day when Bonhoeffer was taken naked out of his cell at Flossenburg Concentration Camp and hanged against a wall along with other conspirators, his last words were: 'For me, this is the beginning of life.' While I am not sure I will be able to say that with such confidence when the time comes, I find these words immensely hopeful. They are the final confession of someone who recognized that our lives are in the hands of the God whom we have seen in the 'face of Jesus Christ'. In Christ, the Alpha and Omega, God has the final word, and that word is 'Yes' to life, the 'Word that was with God from the beginning' and who brings everything to completion.

Hope and love are the two most enduring qualities of being truly human. They are an everlasting protest against nothingness and despair, against cynicism and hatred. Love is

---

4 Mayne, *Learning to Dance*, p. 236.
5 Mayne, *Learning to Dance*, p. 237.
6 Bonhoeffer, *Ethics*, p. 79.

affirmation of the human against its denial; a proclamation of the resurrection of the body against a chaos that has no ultimate pattern, the cement that binds us to each other in enduring relationships in the 'body of Christ'. As Christians we witness to God's love story, and seek to live our lives on the basis of the narrative that calls it to mind in Scripture and eucharistic worship. And we do so in hope, for it is this quality perhaps above all that should characterize those who believe in God. Inseparable from love, hope is nevertheless different. 'Hope', writes Tina Beattie, 'is love's commitment to the future.' It is

> something subtle, perhaps not even recognizable. It refuses to yield to despair but offers no platitude, no false word of comfort, no response other than its own elusive presence. And sometimes it must declare its presence not even as future eventuality but as love here and now, before and beyond the terror of death.[7]

We return to the images with which we began: the 'Vitruvian Man', symbol of human perfection and well-being, humanity in the 'image of God'; the crucified Jesus of Nazareth, the embodiment of God become 'fully human' so that our humanity may be restored and brought to wholeness; and the *Shona* sculpture, the maternal image of relationships that embrace us from conception and birth, keeping us human. All three are important and true. The first two portray arms outstretched, the one revealing that we are wonderfully made; the other, that we are redeemed at great cost. The third image speaks to me of the eternal Parent embracing the prodigal and welcoming me home.

---

7 Tina Beattie, *Eve's Pilgrimage: A Women's Quest for the City of God* (London: Burns & Oates, 2002), pp. 207–8.

Index of Names and Subjects

John W. de Gruchy is Professor Emeritus of Christian Studies at the University of Cape Town, South Africa. General Editor of the Making of Modern Theology series (Fortress Press), de Gruchy also has translated, edited, and served on the Board for the English-language edition of Dietrich Bonhoeffer's Works. He was awarded the Karl Barth Prize in Berlin in 2000. His published works include:

Bonhoeffer and South Africa: Theology in Dialogue, 1984

Theology and Ministry in Context and Crisis: A South African Perspective, 1987

Dietrich Bonhoeffer: Witness to Jesus Christ, 1991

Liberating Reformed Theology, 1991

Christianity and Democracy: A Theology for a Just World Order, 1995

Bonhoeffer for a New Day: Theology in a Time of Transition, editor, 1997

Dietrich Bonhoeffer's *Creation and Fall*, editor, 1997 (vol. 3 of Dietrich Bonhoeffer Works)

The Cambridge Companion to Dietrich Bonhoeffer, editor, 1999

Christianity, Art, and Transformation: A Study in Theological Aesthetics, 2001

Reconciliation: Restoring Justice, 2002

The Church Struggle in South Africa: 25th Anniversary Edition, revised and expanded, with Steve de Gruchy, 2004

Daring, Trusting Spirit: Dietrich Bonhoeffer's Friend Eberhard Bethge, 2005